# The Chinese
# Agricultural Economy

# About the Book and Editors

*The Chinese Agricultural Economy*
edited by Randolph Barker and Radha Sinha
with Beth Rose

Although the People's Republic of China is well known for its policy of emphasizing self-reliance in rural areas, recent reports indicate that serious problems remain to be overcome. Despite overall improvements in agricultural production and average rural living standards over the last three decades, many localities in China remain desperately poor. For this reason Western assessments of the past performance and future potential of the Chinese agricultural economy are mixed.

In this book, the authors present an array of views analyzing past successes and failures of China in its efforts to increase agricultural production and improve its people's economic standard of living. Although the focus of the book is on the post-1949 period, introductory chapters provide historical, social, and geographical settings that serve as a backdrop for the agricultural development of the PRC. Subsequent chapters document and discuss the significance of recent important changes in agricultural policy and in the rural economy. Throughout their discussions the authors emphasize that the economic development of China is dependent on many factors, including social institutions, natural resource potential, technological development, and government policy and its implementation. Information on these factors is presented along with a view of Chinese agricultural development in a comparative international context.

**Dr. Barker** is a professor of agricultural economics at Cornell University. From 1967 to 1978 he was head of the Department of Agricultural Economics at the International Rice Research Institute. **Dr. Sinha** is reader in political economy at Glasgow University. His many books and articles on agricultural economics include *Food and Poverty*. **Ms. Rose** is a research assistant at Cornell University.

# The Chinese Agricultural Economy

edited by Randolph Barker
and Radha Sinha
with Beth Rose

Westview Press • Boulder, Colorado
Croom Helm • London, England

*This volume is included in Westview's Special Studies on China and East Asia*

Published in 1982 in the United States of America by
  Westview Press, Inc.
  5500 Central Avenue
  Boulder, Colorado 80301
  Frederick A. Praeger, President and Publisher

Published in 1982 in Great Britain by
  Croom Helm Ltd.
  2-10 St. John's Road
  London, S.W. 11

Library of Congress Catalog Card No. 82-8549.
ISBN (U.S.) 0-86531-253-2
ISBN (U.S.) 0-86531-342-3 (pbk.)
ISBN (U.K.) 0-7099-0682-X

Printed and bound in the United States of America

# Contents

# Figures and Tables

# Preface

This book originated in a workshop held in May 1979, "Agricultural and Rural Development in the People's Republic of China." A number of social and agricultural scientists met at Cornell University to discuss the impact of recent policy changes on agricultural and economic development in China. It became evident in these discussions that although much has recently been written about China, there have been only a few comprehensive books on the Chinese agricultural economy, most of which were written in the 1960s and therefore do not cover the more recent developments. Given the obvious need for such a volume, we had little difficulty in soliciting chapters from a number of knowledgeable China scholars.

The first four chapters of the book provide the setting. They include an overview of current issues, a historical look at Chinese agricultural development, and a description of the physical environment and resource endowments. The remaining eight chapters, which focus on priorities and policies since the founding of the People's Republic of China, explore a wide range of topics. The emphasis is on the period prior to the death of Mao, but attention is also given to the implications of recent policy changes.

The book has been written for the general reader and for students of agricultural and economic development. A list of supplemental readings is provided at the end of each chapter (except Chapter 1). Appendix A contains national-level statistical data on population, agricultural production, and major agricultural inputs. The Pinyin system of romanization has been used throughout.

Funding for the book was provided by the Program in International Agriculture and the Department of Agricultural Economics, Cornell University. The research on which several of the chapters are based was supported by the Henry Luce Foundation, which deserves much credit for encouraging recent scholarly work on China.

The reader, of course, should be aware that conditions often change between the time a chapter is written and its publication, and statements made at the time of writing may not reflect the current situation or policies.

Finally, we would like to acknowledge the invaluable assistance of Judy Wiiki, who was responsible for typing all but the initial drafts of the manuscript.

*Randolph Barker*
Cornell University

*Radha Sinha*
Glasgow University

# Chronology of Recent Historical Events

| | |
|---|---|
| 1912 | Sun Yat-sen; Republican China |
| 1921 | Founding of the first congress of the Chinese Communist Party (CCP) |
| 1928–1937 | Warlord period; Kuomintang Nationalists led by Chiang Kai-shek |
| 1934–1935 | Communist Long March to Shaanxi Province |
| 1937–1945 | Japanese domination of China |
| 1946–1949 | Civil War |
| 1949 | Founding of the People's Republic of China |
| 1950–1953 | Land reform |
| 1950–1953 | Korean War |
| 1950–1960 | Period of Soviet aid |
| 1956–1957 | "Let a hundred flowers bloom" |
| 1958–1961 | Great Leap Forward |
| 1966–1976 | Cultural Revolution period |
| 1972 | Nixon visits China |
| 1976 | Zhou Enlai and Mao Zedong die; arrest of "Gang of Four" |
| 1977 | "Four modernizations" program |
| 1978 | New agricultural policies announced |
| 1979 | Sino-Vietnamese War; diplomatic relations established with United States |
| 1981 | Trial of "Gang of Four" concludes; United States grants China most-favored-nation status |

# 1
# Chinese Agriculture: Some Major Issues

*Randolph Barker*
*Radha Sinha*

The Chinese agricultural economy is undergoing a number of changes. The apparently more serious commitment to "agriculture first," demonstrated by recent policy changes designed to encourage agricultural production and increase productivity, has raised the expectations of the Chinese leadership and of many foreign observers. Whether or not government policy can accelerate agricultural production and help achieve a higher standard of living for the people is subject to debate.

Accurate statistics with which to measure the performance of Chinese agriculture are still lacking. Nevertheless, the time seems appropriate to compile a set of articles presenting the many facets of the Chinese agricultural economy — the historical antecedents, the priorities and policies since 1949, the achievements, and the prospects for future growth. This book focuses on the years under communist rule, giving special attention to changes that have been occurring since the death of Mao and what these may portend for the future. In this introductory chapter we present an overview of the Chinese agricultural economy, highlighting many of the issues that are treated in more depth in the following chapters. Although the chapters do not have a common perspective or interpretation of events, we will point out some of the shared viewpoints without attempting to judge the correctness of the various positions taken or the conclusions reached.

On the other hand, it must be recognized that economics as such is not "value neutral." Any development model that does not easily fit Western perceptions is often suspect. Recent policy changes in China would seem to have brought the Chinese development model nearer to Western preconceptions of an appropriate development strategy. It becomes easy for Chinese and Western scholars alike to reject the past as a period of mistaken policy directions, of neglect of economic forces. Our view is that

*1*

· recent changes in agricultural policy, although important, do not reflect a radical break from the past, but rather an evolution in the process of Chinese agricultural and economic development.

## The Setting

Chinese agriculture, developed over a period of several centuries under conditions of land resource constraint and labor surplus, reached a high state of technical development in the premodern period. The technological advances made during this period (Chapter 2) probably permitted a long-term growth in agricultural output equal to concurrent population growth. Notwithstanding crop failures resulting from the vagaries of weather, such as recurrent floods and droughts, by all accounts premodern Chinese farming was remarkably productive on a per hectare basis. Despite comparatively high yields, there is no indication of a significant gain in agricultural productivity as measured by the ratio of output to population. Data on other inputs simply do not exist.

By the mid-twentieth century, most of China had exhausted the possibilities for further agricultural growth using traditional inputs—land, water, and labor. In the fertile lands of southern and eastern China the cropping index already exceeded 150. Agriculture in these areas, as described by Elvin (Chapter 2), was a sort of horticulture requiring intensive management to achieve high yields. Given the serious topographic and climatic limitations, the scope for bringing new land into cultivation elsewhere in the country, with the exception of northeast China, was extremely limited (Chapter 4). Substantial and sustained increases in agricultural output presumably could be attained only by using modern inputs, such as chemical fertilizers or pesticides, supplied by the nonagricultural sector. At the turn of the century such a system of modern agriculture was gradually materializing in Japan. The system was based on (1) a formal agricultural research system, (2) an industrial sector capable of producing inputs such as chemical fertilizers, and (3) a transportation and communication network to insure that these inputs could be supplied to the farmer. Following World War I, Japan extended this system of modern agriculture to her colonies, Korea and Taiwan. Both the political situation and the state of economic development in China precluded a comparable opportunity for modernization of Chinese agriculture until 1950. Throughout the first three decades of the century, prior to war and revolution, Chinese agricultural output continued to grow in the traditional mode, feeding the growing population at or near the subsistence level. Whatever surplus remained above subsistence was appropriated by the landed gentry and the state apparatus, leaving little for direct development purposes.

In 1949 the new communist government found itself in a unique position among the countries of South and East Asia with regard to agricultural development. Even though China shared a long history of population pressure, including a very unfavorable man-land ratio, with Japan and Korea, it lacked the industrial, educational and transport underpinnings necessary for agricultural modernization. Efforts had been made during the Republican Period (1912–1949) to establish an agricultural research system, but continuous war seriously disturbed such work. The industrial sector—except in Manchuria, which was under Japanese rule—largely consisted of consumer goods industries and was grossly ill-equipped to produce inputs such as chemical fertilizers or tractors. Transport and communication networks were extremely disorganized and deficient. The vast and rugged terrain of China was a primary constraint in the development of roads, railroads, and waterways.

Like its neighbors to the south, China lacked many of the preconditions for agricultural modernization. But, unlike China, the countries of South and Southeast Asia had some additional land left and could depend on further exploitation of traditional inputs for a large share of agricultural growth in the decades immediately following World War II.

Most scholars agree that with the expansion of agriculture through use of traditional inputs essentially exhausted, and with population growing at a rapid rate, modernization of agriculture was urgently needed to avoid a deterioration in per capita production and the standard of living. Yet China lacked the industrial base and transportation network needed to follow the pattern of East Asia, nor could such a vast country rely, even temporarily, on the importation of modern inputs. Imported agricultural technology—another possibility—almost always requires adaptive research, and China lacked a functioning research system. As Dernberger (Chapter 5) and Rawski (Chapter 8) note, when the communists came to power they initially attempted to solve agricultural problems using traditional inputs in combination with significant social change, including mobilization of peasant labor.

## The Collectivization of Agriculture

A series of major institutional changes, culminating in the collectivization of agriculture, reshaped the basic structure of the rural economy after the founding of the People's Republic of China. As Stavis (Chapter 6) indicates, these institutional changes were designed to promote the goals of equality, growth, and industrialization. To the present day there has been a

continuing political debate about the most appropriate institutional structure necessary for achieving these goals. Institutional modification has been
a frequent consequence of political and economic changes in China. Two
related issues in this debate have been the degree of priority awarded to
agriculture over industry and the degree of freedom given peasants in production decisions.

Land reform, carried out from 1950 to 1952, destroyed the power of the
rural elite and at the same time provided some land to every rural family.
However, shortages of capital and agricultural inputs continued to be a
pressing problem. In the period from 1954 to 1958 Chinese agriculture was
collectivized and by stages reached the now familiar structure of commune,
brigade, and production team. Radical departures from the traditional
social system initially resulted in a loss of producer incentives. Much of the
sharp drop in agricultural production during the Great Leap Forward
(1958–1961) was the outcome of these changes, although weather was also a
contributing factor. A series of modifications in commune structure followed the disaster. Responsibility for the division of profits was gradually
decentralized from the commune level down to the production team. Some
attempts were made to restore the unit of accounting to the brigade level
during the Cultural Revolution, but since 1976 the trend has been in the
opposite direction.

Dernberger (Chapter 5) discusses the debate on the strategy for the
development of rural institutions and collectivization of agriculture. He
argues that, despite the good intentions of left-wing Chinese leaders, collectivization has led to the "exploitation" of agriculture for industrial development. With the stress on self-reliance, resources were mobilized in rural
areas with limited direct investment by the state. Grain production was emphasized, and the surplus extracted through taxes and quotas at unfavorable producer prices. It should be noted, however, that an urban and
industrial bias has been characteristic of the policies of most developing
countries whether communist or noncommunist. Collectivization undoubtedly facilitated the extraction of surplus from the rural areas. Most of
the capital gained in this way was directed toward key development projects
in the nonagricultural sector.

In the process of modernization of agriculture, was collectivization
necessary or was the earlier land reform sufficient to insure the goals of
equity and productivity? This question is raised by Myers (Chapter 3), who
emphasizes that under East Asian conditions there are few economies of
scale to be realized from large-scale agricultural production. However,
beyond the production and land equity issue per se are the important questions of labor absorption, capital accumulation, and the extraction of
agricultural surplus for industrial development that Dernberger (Chapter

5), Rawski (Chapter 8), and Stavis (Chapter 6) view as important objectives of the collectivization process.

In the absence of modern inputs from the urban industrial center, surplus labor was mobilized under the commune structure for capital investment in agriculture (e.g., irrigation development, land improvement, organic fertilizer production) and for development of small-scale rural industries (e.g., chemical fertilizers, cement, machinery) to supply badly needed inputs for the rural areas (Wong, Chapter 9). Rawski (Chapter 8) observes that China's farm sector succeeded in absorbing nearly 100 million new workers beween 1957 and 1975, amounting to an increase of 40 percent in the agricultural labor force. Despite this, the annual labor input per worker also rose by at least 40 percent.

Not all cultivated land was collectively farmed. Approximately 5 percent remained under private family control, except during the Cultural Revolution when some attempts were made to withdraw this privilege. The private sector specializes largely in the production of highly valued vegetable and meat products. Its contribution, estimated at about 20 percent of agricultural income, is a much larger percentage than its share of total land.

Immediately after 1949 there was a high payoff for mobilization of labor to increase multiple cropping, gather organic fertilizer, and improve irrigation facilities. After three decades it is apparent that the marginal productivity of labor for capital investment in commune agriculture has decreased relative to the profitability of labor in public and private sideline activities. This fact and the short supply of vegetables, fruits, and livestock products are among the underlying reasons for the current interest in creating a more flexible rural commune structure with greater private and small-group initiative in decision making.

## Modernizing Agricultural Production

Chinese agriculture can scarcely be viewed as modern by Western standards, yet the three decades since 1949 have been a period of very rapid modernization. We begin by reviewing the performance of Chinese agriculture in this period and then examine the process by which modernization has taken place.

Measuring the performance of Chinese agriculture is an extremely difficult task. From the end of the Great Leap Forward to the end of the Cultural Revolution almost no statistical information was provided on production. Since the mid-1970s more information has gradually become available, but only very recently has it been possible to make any assessment of regional differences in performance.

For the period 1957 to 1979 grain production in China increased at an annual rate of 2.4 percent, and total agricultural output grew somewhat more rapidly. These growth rates are very consistent with those achieved for India or for the developing countries of South and Southeast Asia. However, there is a considerable variation in performance among Chinese regions, just as in Indian regions.

Broadly speaking, we can say that production in north and central China grew more rapidly than in south and west China, output in nonrice areas grew more rapidly than in rice regions, and that production in the areas of better soil and water conditions grew more rapidly than in the marginal agricultural areas. Of course, there are major variations both among and within regions, as discussed by Barker, Sisler, and Rose (Chapter 11). The growth in grain output was most rapid in northeast China (formerly Manchuria) where cultivated area expanded and hybrid corn varieties were substituted for lower yielding millets, sorghum, and soybeans, and in north China (the North China Plain) due principally to the expansion of tubewell irrigation and the extension of improved varieties of wheat. Yield level and rates of growth in north China have been comparable to those in north India. By contrast, in south China, where rice is the primary crop, grain production between 1957 and 1979 grew at less than 2 percent despite the widespread adoption of modern, fertilizer-responsive, semi-dwarf varieties of rice.

The growth in agricultural production has been accompanied not only by the adoption of modern inputs, but also, as mentioned, by a significant increase in the use of human labor. Rawski (Chapter 8) shows that this has been achieved without a decline in the gross value of output per man-year, although there has been some decline in output per man-day. Also, total productivity, as measured by the ratio of total agricultural output to total inputs, has probably declined. Wiens (Chapter 7) points out that despite the slow gain in factor productivity, there has been substantial technological progress. It is evident that any developing country committed to full employment of surplus labor and achievement of an annual growth in output of 2 to 3 percent cannot initially expect to achieve a significant growth in total factor productivity. Free market economies might be expected to register more rapid growth in productivity at the expense of a higher level of under- and unemployed in the rural economy.

Modern inputs have taken many forms. Pumps replaced hand-powered irrigation lifts to improve efficiency in irrigation and drainage, threshers saved labor at harvest time, and chemical fertilizers in combination with organic fertilizers raised yields. These and many other inputs were produced by small-scale rural industries. As Wong (Chapter 9) illustrates, rural industries varied in terms of economic efficiency, but nonetheless played a vital role in agricultural and rural development. Lacking the capacity to build modern plants for production of fertilizer, cement, iron, steel, farm machinery, and electricity, and to deliver the final product to the farmer, China adopted technologies that, although inefficient by Western standards, seemed appropriate to its conditions.

The development and dissemination of biological technology in agriculture depends to a large degree on public investment in agricultural research and extension. This is true for both free market and centrally planned economies. It is difficult to judge the capacity of the Chinese research-extension system. As in most other developing countries, there is a lack of trained professional researchers, particularly at sophisticated levels. Nevertheless, the low level, applied research-extension system seems superior to that of other developing countries. The so-called "four-level" research network — county, commune, brigade, and production team — has potential for rapidly extending new technologies to the local level. However, there have been instances where political pressure or commandism forced the adoption of inappropriate technologies.

Despite the occasional undermining of scientific research, particularly during the Cultural Revolution, China has succeeded in developing and disseminating modern varieties of rice, wheat, and corn with yield potentials similar to those developed at the international agricultural research centers (International Rice Research Institute [IRRI] and Centro Internacional de Mejoramiento de Maiz y Trigo [CIMMYT]). In 1977 China announced the release of the first $F_1$ hybrid rice variety ever produced, a significant scientific achievement. Both the successes and the problems in Chinese agricultural research are well documented by Wiens (Chapter 7). Because China's agricultural development depends greatly on its capacity to generate new agricultural technology, the question remains: what are the long-term effects of the Cultural Revolution on agricultural research and how long will it take to overcome these effects?

## Income and Consumption

Attempting to measure the performance of the Chinese economy for income and consumption is even more difficult than for production. Production figures give us some guidelines as to how much food was available, but tell us nothing about the distribution of food among regions or between rural and urban areas. There seem to be considerable differences of opinion concerning the degree of equity achieved. One view is that China has solved her food problem, not through extraordinary production gains, but by a more equitable distribution of food. This view seemed to be widely held prior to Mao's death. An alternative, but increasingly popular, opinion is that a significant portion of the population subsists on a substandard diet, "below the poverty line." What is of particular interest is that this recent reassessment of the situation by many Western scholars has paralleled a shift in Chinese public policy statements. The pronouncements by the present leadership have a distinctly negative tone and emphasize the inequity in consumption patterns and the failures of past policies.

By all accounts the gross value of agricultural output between 1957 and 1978 increased slightly faster than population growth in the rural areas. The current average per capita rural income is estimated by the State Statistical Bureau at 170 yuan ($85) for 1980; for urban areas it is much higher. Most sources cite a one- to threefold differential between rural and urban incomes, and it may be higher in some areas. With divergent growth rates of agricultural output and uneven access to factor-endowments as well as to urban markets, there are income differences between and within communes and even within teams. However, many of the interfamily income discrepancies arise largely from differences in labor power (number of healthy adults per family) and not from unequal access to resources or subsidiary income.

As a result of income differentials it is possible that consumption levels in some regions have not shown significant progress. The much publicized CCP Central Committee acknowledgment of 1977 (deleted in the revised version of the same document), stating that "more than 100 million people in rural areas suffered from lack of grain," has been analyzed by many scholars. The consensus seems to be that total caloric consumption was probably not greatly different in 1978 than it was in 1957. This in itself does not explain the extent of hunger described in the official statement quoted above. Lardy (Chapter 10) shows worsening distribution among regions resulting from differing rates of growth in agricultural output, accompanied by an inability or unwillingness of the central government to alleviate the subsequent maldistribution by transfer from surplus to deficit areas. Without questioning Lardy's observation, it still is difficult to interpret the meaning of this and other public statements that pertain to the degree to which minimum grain needs were not being met for a specified segment of the Chinese population. Many observers believe that the distribution of food grains has been more equitable in China than in India and other developing countries of South and Southeast Asia.

A primary reason for depressed consumption has been the high rate of overall savings and investment. Savings have been utilized to develop rural small-scale industries and services such as health care and schooling. As much of the capital construction was achieved by the mobilization of labor, whose opportunity cost is not easy to ascertain in a labor surplus economy, the exact magnitude of the total investment continues to be a matter of debate. The rural investment in China has been rather high in comparison to that of other developing countries. At the same time, however, there seems to have been an underinvestment in agriculture by the central government, and hence a lack of much needed industrial inputs.

Another important aspect of the income and consumption pattern has been population growth. Here again, a lack of reliable data makes it difficult to analyze the situation. However, it is clear that the rate of population growth has gradually diminished over the past decade from more than 2 percent to between 1 and 2 percent. The present leadership regarded this as too high and in 1978 called for a 1 percent growth rate by 1980. Strong rewards and sanctions have been imposed to enforce the concept of the 1- or 2-child family and the program appears to be meeting with considerable success even in the rural areas where traditionally there has been a strong incentive for larger families.

## Prospects for the Future

China is in a period of political change and consolidation. It is far too early to say what effect this change will have on the rural economy. The rates of growth sustained for Chinese agricultural production and productivity will depend on what policy guidelines are pursued by government leaders and whether the inputs and infrastructure can be provided on the scale required. However, whether recent policy changes will promote a more rapid growth in agricultural production is difficult to predict because the degree to which technical as opposed to organizational and management constraints are binding in the short run, and the speed with which either can be overcome, is not certain.

There appears to be restrained optimism regarding recent changes that are expected to improve the economic efficiency of Chinese agriculture. For example, the new strategy of greater specialization should increase efficiency in resource use. In theory, crops will be grown where the conditions of soil and climate are most favorable. There may also be important economies of scale associated with greater regional specialization, but prices will still be set by the state and may not reflect local production costs or resource availability. In addition, there is unlikely to be a reallocation of resources to the best suited crops or crop mixes. The lack of labor mobility may also become an increasingly serious source of inefficiency.

New strategies appear to allow the production team greater control over resources and decision making. Most observers report, however, that the degree of choice is still limited—grain production targets must still be met and production teams are usually not at liberty to grow whatever crop they choose. In spite of the fact that teams have more freedom to sell above quota products at "private" markets, they will not have much say in determination of prices.

Ultimately, growth in agricultural production and productivity must depend on expanding the technical capacity of Chinese agriculture. This is achieved by investing in research to bring about technological change or by investing directly in infrastructure. The apparent underinvestment in agricultural research and in major government irrigation systems during the Mao period is likely to be a deterrent to rapid growth of agriculture in the immediate future. Although there seems to be some potential for further improvements in the management of existing technology and water resources, most of the easy investments have been made. Future gains are likely to require the development of major projects with long gestation periods.

The productivity of labor for capital investment in such activities as irrigation, land reclamation, and composting has been steadily declining with the passage of time. In many parts of China today the opportunities for profitable investment in collective agriculture, particularly grain production, seem to be limited. In contrast to grain production, both public (including nongrain crops and rural small-scale industries) and private (including private agricultural production) sideline activities are showing pronounced growth. They have responded very favorably to policies of the post-Mao period. Sideline activities hold the greatest hope for more productive employment of the rural labor force. Recent vigor of private agricultural production and marketing once again raises the question of the appropriate balance between private and public control over resources in achieving rapid growth.

The peasants appear to be enthusiastic about the changes brought about by the present Chinese leaders. The rise in prices and greater flexibility in production have meant increased opportunities to raise individual income, at least in the short run.

The new leadership is currently emphasizing the need for equity of income and consumption between agriculture and industry, and among the various regions of China. Yet they would seem to be more inclined than their predecessors to sacrifice equity for production targets. Greater flexibility in production decisions may make it difficult for the state to acquire adequate domestic grain supplies without shifting the terms of trade in favor of grain production. Furthermore, an increased requirement for grain imports may divert scarce foreign exchange resources away from imports of capital and technology, which are essential for the "four modernizations."

Success in achieving a higher standard of living will depend in large measure on the campaign to control population growth. While most experts agree that the Chinese targets are ambitious, their success in this area is likely to set an example for other developing countries. The effect of this policy on consumption and living standards will be felt gradually. But the effect on labor supply and employment will not be realized until near the turn of the century. Finding productive employment for a growing rural labor force will continue to be a major problem.

## Lessons from the Chinese Experience

What are the lessons to be learned from the Chinese experience? Is the Chinese model of development transferable? These are questions frequently raised by those concerned with development. The Chinese leadership today is asking similar questions: What are the lessons to be learned from the West? How can China catch up?

We have emphasized the unique set of conditions existing in 1949 that set China apart from its more advanced neighbors in East Asia and from the less developed countries in South and Southeast Asia. Chinese development strategy and institutional reforms bear the mark not only of communist ideology, but also of centuries of cultural and economic development coupled with population pressure on the land.

Although it lacked the necessary preconditions for agricultural development, China did achieve some measure of success in increasing agricultural production and improving the distribution of food. Despite the recent suggestions of shortages, its record of supplying basic needs to the entire population has been more impressive than that of most developing countries. The collectivization of agriculture and related institutional reforms, which facilitated the mobilization of labor and creation of small-scale industries, were an integral part of the development strategy.

It has long been recognized that institutions, policies, and strategies of development that have proved successful in one country are not readily transferable to another. The recent experience of the "Green Revolution" has also emphasized that the appropriate choice of technology is determined by the institutional and socioeconomic setting. There is always the danger that the lessons drawn from another's experience might be the wrong lessons. This fact notwithstanding, it seems reasonable to expect that such risks of error will be more than offset by the benefits derived from the sharing of experience in agricultural development, even more so since the Chinese experience has many unique facets.

In agricultural technology an active program of professional exchange has been underway since 1975. For example, scientists at the International Rice Research Institute in the Philippines are now studying the Chinese technology that produced $F_1$ hybrid rice. Scientists at the International

Potato Center in Peru are analyzing the Chinese technology for producing potatoes from true seed. Chinese scientists are learning more advanced techniques in breeding for insect and disease resistance from these centers. Scientists and scholars on both sides are interested not only in the technology per se, but also in the institutional organization of research and extension that produced this technology.

A seminar was held in 1974 to review Taiwan Province's experience in agricultural development. In a summary, Walter Falcon wrote: "To me the single most impressive aspect of Taiwan agricultural development has been the delicate manner in which agriculture has been provided with labor intensive technology and modern inputs, while at the same time being squeezed heavily in net resource terms."[1] No one would argue that the PRC's approach to agricultural development has been "delicate," and yet the above statement has a great deal of relevance for the Chinese experience. Chinese efforts in the area of labor absorption and mobilization for capital investment deserve special attention by governments confronted with a severe land constraint and a rapidly growing population of landless agricultural laborers.

The modernization of Chinese agriculture is in the formative stage and events of the recent past are still unclear. A glimpse into the future suggests that the road ahead will be as difficult as that already traveled.

**Notes**

1. Walter P. Falcon, "Lessons and Issues in Taiwan's Development," in T. H. Shen, ed., *Agriculture's Place in the Strategy of Development: Taiwan Experience* (Taipei: Joint Commission on Rural Reconstruction, 1974), pp. 269–284.

# 2
# The Technology of Farming in Late-Traditional China

*Mark Elvin*

The way the Chinese farmed in late-traditional times (1350 to 1900 A.D.) was so different from United States and European agriculture today that an effort of imagination is needed to understand it. Some of the keenest early observers with a comparative perspective were the Jesuit missionaries. Their comments on Chinese farmers in the eighteenth century make an easy and appropriate place to begin this process of mental reconstruction.

In the first place, as they saw it, Chinese farming was more like gardening. It produced high yields per hectare from a multitude of adjustments to local conditions arrived at through a constant empirical experimentation. One missionary wrote:

> Most of the farmers have a refined knowledge of weather and time, or, in other words, of the sequence of seasonal change, each one of them as it applies to his own small area. . . . They analyze indifferently . . . the reasons . . . yet they hardly ever make a mistake. . . . [In] plowing, sowing, planting, watering, and the like . . . a European is disconcerted . . . by the boldness and assurance with which from time to time they will act before the ordinary moment. He admires even more the calm and patience they show . . . in waiting and holding everything up until some change for which they have been hoping has occurred. . . . If we were to begin to describe . . . the heroic and invincible curiosity of certain individuals during the last three dynasties, we should cause a certain sort of reader to laugh too much. . . . That said, . . . it seems that a number of fine discoveries are due to bizarre experiments and simple caprice, or even to negligence and mistakes. . . . The little extra efforts and knacks, inventions and discoveries, resources and combinations, which have caused people to exclaim at miracles in gardens, have been transported on a large scale out into the fields and have done marvels.[1]

Late-traditional Chinese farmers were neither "primitive" nor caught in an unthinking technological conservation, but their methods were not scientific in the modern sense of the term. One may guess that many of them acted in the spirit of the Kangxi emperor who, it is said, once had soldiers guard a single stalk of early-ripening rice in a field so that a new strain could be developed from its seeds. A typical example of the unending flow of minor adaptations was the way in which the peasants of Nanhui county shifted in the nineteenth century from fertilizing their cotton plants with pig manure to using aquatic weeds, having found that this reduced the incidence of pests. Some scholars took ideas from old encyclopedias or from gazetteers describing other parts of the empire and experimented with them on their own lands; but much vital practical knowledge about farming never reached the printed page, or was merely sketched:

> They are not content to determine what sort of manure is suitable for each soil. They go on to desire that account be taken of what has been harvested, and what is to be sown, of the weather that has gone before, and that chosen [for a particular operation]. This is because it is necessary to employ one sort of manure rather than another according to whether the year has been dry or rainy, and whether the winter, the spring, the summer, or the fall is chosen.[2]

The Jesuits also noticed that this garden farming was most productive in small units of operation. The constant managerial decisions needed for fine technical tuning were thus in the hands of those closest to the process of production and most directly motivated to take them effectively. The labor power of the whole peasant family could be most efficiently exploited in such a system, and the costly requirements of animal power were kept to a minimum:

> That which has struck us most forcibly in our observations of the Chinese is that a man who farms one acre instead of three is neither short of time nor overwhelmed with work. . . . It is by these means that heavy toil is kept to a minimum, and the small cares of cultivation become the norm, wherein he is assisted by the women and children. . . . [The lands] of peasant proprietors are of an astonishing fertility, in contrast with the large estates.[3]

Finally, the appearance of the countryside was different. There was no Chinese equivalent to common land, especially pastures and forests, and to the large fields farmed under a collective organization in northern medieval Europe. China was, in contrast, a land of ubiquitous private property, operational individualism, minimal reserves, and cultivational uniformity with intensive and continuous arable farming replacing pasturage wherever possible. As the Jesuits wrote: "In France, the land rests every other year. In many places there are vast expanses of virgin soil. The countryside is broken up by woods, pastures, vineyards, parks, and buildings put up for pleasure. Nothing of all that could exist here."[4]

The picture we have outlined here is of northern China. For the Yangtze Valley and the south, one more element must be added: water, and the countless terraced fields and irrigation ditches through which it circulates.

The pages that follow describe the historical development of this late-traditional system and, by implication, the difficulty of developing it further into anything else.

## Long-term Background Trends

The development of Chinese farming technology is best examined against the background of certain long-term trends. For the purposes of a simple description, we may think in terms of the following five periods:

| | | | |
|---|---|---|---|
| Ancient China | 200 B.C. | to | 300 A.D. |
| Sino-barbarian China | 300 A.D. | to | 600 A.D. |
| Medieval China | 600 A.D. | to | 1350 A.D. |
| Late-traditional China | 1350 A.D. | to | 1900 A.D. |
| Modern China | 1900 A.D. | to | the present |

The criteria for these divisions are mainly political. Ancient China corresponds to the first unified empire covering most of China Proper. Sino-barbarian China was politically fragmented, and much of it was ruled by non-Han peoples. Medieval China saw the reestablisment of the empire, a slow transition from an aristocratic to a meritocratic officialdom, and an economic revolution. Late-traditional China had a more absolutist monarchy and the mandarinate, that is to say officials and local elites selected for their mastery of neo-Confucian orthodoxy in competitive examinations.

## The Changing Distribution of Population

Most of the population of Ancient China lived in the Yellow River valley and was fed by dry-field farming. Sino-barbarian and Medieval China saw a massive relative shift to the Yangtze valley and the far south, where wet-field agriculture predominates. In Late-traditional China a balance between north and south was gradually reestablished. In modern times there has been a large-scale movement of Han Chinese into Manchuria, Inner Mongolia, and even Eastern Turkestan.

In Ancient China the total population fluctuated according to economic, epidemiological, and military conditions, but probably never exceeded 60 million. Medieval China experienced a long-term upward trend that increased population, with only two brief periods of decline (approximately in the latter thirteenth and mid-seventeenth centuries), to about 430 million by 1850. One symptom of this trend was that early in the medieval period the main burden of taxation shifted from people, the original scarce resource, to arable land, the new scarce resource. The continuing pressure of population on land was the cause of massive internal migrations and of extensive land clearance and reclamation in river deltas, up hillsides, and in jungles. It focused technological improvement on increasing yields per hectare rather than per man hour.

## The Expansion of Arable Farming

Ancient China lived on millet. Wheat became an important cereal only toward the end of the Sino-barbarian period with the development of better milling machinery. Rice was the staple food of Medieval China with the rise of irrigation-based cultivation in the Yangtze valley and the south. In Late-traditional China, maize, some form of which had existed for a long time in East Asia, acquired a significant role, probably as a result of strains imported from the New World through the Spanish Pacific trading system. Peanuts and sweet and white potatoes came in by the same route at the same time. By about 1700 Chinese agriculture had assumed its final premodern pattern: a basic division into a northern wheat region and a southern rice region, with a variety of other crops being grown on the poorer lands away from the alluvial plains and valley floors.

The expansion of arable farming had two major consequences. First, it ate into land previously used for pasturage. During the medieval period there were still large herds of cattle and sheep in some parts of north China. By late-traditional times it is true, in a broad sense, to say that extensive stock raising began only where the Han Chinese culture area stopped. Sheep, goats, cows, horses, camels, and yaks remained the economic basis of much of the non-Han world of Manchuria, Mongolia, Turkestan, and Tibet into early modern times. China Proper was always short of animal power and animal manures. Its typical livestock in late-traditional times were scavengers: ducks, poultry, and pigs. Whether one looks at transport, machinery, or fertilizer, human effort often supplied what could have been more easily and abundantly provided by animals.

Second, the Chinese natural environment was degraded. The stripping of timber began even before ancient times, but reached its peak in Medieval China when swift economic growth produced a demand for charcoal, houses, and ships that made the commercial growing of forests good business. The destruction of trees caused Late-traditional China to suffer from erosion, as well as rising costs for fuel and building materials. The draining of wetlands also led to frequent floods and droughts by removing the vegetation that had acted as a natural sponge. The wildlife that had provided game became almost extinct, and turning reed swamps into paddy fields removed an important alternative source of fuel. In a sense, Modern China has suffered from the thoroughness of her pre-modern development.

## The Changing Pattern of Land Tenure

The history of land tenure is a controversial subject, but there are four guiding principles that help to make sense of the main variations across time and space.

1. There was a long-term conflict between the state apparatus and the more powerful members of society in their private capacity for the surplus that could be extracted from farmers, whether as taxes or as rents. Relative advantage in this competition varied, depending on such factors as the efficiency of the administration and the extent to which the weight of taxation drove peasants to seek protection from local magnates against the tax collector. Small-scale ownership was in the state's interest, because it made the levy of revenue easier. Further, when the social elite had good alternative sources of income in local politics, trade, money lending, and urban real estate, they became less interested in struggling for the direct rural surplus. This was notably the case in the late-traditional period after about 1700.

2. Large-scale managed farming paid better when large-scale development and reclamation were called for. The opportunities for this decreased during late-traditional times, and the fine tuning of the small-scale operation acquired a comparative advantage. The family farm, whether owned or rented, had always played an important role, but now it completely replaced the managed estate, first in north China, and then in the center and south.

3. Owning land for the sake of extracting rent was more attractive the more fertile the land. The incidence of tenancy in China at the beginning of the modern period varied roughly in accordance with per-hectare yields. Presumably this pattern can be extrapolated some way back into the past.

4. Chinese partible inheritance (as contrasted with European primogeniture, or Japanese inheritance by a single heir) was forever breaking up accumulations of land and forcing each generation, to some extent, to start again.

These four principles are not, in themselves, adequate to account for the remarkable micro-variations in local tenure patterns, even as between counties, nor for such regional peculiarities as the corporate land holdings of lineages in the far south. They do provide the basis for a general understanding of what happened in China during imperial times, at different rhythms in different areas. In particular they predict mixed rather than uniform patterns of management and tenure, owing to the complexity of the causes involved. They predict that the rise of a commercialized economy will be accompanied by a relative shift away from the managed estate toward the family farm, and the withdrawal of elite investment capital from agricultural improvement (as contrasted with the holding of land for prestige or security). As this process of commercialization takes place, they point to smaller holdings of land, once elite fortunes are less used to reassemble large holdings broken up by inheritance, and also to the fragmentation and scattering of land owned by nonfarming landlords who are interested only in rents and not in management. They also suggest the likelihood of intermittent politically inspired disruptions of national or regional tenure patterns, as when the first Ming emperor "nationalized" most of the land in Suzhou and Songjiang because the landowners of these prefectures had opposed him. Above all they provide a good part of an economic explanation as to why serflike conditions of tenure, closely linked to the managed estate, virtually disappeared during the seventeenth century. This is important for our subject, since personal freedom can be an important input in production.

## Crops

If crops are classified by end use, we may distinguish cereals, vegetables and tubers, fruits and nuts, condiments, stimulants, drugs, edible oils, fodder, fibers, fertilizers, fuels, preservatives, and materials for handicrafts and building. In fact, of course, most plants were used for a variety of purposes. The stalks of scented rice served as winter fodder for cattle or, with the pith removed, as material for plaited shoes or ropes; they were also made into paper and served as an ingredient in several medicines. Tong trees were grown primarily for their oil, which could serve both for waterproofing and killing insects. The flowers were also mixed into pig feed. The exploitation of a variety of such interlocking end uses was fundamental to the Chinese peasant economy.

China's staple crops were wheat and rice. In ancient, Sino-barbarian, and medieval times clothes were made mostly from hemp or ramie fibers. Later they were made from cotton, which was introduced from South or Southeast Asia, or from both. Outside these basic items, the Chinese repertoire was extensive and distinctive: water chestnuts, snow peas, bitter melons, Chinese cabbage, lychees, longans, tea, silk, tong-tree oil, soybeans, lacquer, and bamboo. Apart from the vegetarian diet of strict Buddhists, and the Moslem ban on pork, the Chinese had no food taboos. Their open-minded, almost experimental, attitude to eating may have helped to widen the range of crops (and animals) of which they made use.

The logic underlying crop use and crop development was to strike a balance between a variety of environmental and economic factors. The Chinese farmer had to be a virtuoso in deciding what to grow, and where and when to grow it.

The falling ratio of land to labor in the medieval period led to the use of multiple cropping to increase per-hectare yields. A quick ripening rice was borrowed from what is now Vietnam, and two cereal harvests were grown each year: rice in both harvests in the south; rice and wheat in the center. Often vegetables formed a third crop. The need to reduce the risks from natural disasters and to spread the use of labor smoothly through the year prompted the use of types of rice that could be planted and harvested at staggered intervals.

A special salt-resistant strain of rice was developed early in the late-traditional period for the semisaline paddy fields of the southeast coast. In areas of low or uncertain rainfall millet was preferred to wheat because of its superior resistance to drought. Maize was another crop that did well in dry and barren places. Peanuts were planted in sandy soils. Transport costs could also shape cultivation patterns. Thus opium, whose high value for weight made it profitable in remote regions, played an important part in the initial development of the southwest and Manchuria at the beginning of the modern period.

The overriding concern was to enhance what was called "the power of the soil." Beans and rape were often grown in alternation with cereals to preserve soil fertility. Pest prevention dictated the same course with cotton, where possible. On hillsides, which could only be farmed intermittently, turnips and yams were often grown to prepare the land for grains like maize and sorghum. Millet was thought to exhaust the soil more than wheat or pearl barley, so avoiding two successive crops of millet was proverbial peasant wisdom.

*Lu* beans were praised because "they neither harm the land nor exhaust the people," but sometimes there was a trade-off between economizing labor and depleting fertility.[5] Thus one nineteenth century agronomist said of *su* millet that "it is most consuming of the land and also gives poor harvests, but does not use up much human effort."[6]

Symbiotic cultivation and intercropping were both practiced. Beans were grown around mulberries to help the trees. Garden peas were sometimes sown amongst wheat and harvested at the same time. Cotton was sown under millet for later harvesting. *Lu* beans could be planted in similar fashion under rice, and sometimes a second rice crop was sown about ten or fifteen days before the first crop was harvested, in among the standing stalks. Fallowing was used when there was plenty of land, or on vulnerable hill-slopes, but it was uncommon. The use of green manures, spaded back directly into the soil, was also known. In respect to rotations and cropping patterns, Late-traditional Chinese practice was probably slightly ahead of the first agricultural revolution in Europe. Although proper information is not yet available, it seems likely that Chinese seed-to-yield ratios were two to three times higher for wheat in the early eighteenth century than the one-to-five that was the average for Europe.

## Land

Farmland in Late-traditional China can be thought of as a form of fixed capital. It was not a given resource but a means of production created by human effort. This is most obvious where there was terracing, or where water control required the leveling of land and the building of dikes and channels. Land in constant use lost its productive power swiftly unless fertilized. It may be noted that one reason why landlords usually granted tenants a substantial period of tenure was that otherwise there was little incentive for the cultivator to preserve the quality of the soil.

Chinese methods of handling soil were refined, but within the limitations imposed by prescientific knowledge. Fields were sometimes double plowed to promote the retention of moisture. Contouring and the partial preservation of the original vegetable cover were used on hillsides to limit erosion. In Hebei "strong and somewhat dry lands" intended for cotton were kept flooded over the winter. Beds of rice seedlings were prepared by burning a mixture of rotted leaves, dried stalks, and chopped-up desiccated roots on them in winter. In dry weather, vegetables growing in pits were watered indirectly, from a ditch around the pit, lest the water "wash away the power of the fertilizer." The transplanting of taro was justified on the grounds that "plants all like a change of soil — and receive added fertilizing power therefrom." The most laborious of all such operations was the inverted transplantation involved in exchanging the soil around mulberry trees with that from rice fields.

Ideally, paddy fields were prepared for the transplantation of rice shoots by the use of the plow, the heavy harrow, and the fine-toothed harrow in succession. When animal power was not available, a heavy four-pronged hoe was used to break up the earth. Repeated weeding, the most irksome of all routine tasks, was essential for good yields. It was often done crawling, with pads covering the knees and metal tips covering the fingers, although a weeding rake was invented at the end of the medieval period. At its most delicate, weeding was performed with bamboo chopsticks. The plucked weeds were pushed back into the soil to serve as fertilizer and often the soil around the roots of the rice plants was loosened at the same time.

There were five main types of fertilizers. Pressed cakes were made from the casings of cottonseeds, rapeseeds, and various sorts of beans. Crops like clover and astragalus (Chinese milk vetch) were spaded back into the soil as were the ashes of reeds and grasses. There was canal and river mud and, lastly, there was manure from cows, pigs, humans, and other animals. Human excrement was prepared in various ways. It could be diluted in water and mixed with urine and cow-dung for sprinkling on the fields. Or it could be compounded with one-third part of earth and formed into flat briquettes, which were allowed to dry and were spread by crumbling and scattering. Lime and feathers, when available, were also used to improve the condition of the soil.

Chinese farm tools included some sophisticated items. One of the most interesting was the multiple-row seed-drill, with a hopper of silkworm dung that covered the seeds after they had fallen into the furrows. There were wind-breaks, necessary on the open plain of north China; dark cloches, placed over ramie in the early stages of its growth and removed during dull days and nights; low sheds to protect pine saplings from the summer sun; and many others, often very local in their use.

Not many Late-traditional Chinese farming operations would have been easy to mechanize. The high per-hectare yields achieved by the methods of the dedicated gardener were a trap. Further labor saving through the techniques of mechanized farming would have meant lowering these yields in a country where land was in short supply, and hence, probably, lowering total production. Increased production was only possible, outside frontier areas like Manchuria, by using inputs characteristic of the *second* European agricultural revolution: chemical fertilizers, powered water pumps, and the like. A point of technological discontinuity had been reached in Chinese agriculture by the end of the late-traditional period that could not be crossed by the efforts of the agricultural sector on its own.

## Water

The control of water in some form or another affected about half of the total crop area in Late-traditional China. Hydraulic work may be broadly divided into that dealing with irrigation and that with defense against floods. The first type was usually managed by groups of individuals, communities, or collectives, which were typically associations of from half-a-dozen to a hundred villages, or by gentry managers acting with community support and state approval. The role of the government was usually confined to supervision and the arbitration of quarrels that could arise between rival systems or within a system over the sharing of water. The second type was characteristically large scale, involving the building of dikes against floods or the maintenance of channels for drainage, and was normally managed by the authorities. The reasons for this were the high cost, the need for coordination over a wide area, and, in some cases, the separation of the places that did the work from the places that received the benefit.

A more refined classification may be devised as follows.

1. *Irrigation based on aggregates of point sources.* This would include the wells of Hebei, where well associations, modeled on revolving credit societies, would provide their constituent families with wells, the order being determined by lot. Also in this category are the rainwater reservoirs built in the depressions between the hills in Sichuan.

2. *Lake irrigation systems.* Their special feature is a reliable but fixed supply of water. They are little prone to disputes, but do not have much scope for expansion.

3. *River irrigation systems.* In their simplest forms these need only the digging of distributory channels and some method of controlling the amount of water diverted through each channel. The Min River complex in Sichuan is basically of this elementary sort. Where seasonal flows are highly variable, retention reservoirs are also necessary. Systems that discharge into the sea require downstream barrages to prevent saline water backing up into the channels at high tide. Both simple and advanced river irrigation systems need to be periodically closed, by the manipulation of sluices or by the construction of temporary cross dikes, and drained, so as to allow the removal of silt. Riverine networks are characterized by quarrels over shares of water, typically between farmers upstream and those downstream in dry years. Rights in land and water tend to become somewhat separated. In Baotou, early in the nineteenth century, there was even an irrigation scheme run by a garden guild that was so commercialized that shares in water were bought, sold, and borrowed quite independently of the ownership of land.

4. *Polder systems.* There were areas wholly enclosed within dikes, usually at the edge of lakes or in delta lands near the sea. For at least part of each year their interiors were below the level of the surrounding water. They thus combined an irrigational aspect with a defensive one. Whereas lake and river systems exploited gravitational flow down natural gradients, polders required pumps worked by men, animals, or the wind. Because most settlements were also within the dikes, social solidarity and mutual help were highly developed. If any sector of the outer wall were breached, all those inside were to some degree imperiled; gongs would sound and everyone come rushing to repair the damage.

5. *Levees and seawalls.* Good examples are the dikes just below the Yangtze gorges, where seventy counties had to combine their efforts to prevent flooding summer and autumn high water, and the long defensive perimeter that ran from the southern mouth of the Yangtze along the seacoast to Hangzhou.

6. *Drainage.* Channels running through delta lands could become so silted up that areas further inland would be flooded by water unable to find an outlet. This happened periodically in the Taihu lake area south of the mouth of the Yangtze. Under these circumstances the State would mobilize many thousands of peasants, usually by conscription, to do the necessary dredging.

The foregoing classification can be viewed in terms of three criteria: the extent to which water was desired as a precious commodity rather than feared as an enemy, the degree of direct personal welfare gained from the work by those doing the work, and the intensity of the sanctions required by the authorities coordinating the operations. A more detailed account of the policies of water management is beyond the scope of this chapter. Here it is necessary to draw attention only to the central organizational paradox of Late-traditional Chinese agriculture, with which these water-management policies were closely related. Considered from the point of view of working the land, Chinese farming in this period was family based, small scale, and largely composed of individual units. Considered from the point of view of the control of water it was collectivity based, large scale, and characterized by the interdependence of the farming units. The only commonly owned lands and properties in the Late-traditional Chinese rural economy (excluding lineage estates) were those belonging to water control organizations, who used the revenue therefrom to pay part of the cost of their personnel and installations.

During the late-traditional period the organization of systems of types 2, 3, and 4 changed. Broadly speaking, consortia of large landowners were replaced by collectivities of the actual cultivators (whatever their tenurial status), or by publicly selected gentry managers, or by a combination of these two. One symptom of this change was that water control bodies often had difficulty in extracting from absentee landlords the contributions they were supposed to make to hydraulic works. At the same time new and worthwhile projects became more and more difficult to find. Overbold irrigation could lead to salinization through leaching. In polder areas, floods sometimes resulted when dikes were squeezed too close together and drainage channels were constricted. In Modern China, the use of metal pipes, powered pumps, concrete, underground irrigation, and other new techniques has transformed the picture. Where capital and labor have been available, large improvements in per-hectare productivity through new irrigation schemes have been proven possible. The requirements of scale have intensified the integration of administration characteristic of water control. State-run water systems now typically cover several communes, and often more; and the relationships between their administrations and that of the communes and brigades seem to be a problem that has not been fully solved.

Another approach to water control lies through the methods used to move water. These were basically four: (1) gravity, (2) man- and animal-powered pumps, (3) water- and wind-powered pumps, and (4) in modern times only, gas, diesel, and electric pumps. The most primitive Chinese water-moving machine was the well-sweep, a counter-balanced bailing bucket suspended from a pole or frame. A variant of this was the water shuttle, a suspended beam with a channel cut along it, down which the water ran from a scoop at one end. More sophisticated was the "dragon's backbone pump," in which a chain of linked rectangular pallets was drawn up a sloping trough. It was usually worked by foot, by pedals like those of a rudimentary bicycle, and was ergonomically efficient in that it used the heavy muscles of the leg. The Archimedean screw, which the Chinese termed the "dragon's tail pump," was known on paper at least since the early seventeenth century, thanks to the Jesuit writings in Chinese on Western hydraulics. It was experimented with in the nineteenth century, but never found much, if any, practical use. The paternoster pump, consisting of a pipe up which water is drawn by balls spaced out along a circulating chain, was unknown in Late-traditional China. Such man-powered pumps, with the exception of the last two, were used in the flat lands in the lower valleys of the great rivers. Their high demand for labor when the rice fields had to be flooded or drained was a key constraint on the total production of a farming household.

In upland areas where there were strong currents, it was possible to use norias moved by the same streams that fed them. These were huge wheels with pots mounted around their circumference, and canted so as to pick up water at the bottom of each revolution and to pour it into a flume just beyond the top of each revolution. Chinese wind pumps were invented early in late-traditional times, and likewise had a limited geographical range. Only in coastal areas were there adequate winds to justify their construction. In shape they resembled large horizontal turntables with masts and sails mounted around the periphery. When the wind was abaft, the sails swung out sideways to the limit allowed by fixed sheets. When it was ahead they swung into an end-on alignment that offered the minimum resistance. They are said to have been effective in light breezes, but easily damaged by gales.

Powered pumps appeared early in the present century. Sometimes they were mounted on so-called "dragon boats" that went around the canals pumping water in and out of fields for a fee. The very gradual spread of the use of concrete has also begun to reduce the annual burden of maintaining the soft earth dikes that surround the individual fields.

## Animals, Fish, Poultry, and Insects

The economic exploitation of the animal kingdom by the Chinese was multifaceted and often original. Among the more unusual aspects was the use of trained cormorants and otters for fishing. The cormorants had rings around their necks to prevent them from swallowing their catch. The otters were on long leashes, and frightened the fish off the river bottom into their masters' nets. Biological pest controls were appreciated: ducks to eat locusts in the crawling stage of their development, and ants to control the insects that infest orange trees. In Manchuria and Mongolia there were small dog farms that raised and killed these animals for their skins.

Leaving aside these curiosa as testimonies to Chinese ingenuity and versatility, the main distinction to be drawn regarding the use made of animals and other living creatures in late-traditional times is between Han China and the vast but thinly populated non-Han periphery. This outer area was a world of herds: of cattle, yaks, cattle-yak crosses, sheep, goats, camels, and horses. Meat, milk, fibers, hides, and transport were provided by a range of breeds and hybrids finely adapted to altitude, aridity, and other local conditions. In contrast, the Han core was a world where the larger animals were kept singly or in small groups. Their chief value was power, for plowing, turning machinery, and transport. The so-called "yellow cow" predominated in the north. The central and lower Yangtze and the south were the domain of the water buffalo, which not only tolerated but enjoyed mud and wet conditions. There were modest numbers of horses, donkeys, mules, and hinnies, used almost entirely for transport. Meat was provided by pigs, pariah-type dogs (in the south and along the Korean border), ducks, chicken, and geese. Fish were raised in specially constructed pools. Fibers came from small groups of sheep, reared in pens and fed by hand with cut grass and leaves, and from silkworms.

Early in the modern period, crossing with breeds from other countries began to modify most of the late-traditional types of Chinese livestock. Today many of the old strains have all but vanished in their pure form. The alertness of Chinese breeders to the advantages of Friesian and Holstein cattle, Berkshire and Landrace pigs, Merino and Rambouillet sheep, and Leghorn chickens was a continuation of the same sensitivity to variation and flair for selection that had earlier produced the goldfish from the carp, and bred the Pekingese dog to look like the spirit lion of Buddha. The guess may be hazarded, however, that cattle- and buffalo-breeding in late-traditional times suffered from the lack of large herds. A village would typically have had one or perhaps two hundred cattle, with most of the males castrated to make them docile. The practical range of choice for a peasant seeking to have his cow covered cannot have been large; and any systematic, long-term breeding policy would have been impossible in conditions of fragmented ownership.

There was a significant contrast between best practice and common practice. The words of the Song agronomist Chen Fu are eloquent on this subject:

> Those who look after cattle must first learn to feel affection for them. . . . They must regard hunger and thirst in an ox as if it were their own hunger and thirst. They must look on misery and an emaciated condition in an ox as if they suffered from these afflictions themselves. They must view an ox's sickness as they view their own. And when a cow has given birth to a calf, they must treat it like their own child. If this can be achieved, the cattle will increase and multiply. . . . At the start of spring, all the straw and manure that has accumulated in the cattle pen must be mucked out. And not just in the spring, either, but every ten days, to prevent the steamy fug of contaminated ethers that cause diseases. If hooves become sodden with water, sickness can also easily occur. . . . In the spring and summer when the grass is lush, let them eat their fill without restraint when you put them out to pasture. But before you do so, they must have a drink of water, and only be given grass after that, lest their bellies should become swollen.
>
> . . . Around three o'clock in the morning, take advantage of the fact that the sun is not out and the air is cool to put them to work. Their strength will be twice the normal, and a day's work can be done in less than half a day. When the sun is high in the sky and they are panting with the heat, let them rest and do not overtax their strength, and so bring about their exhaustion. . . . Do not work them too hard — that is the essential point to observe. . . . The reason why oxen get tired and thin is that people think only about immediate emergencies and forget to show them compassion. . . . What is more, when fields were divided up in ancient times, it was the system always to have some fallow land for pasture. . . . In this way stock raising and grazing were properly provided for. The animals were large and fat, and did not suffer from skin infections. . . . In later times there have been no fallow lands for pasturage, and since then [cattle] have not been properly provided for.[7]

The maintenance of animal power was something of a weak link in the Late-traditional Chinese economy.

Differential access to such power was a source of variation in productivity and prosperity. It was not just a question of plowing hard soils and clearing new land. In many agricultural industries, such as crushing sugar-cane, animal power was indispensable if water power was not available. In some areas there were "ox-lords," comparatively well-to-do persons who hired out cattle in somewhat the same way that a landlord rented out land. An alternative system was for peasants to raise cattle or buffaloes on behalf of their owner, giving him three calves out of every four and labor services as payment. The distribution of the ownership of animal power was in the main aligned with land-owning status, but could diverge quite remarkably in particular localities. The strongest breeds of buffalo could plow up to 0.5 hectares in a day. Since the median annual crop area of Chinese farms early in the modern period was only 1.5 hectares, the renting of oxen was thus more or less built into the structure of garden agriculture.

Wealth in the form of animal power was more precarious than wealth in land. Epizootics took a severe toll of livestock, and loss of draught animals could bankrupt a household or even ruin a village. To guard against theft, cattle were often kept in a family's living quarters. In spite of the insistence of traditional agricultural theorists on cleanliness, they were closely confined to ill-ventilated and filthy conditions, and frequently housed with pigs. Since at least Song times the Chinese had understood that infection often spread from sick animals to well ones, and had tried to separate the ill from the healthy by various means, such as a ban on cattle markets at times of animal plagues. Chinese premodern veterinary medicine, which was mostly herbal, seems to have been at best of limited effectiveness.

The Chinese methods of raising pigs, sheep, poultry, fish and silkworms had in common the creation of a controlled artificial environment for at least part of the animals' life cycles. To this extent they may be seen as a premodern approach to factory farming. One consequence was that the peasant was made aware of the cost of his inputs, many of which had to be bought in the market. In some areas, such as the supply of baby fish, part of the production process was almost entirely commercialized and not in the hands of the individual peasant household.

An obvious example is the use made of incubators for hen, duck, and goose eggs. The largest of these handled over a thousand eggs at a time. Basically, they were double walled earthenware jars, with charcoal heating between the two walls. Control of the varying temperatures required was a refined skill. The incubator operators were specialists who bought their eggs from the peasants and sold live chicks back to them.

The management of the covered pig pen was also an art, although not a separate profession. Small individual pens kept the pigs inactive and made them fatter. Female piglets had to be separated from their mothers after weaning or they frolicked about and did not eat enough. Filth in the pig pens was a good thing as it (allegedly) kept them cool and so free from sickness. Pens were, however, warmed in winter. The boars were castrated to make them gain weight, and there were several traditional fattening mixtures said to bring them to peak condition in a few days.

The design of fishponds was meant to include a number of islands to make the fish swim in circles, as sudden turns at the end of the pond were thought to make them uncomfortable. Also, the depth of the water had to vary. New fish had to be put into the water silently. An old popular belief prescribed that freshwater turtles should be kept in carp pools, to stop the fish from flying away led by a dragon. The evaluation of the usefulness of these practices awaits research. Species other than carp had to be fed. It was reckoned that a thousand fish needed about 200 kilograms of hay a day, except in winter, when the fish were dormant on the bottom of the pond.

Raising silkworms was a delicate art. The essential stages were the selection and mating of the moths; the laying of the eggs on heavy paper sheets and their storage; the selective killing of weak eggs by dipping the sheets in brine or exposing them for a time to the winter weather; the hatching and constant feeding of the larvae in bamboo trays filled with mulberry leaves; the spinning of the cocoons on frames covered with straw cocks; killing and preserving some of the cocoons for later reeling by dry or wet salting, or by heating with fire, steam, and sunlight; and killing the others in nearly boiling water, and reeling off the filament in the brief time before the new moths broke through and spoiled the silk. Uninterrupted and wearisome attention was needed for four to six weeks for a crop of cocoons. There were many hazards, including disease, rats, and a shortage of leaves. Not surprisingly, production was surrounded with social taboos and superstitions.

The silkworm house was another example of a carefully controlled environment. The larvae needed warmth, dryness, and light, and an absence of drafts, smoke, and latrine smells. The following is a description of such a house quoted in a late-traditional book on farming:

> There are roll-up blinds on all sides. In the center is sunk a mature fire [consisting of alternate layers of tightly packed dried ox dung and broken up dried firewood in a deep brick-lined pit, allowed to smolder for some days before the hatching of the larvae, the smoke being cleared from the house at the last minute]. If the weather is cold and the worms desire warmth, close the straw blinds and the cold will not enter from outside, while inside they live in a comfortable atmosphere. . . . If the weather is warm and the worms desire cool, damp down the fire and roll up the straw blinds, so that the heat inside grows less and the cool airs enter. If the heat is so great that even with the blinds entirely rolled up it cannot be overcome, remove the paper covering the windows, roll up the skylights [?] and open the wind-vents below. On silkworm frames outside the windows sprinkle fresh water, and the cool airs will

penetrate everywhere. When the heat has passed, paste up the windows again, and close the wind-vents, so that from beginning to end the worms suffer from neither heat nor cold.[8]

These techniques of environmental control had something in common with those used in the traditional Chinese greenhouse, supplied with paper windows, blinds, braziers, and pans of water to increase humidity, and with the damp underground spinning cellars used to stop cotton yarn snapping in the dry North.

## Labor

The supply of labor power in a peasant household was largely a given factor at any one time. This is of course the basic difference between the textbook peasant and the textbook capitalist entrepreneur, who varies inputs of both capital and labor as profitability dictates. For a peasant, the fundamental economic decisions revolved around the question of how to make the best use of the labor available in his family. An example from late-traditional times may be found in *Mr. Shen's Book on Farming*, which was written in the seventeenth century. It shows clearly the rational and calculating mentality of the peasant of these times, and the matter-of-fact reliance on the market in long-range forward planning:

When Xing Suzu died, his mother was old and his [two] sons were young. He bequeathed to them only ten *mou* [0.7 hectare] of farmland, a pool, and a house a few columns wide. . . . Regarding their inheritance, I would plan as follows:

If a family farm ten barren *mou* themselves, these will provide them with all the food they need. If they hire others to farm it for them, it will be no different from owning fields of stones. Renting it to others will furnish only enough in rent to meet taxes and labor services. . . . A plan must be made for circumstances in which there is not enough labor power for arable farming. . . . It would be best (1) to plant three *mou* with mulberry trees. (Green vegetables should be planted under the mulberry trees in winter, and beans and taro all around them. . . .) (2) To plant three *mou* with beans. (When the beans are up, plant wheat or, even better hemp. The reason for not planting rice is to economize on labor power . . .) (3) To plant two *mou* with bamboos. (Plant an assortment of large and small, and of those with early- and late-ripening shoots, all of which can be traded for rice.) (4) To plant two *mou* with fruit. (For example, plums, pears, jujubes, and oranges, all of which can be traded for rice. . . . Take into account their natures: some do well in rich soil, some in poor. Below those that like rich soil plant melons and vegetables . . .) (5) To rear fish in the pool. (The rich mud from it should be put onto the bamboos' soil, and the rest used to bank up the mulberries. At the end of the year the fish can be exchanged for rice.) (6) Keep five or six sheep to provide manure for the mulberry and other trees. (Lambs can also be exchanged for rice. Rearing pigs requires a capital outlay, whereas sheep can be fed on nothing but grass.)

All their fields are high up, and so rice cultivation will always be in difficulties because of water. Since growing beans and mulberries takes less labor, it is possible to manage them, given an effort; and there will be no anxieties about drought. Although bamboos and fruit are not basic farming, once the initial exertion has been made, there is no more hard work, and their benefits may be enjoyed within five years. (I estimate that the mulberry harvest should feed 24 trays of silkworms, and that when the worms have matured 40 pounds weight of silk thread may be obtained. . . . When the beans and wheat come up, I estimate that they will feed two people. Hemp is twice as profitable, but it also requires twice the labor. If one is short of labor power, it is best to grow wheat. Once the bamboos are grown, each *mou* will support one or two people. When the fruit trees are mature, each *mou* will support two or three persons, and there will still be some profit left over. If the fish do well, each *mou* [of pond] will support two or three persons, but only half that number if a miscellaneous assortment of fish is reared.) . . . When the boys are grown, they will be capable of handling cereal growing, and buy several additional *mou* of land with their surplus profits.[9]

Farm technology has thus always to be considered in relation to the labor available, and the pattern of work changed as a family moved through the cycle of reproduction, aging, death, and division, with its changing assortment of hands to work and mouths to feed.

The planning of the farming year, with its interlocking activities, was a related challenge. A relatively simple calendar of work for south China is given in Table 2.1. It comes from Bao Shichen's book on agriculture, written in the first half of the nineteenth century. More complicated schedules can be found in the pre-Modern Chinese literature, some with distinct tasks listed for bright and for rainy weather; but this calendar, although it omits such important operations as the maintenance of the irrigation system, conveys a good general picture.

The variations in the need for labor power across the year are evident. There was a period of feverish activity in May and June, in which planting, transplanting, harvesting, and sericulture were all going on simultaneously. Counterbalancing this was a slack season from November to February. The other months contained an intermediate amount of work, either planting or harvesting, or both, with a partial hiatus in mid-July. The imbalance was more pronounced still in the north. Broadly speaking, the use of labor in late-traditional farming was caught between two constraints: high requirements during key operations that had to be done within a limited span of time, notably transplanting, irrigating, and harvesting; and the absence of enough work for the peak-period labor force at other times. J. L. Buck, including subsidiary work in his calculation, estimated the average idle time of an able-bodied male farm worker at 1.7 months a year around 1930, more than half of it in December and January.

Three observations are called for on this last point. First, some of the spare time, which, in aggregate but not in distribution, was the equivalent of having Sundays off, must have been needed for rest and recreation and for festivals, visits to shrines and graves, and generally for social life. Second, the use of labor in the Chinese peasant economy has to be considered in the context of the market for handicrafts, local industries, and services that could provide jobs in the off season. This premodern commercialization expanded in the late-traditional period. The result was a complex pattern of interlocking agricultural and nonagricultural use of labor. Third, the more intensive specialization and industrialization of the modern period has tended to destroy the nonagricultural part of this pattern. (One example that will serve for many is the ending of part-time coal mining from shallow deposits by farmers.) Farming has been forced to become more specialized. Unless this is counterbalanced by other developments that can flatten the seasonal curve of demand for manpower, this leads in the Chinese context to an increasing underuse of rural labor.

Lastly, peasants have a significant level of leisure preference. Hence it is reasonable to suppose (following Chayanov) that an economically free peasant will work until such a time that the irksomeness of the input of extra labor at the margin is balanced by the utility of the extra labor at this margin. If part of his output is now taken away from this peasant in the form of rent or taxes, it is also reasonable to suppose that he will work in the altered situation for a certain quantity of *extra* time, such that a new equilibrium is reached between the irksomeness of his toil at the margin and the marginal gain in output, net of rent or tax deductions, that he can actually enjoy. The peasant loses twice: He works longer hours and he eats less. However, total farm output is greater. This could be expressed epigrammatically by saying that exploitation can be a form of fertilizer. That there can also be serious negative effects, especially if the diet of the peasant is reduced to the point where his labor power is impaired, does not affect the general thrust of the argument. Historically, this process of exploitation was probably a major means whereby the growth of state power (and military and administration requirements), and the growth of cities

Table 2.1. Simple Calendar of Farmwork for South China, Early Nineteenth Century

| | |
|---|---|
| Feb. 5–Feb. 18 | Repair farm tools. Bathe silkworms [to kill weak ones]. Hoe wheat and barley. Weave straw shoes. Weave straw mats [on which silkworms will spin]. Cut tree branches and burn them on land on which crops are to be grown. |
| Feb. 19–Mar. 4 | Transplant and cut pines and bamboos. Repair fences. Transplant mulberry seedlings. Muck out cow manure [accumulated in the winter in the byres]. Pinch off rape flowers. |
| Mar. 5–Mar. 19 | Layer mulberry branches [to produce new saplings]. Fertilize rape. Put fish fry [into pools]. Insert willow shoots. Make beancurd. |
| Mar. 20–Apr. 4 | Manure barley. Hoe garlic. Plant scallions. Plant tea. Plant yams. Plant early taro. Plant red hibiscus. Soak [rice] seeds [in a nutrient solution before planting]. Plant indigo. Mate cattle and horses. Warm silkworms. Put ginger seeds in mounds. Plant melons and gourds. |
| Apr. 20–May 4 | Plant rice and green vegetable seeds. Brush newly hatched silkworms. Plant ramie. Plant eggplant, edible greens, and lettuce. Pound the threshing floor. Gather elm seeds. Plant rushes, millet, and maize. Plant sweet potato sprouts. |
| May 5–May 20 | Reap barley. Prune mulberry trees. Plant ginger. Irrigate beans. Harvest mulberry fruit. Fell trees. Transplant rushes, millet, and maize. Harvest peas and broad beans. Plant late taro. Pull up garlic. |
| May 21–June 5 | Harvest wheat. Transplant early ripening rice. Plant cotton. Plant linseed. Harvest rape. Put silkworms on straw mats [on frames]. |
| June 6–June 20 | Transplant intermediate ripening rice. Plant millet. Weed early ripening rice. Harvest ramie. Transplant indigo. Pull up red hibiscus. Reel silk off cocoons. |
| June 21–July 6 | Transplant late ripening rice. Plant mulberry fruit [to grow new saplings]. Plant hemp. Weed intermediate ripening rice. Plant later ripening red hibiscus. Cut and insert sweet potatoes. |
| July 7–July 22 | Weed late ripening rice. Harvest "cocoon rice." Fell bamboos. |
| July 23–Aug. 6 | Plant second crop rice. Pick green lentils. Reap ramie. Gather firewood. Dry everything in the sun. Harvest early ripening rice. Plant buckwheat. Gather cotton. Harvest locust tree flowers [for their yellow dye]. Cut the varnish tree [to draw off lacquer]. Pound the threshing floor. Plant cabbages and turnips/carrots. |

*Table 2.1 continued*

Aug. 23–Sept. 7    Plant *lu* beans and soybeans. Pull up indigo.

Sept. 8–Sept. 22   Transplant cabbages, turnips, and carrots. Gather jujubes.
                   Harvest intermediate ripening rice. Harvest maize. Pluck
                   second crop of red hibiscus.

Sept. 23–Oct. 7    Plant early ripening wheat. Repair granaries. Harvest reeds
                   and millet. Harvest millet. Reap ramie. Gather mulberry
                   leaves [and store in earthenware jars].

Oct. 8–Oct. 23     Harvest late ripening rice. Harvest linseed and soybeans. Plant
                   rape. Gather juniper seeds [for oil]. Gather lotus leaves. Plant
                   peas and broad beans.

Oct. 24–Nov. 6     Dig up taro. Dig up ginger. Pluck cotton. Pluck up sweet
                   potatoes. Make stooks of rice straw. Keep back turnip and
                   carrot seeds [for future sowing]. Plant garlic.

Nov. 7–Nov. 21     Dig up turnips and carrots. Dig up yams. Harvest winter
                   melons. Salt vegetables. Plant late wheat. Store seeds for all
                   grains and vegetables. Plant black cabbage. Reap rushes.

Nov. 22–Dec. 6     Weed wheat and barley. Plow the paddy fields. Manure the
                   hemp fields. Reap rushes [for making mats]. Bind various
                   trees [in the sapling stage with straw to stop them suffering
                   from cold]. Make lime by burning.

Dec. 1–Dec. 20     Ferment wine [from glutinous rice]. Harvest the fruit. Scoop
                   up mud from the waterways [to use as fertilizer]. Weave
                   rushes [into mats].

Dec. 21–Jan. 5     Manure wheat. Bury various sorts of grain to forecast the
                   coming year. Drain the fish pools. Fell timber. Collect bamboo
                   stems.

Jan. 6–Jan. 20     Chill silkworm eggs. Collect snow-water. Pluck mulberry
                   leaves.

Jan. 21–Feb. 4     Hoe green vegetables and wheat and barley. Dig pits for
                   melons and ginger.

The planting of other vegetables (such as onions and leeks), and the repair of
other equipment (such as the weaving of storage containers and the twisting of
ropes) are done during the moments of leisure from farming. There are no fixed
seasons.

[Dates are Western.]

---

Source:  Bao Shichen, *Qimin sishu* (Four Techniques for Ruling the Com-
         mon People), early nineteenth century, in *Anwu sizhong* (First published
         1844, n.p.: Zhuqingtang, reprint of 1872), ch. 25, pp. 29a–30a.

(where high-spending landlords lived), promoted technical advance in agriculture.

## Conclusion

This outline account of late-traditional farm technology in China has left out important aspects. The cultivation of trees, apiculture, tea, the use of insect- and bird-repellents, storage and storage strategy to cope with annual variations in the size of harvest, the use of wild plants for survival when famine did strike, the wastage of land through the overdivision of fields in dry farming areas are all obvious examples of these omissions. Other topics have been touched on only lightly. The provisional conclusion should, however, be clear. The best late-traditional Chinese farming was remarkably productive per hectare, by any premodern standards. How far the average fell below the best must remain at present an unanswered question. The chief immediate constraint on productivity per worker in China Proper was the shortage of good arable land. Where this constraint did not exist, as in Manchuria during the first half of the twentieth century once the old imperial prohibition of Han Chinese migration there had been lifted, the premodern techniques could and did produce a substantial marketable surplus. With the exceptions of moving water (by using valve-and-piston pumps), more hygienic care of cattle used for draught purposes, and the consolidation of fields in dry farming regions, there were hardly any easily available ways of increasing agricultural output at the beginning of the modern period. This was a task that, fundamentally, called for industrial and scientific inputs.

## Notes

1. *Mémoires concernant les Chinois* (Paris: Nyon, 1776–1814), 14 vols., "Par les missionaires de Pékin," vol. 11, "Observations sur les plantes de la Chine," pp. 210–226.

2. *Ibid.,* vol. 11, p. 228.

3. *Ibid.,* vol. 11, p. 236.

4. *Ibid.,* vol. 4, "Mémoire sur l'intérêt de l'argent en Chine," p. 320.

5. *Lu* bean or "mud-yellow bean" (ni huang dou) was commonly used as animal feed or fertilizer.

6. Bao Shichen, *Qimin sishu* (Four Techniques for Ruling the Common People), in *Anwu sizhong* (first published 1844, n.p.: Zhuqingtang, reprint of 1872).

7. Quoted in Oertai et al., eds., *Shoushi tongkao* (Complete Investigation of the Transmission of Seasonal Practices in Agriculture) (Peking: Zhonghua shuzhu, 1956 reprint), vol. 2, ch. 41, pp. 903–904.

8. *Ibid.*, vol. 2, ch. 72, pp. 1651–1652.

9. *Shenshi nongshu* (Mr. Shen's Book on Farming) (Beijing: Zhonghua Shuzhu, 1956 reprint), ch. 2, pp. 47–48.

## Readings

Buck, John L. *Land Utilization in China,* vol. 1. Nanking: University of Nanking, 1937; New York: Paragon (reprint), 1964. The easiest first reference for facts about Chinese farming in the 1920s and 1930s.

Elvin, Mark. "On Water-Control and Management during the Ming and Ch'ing Periods," *Ch'ing-shih wen-t'i,* vol. 3, Nov. 1975. A brief introduction to a vast subject inadequately covered by the Western literature.

Epstein, H. *Domestic Animals of China.* Farnham Royal: Commonwealth Agricultural Bureau, 1969. A descriptive account based on present-day information.

King, Franklin. *Farmers of Forty Centuries.* London: Cape, 1972; revised edition, 1949. The basic text for anyone trying to develop a feeling for traditional Chinese agriculture.

Motonosuke, Amano. *Chūgoku nōgyō-shi kenkyū* (Studies on China's Agricultural History). Tokyo: Ochanomizu shobo, 1962. The basic reference for the historical development of Chinese farm technology. In Japanese, with extensive citations in Chinese.

Perkins, Dwight H., et al. *Agricultural Development in China 1368–1968.* Edinburgh: Edinburgh Publishing Co., 1969. The most comprehensive historical survey. Very valuable, although the premodern statistics should be treated with caution.

Rawski, Evelyn S. *Agricultural Change and the Peasant Economy of South China.* Cambridge, Mass.: Harvard University Press, 1972. Two regional surveys, of Ming Fujian and of Qing Hunan. Excellent on technology and marketing, less satisfactory on the social organization of farming.

Shiba, Yoshinobu. *Commerce and Society in Sung China.* Ann Arbor: Center for Chinese Studies, University of Michigan, 1970. Although not explicitly on agriculture, contains a wealth of incidental material on specific products and techniques of production.

Shi, Minxiong. *The Silk Industry in Ch'ing China.* Ann Arbor: Center for Chinese Studies, University of Michigan, 1976. Covers both traditional sericulture and early modernization.

# 3

# Land Property Rights and Agricultural Development in Modern China

*Ramon H. Myers*

Land distribution in China during the 1930s was extremely unequal. A 1935–1936 Nationalist government survey of 1.8 million rural households in 22 provinces showed that about 80 percent of the farming communities owned only 40 percent of the land.[1] Many village surveys also indicated that one out of every three or four households did not own any land. Although figures vary, it is clear that land ownership was concentrated amongst a small proportion of the rural households. Examining the character of China's land tenure system and analyzing how this system influenced rural development is an issue of overwhelming importance.

Although many perceived the distribution of land and rural income as unequal, were conditions in the countryside really as they seemed? If faulty sampling and survey procedures produced results that distorted the true distribution pattern of land and income, might the distribution pattern have been more equitable or less? How did inequalities of land and income distribution actually influence agricultural development over the long term in China? Alternatively, did the pattern of agricultural development influence the distribution of land and income?

The investigation of land tenure systems shows that a large number of apparently tenant households were actually bona fide landowning households. If this is so, the estimated number of tenant and part-tenant households renting land during the 1930s should be readjusted.

During the early twentieth century Japan and Taiwan achieved rapid growth rates for agricultural production even with land distribution that was as unequal, or more so, as that of China. To resolve this paradox we must focus upon the complex interaction between agricultural technology, family farm decision making, and rural market forces. We will study the path of agricultural development from 1870 to 1937 in the context of regional patterns of land distribution. We hope to clarify connections that may exist between land tenure systems and the process of rural development.

## Land Tenure Systems

There were five ways for tenants to pay landlords for land use. Although these land tenure systems were found in diverse areas, a definite relationship existed between the particular tenure system and the physical characteristics of the region, as outlined below.

In a *labor tenancy* arrangement the tenant supplied a specified number of days of labor to the landowner in exchange for the right to farm some land. This system was rather rare by the second quarter of the twentieth century, but it existed in Hebei, Shandong, Henan, Shanxi, Jiangsu, Hubei, Sichuan, Fujian, Guizhou, and Ningxia.[2] Both parties agreed on the number of days of work per unit of land (usually 1, 2, or 3 days per mou). Sometimes the tenant even agreed to pay a certain amount of the harvested produce to the landowner, but labor was the major payment made.

The contractual *crop-sharing tenancy* existed everywhere in China and was referred to by many different terms. In this tenure system the landowner and tenant agreed to share a certain percent of the total harvest. Three main variants of this system existed. The first involved the landowner supplying seed, fertilizer, and tools to the tenant. Under this system in Xiao County of Jiangsu the tenant received 20 percent of the harvested crop and the landowner the remaining 80 percent.[3] The more common crop-sharing arrangement was for the owner to supply bare land and leave its management entirely to the tenant who supplied his own labor and capital. Under such contracts tenants usually received 50 percent (in Hebei) to 75 percent (in Shaanxi) of the crop. A third arrangement was for several households to collectively farm a landowner's land and pay him a certain percentage of the harvested crops. In many areas of north China, villagers used the crop-sharing contract because it was regarded as the safest system, given the extreme variability of local weather. Under this contract both parties were guaranteed some share of the harvested crop, even if weather conditions reduced the harvest far below the normal level.[4]

Generally, once the contract was concluded, the landowner did not interfere with tenant management. This could change if the landowner advanced farming capital to the tenant. Share-crop rent contracts usually ran for between one and three years, but were renewable if both parties agreed upon renegotiating. A few written contracts have survived, but village surveys report that farmers usually made oral agreements. The landowner generally terminated the contract if the tenant delayed paying the rent or failed to fulfill certain contractual agreements to the landowner's liking.

Then the landowner merely replaced his former tenant with a new one. The share-rent system did not make any allowance for reducing rent even when the harvest had been poor. North China village survey evidence shows that crop-sharing contracts were used most often by landowners who had poor soils that gave low yields.

The *fixed-rent tenancy* system was frequently referred to by terms like "guaranteed rent" or "fixed amount of rent." Under this system a fixed amount of the crop was paid as rent for the right to farm a unit of land. There were some areas where landlords commuted fixed-crop rents into cash payments. This variation existed mainly in southeast China, but not in the north where payments in kind were customarily made each cropping season. As under the crop-sharing system, landowners could invest capital in the farmland if they wished. Under the fixed-rent system the crop rent was supposed to remain unchanged over time. However, not only did many landowners permit their tenants to delay paying rent if the harvest had been poor, but in actual practice perhaps as many as four out of five landowners permitted some form of rent reduction. Surveys in the north reported that landowners used the fixed-rent system primarily for land with fertile soils. Landowners usually were unable to personally farm the land and wanted to make certain tenants would manage the land well. A fixed-rent gave the tenant considerable incentive to invest in land improvements with a view to raising yields.

In some parts of the countryside landowners leased their land in exchange for a rent paid in cash. This system was called *money-rent tenancy*. Tenant farmers usually grew nongrain crops like cotton, tea, silk, fruit, vegetables, or bamboo. Money-rent tenancy flourished in the outskirts of large cities. In Jiading, a cotton district outside of Shanghai, farmers sold cotton for cash to buy rice. Virtually every farmer renting land in the area paid cash rent. Tenant farmers renting land from the state, temples, or schools, also paid cash rent. In other cases tenant farmers paid cash when renting land leased by a creditor who had obtained the land as a mortgaged asset. Finally, where landowners lived some distance from the land they often insisted upon a rent payment in cash. In 1935 a tenancy survey reported that highest rents were paid in agriculturally productive areas of China like Shandong, Jiangsu, and Anhui. Lower rents were paid in marginal areas like Shaanxi, Shanxi, and Qinghai.

In north China tenants generally paid their rent money before the crop was planted. This practice guaranteed landowners a cash rent even if yields were low or the crop failed, as often happened in marginal areas. In villages where landowners accepted cash payment after the harvest, the rent per unit of land was higher. In such cases tenants often paid their cash rent in several installments, sometimes paying a premium at the last cash installment as a small reward for the landowner's wait. As in other tenancy systems, the period of lease usually lasted only a year or two, and written contracts were rare.

The *permanent tenancy* system existed everywhere in China. It accounted for roughly 40 percent of the tenancy contracts in Jiangsu, 30 percent in Zhejiang, 44 percent in Anhui, 78 percent in Tsi-tsi-har, and 94 percent in Suiyuan.[5] Landowners of large tracts of unreclaimed land often contracted with tenant households to clear and farm land in exchange for long-term tenancy rights. The annual rent was fixed over a long or indefinite period. If the tenant improved the land any increased yield accrued to him alone. Landowners sometimes awarded permanent tenancy rights to those that had greatly improved land. Permanent tenants had exclusive rights to the top soil. This form of tenant contract gave the tenant property rights similar to those held by the landowner. Tenants could mortgage tenure rights for credit. Permanent tenant rights could be bought or sold (also by landlords). All or part of a tenure right could be transferred to male heirs. For these reasons we can consider permanent tenants as quasi-property owners. The landowner's sole responsibility was the land tax. Even though a landowner might sell his property, permanent tenants had continued rights to farm the land. Landowners could not legally replace tenants unless they had not paid rent for a three-year period. Land owned by the state, Manchurian banner families, or temples frequently was leased on a permanent tenure basis.

### Distribution of Land Property Rights

The best survey of land tenure was undertaken by the Nanking Government's Land Commission (Tudi Weiyuanhui) set up on August 2, 1934.[6] Altogether, the Land Commission employed over 3,000 persons from government agencies and universities to carry out its research and survey work in 22 provinces. The commission's survey selected at least 20 percent of the counties in each province from which 20 percent of the rural households were surveyed according to household land, income, expenditures, etc. The full particulars of the survey, except summary tables of general findings, were never published because of the outbreak of war with Japan.

The survey's sampling technique produced results that probably reflect the general land tenure conditions in the countryside during the mid-1930s. The regions most heavily sampled — the north, central, east, and southeast — contained 95 percent of all rural households surveyed. These regions produced the largest proportion of the country's food and industrial crops. The areas of highest tenancy concentration were the central, east, and southeast provinces, with around 558,000 full- and part-time tenant

Table 3.1.  Land Tenure Conditions, Tenant Households, 1935–1936

| Land Tenure Conditions | A | | B | |
|---|---|---|---|---|
| | Households (Thousand) | Percent | Adjusted households* (thousand) | Percent |
| Owner-farmers[a/] | 831 | 48 | 1202 | 69 |
| Tenant households[b/] | 704 | 40 | 333 | 19 |
| Landlords, agricultural laborers without land, other rural households without land[c/] | 210 | 12 | 210 | 12 |
| Total rural households | 1745 | 100 | 1745 | 100 |

*Adjusted column B moves 350,000 part owners and 21,000 permanent tenants from the tenant household to the owner-farmer category.

a/  This category of owner-farmer contains only those households owning and farming all of their land.

b/  Tenant households include households that own some land and rent land, that farm rented land, and that rent land and also work as farm laborers.

c/  This category includes (i) landlord households leasing out all or part of their land, (ii) households neither owning land nor farming rented land—their income came entirely from wages, and (iii) households earning income from non-farming occupations.

households, accounting for around 32 percent of the total tenant households. Tenancy was not very widespread in the north. The category of tenant households, with about 704,000 members, included nearly 350,000 households that owned land but still rented some land. However, most of these farms could have been considered bona fide owner-cultivator farmers. If we shifted owner-renter households into the owner-farmer category, the number of pure tenant households would be reduced to around 354,000 households, or about 20 percent of the total rural households. In addition, as previously discussed, permanent tenants had lawful rights to tenant land although they paid annual rent. Should the permanent tenants therefore be considered quasi-owners, and these households relegated to the owner-farmer category? If we readjust the tenant category to exclude permanent tenants we find that the number of tenant households is reduced from 40 to 37 percent, which raises the owner-farmer share from 48 to 51 percent. These two adjustments combined lower the tenant households to 19 percent of total households surveyed (Table 3.1, column B).

One out of every three rural households had to rent some land. This was undoubtedly caused by China's rising rural population and scarcity of cultivatable land. To improve this situation much could have been done to extend property rights to the 37 percent who still negotiated short-term rent contracts with landowners. The state could have extended full property rights to these tenants by initiating post–World War II land reforms like those carried out in Japan and Taiwan, where the state paid landowners to relinquish ownership to their land above a certain legally prescribed ceiling and granted long-term loans to tenant households to buy this land. Such a reform could have created a solid class of family farm proprietors like that in Japan and Taiwan. Whether the Nanjing government would have committed its resources to surveying the land and carrying out a land transfer to expand the ranks of owner farmers is difficult to say. The communists did carry out land reform, but they quickly confiscated all property and transformed households into teams to farm the collectivized land.

In the seventeenth and early eighteenth centuries land distribution was even more unequal than in the 1930s. In 1700 around 45 million hectares supported 90 million people, and of this, 40 million hectares were privately owned. By 1900 cultivated land had increased to 55 million hectares, a mere 38 percent, but population had grown by 287 percent to around 500 million people. Private holdings in 1900 totaled around 49 million hectares and the real growth of private land was only 22 percent. There is some evidence that suggests the fraction of rural households that were tenants in 1700 exceeded 37 percent, which was roughly the proportion of tenant households in the 1930s. We can conclude that over this two-century period farm land only slightly increased, rural population greatly increased, and the share of tenant households remained the same or slightly declined. China's land tenure system enabled villages to absorb more rural households without the share of tenant households rising.

In the late seventeenth century the Qing dynasty (1661–1911) seized vast tracts of land for its military troops, the nobility, and the imperial household treasury. During the next two hundred years much of this land reverted to the hands of private individuals through market sales and mortgages that were never reclaimed by former owners. As the urban population remained constant at around 6 percent from 1850 to 1930, population density in the countryside increased roughly threefold. If the rate of tenancy declined as population density increased, how did this happen? It can be surmised that the flexible contractual arrangements developed by families enabled those with few resources to obtain a toehold in agriculture and gradually establish small claims to land. At first farm families rented some land while working as farm laborers. Later they purchased some land or a permanent tenancy right. This asset became part of the household's corporate estate and generated a stream of income for the rural family until it was mortgaged, sold, or transferred to a male heir.

## Agricultural Development and Land Tenure

Statistics for Chinese agricultural development before 1949 are virtually nonexistent. The general evidence for the 1870 to 1937 period suggests that farm production expanded at the same rate as population. Food grain output data for the 1930–1937 period show an index of virtually no growth. Rural labor expanded at roughly the growth rate of population, as did farm capital. The cropping index rose slightly, but scarcely any new technological advances were introduced. The growth of total factor inputs seems to have matched that of output until 1920. Thereafter, total factor productivity probably became negative, especially during the 1930s. Meanwhile, the land tenure system remained stable between 1870 and 1930. In the early 1930s a slight increase in the number of land-renting households took place. This was caused by an unusual increase in distress sales and mortgaging of land caused by the deflationary impact of the world depression upon the Chinese economy, and by regional trade dislocations suffered by Japan's seizure of Manchuria. Although modern agricultural development never took place, the land tenure situation did not worsen.[7] Instead, population growth continued its relentless, slow increase. China's rural population absorbed more households because the land tenure system permitted renting and then purchase of permanent tenancy rights.

## Family Farm Behavior

During the period under study, eight or nine out of every ten families resided in villages. The village communities ranged in size from as few as 20 to 30 to as many as several hundred or more households. Villages consisted of clusters of households grouped together. Most households farmed the land, but even these supplemented their farm earnings with incomes from selling services or handicraft articles and from trade. Farmers managed plots of land that were separated by some distance instead of the consolidated units like those of Western farmers.

Family farms used different cropping systems depending upon the climate, soil, and local technology. The first cropping system, used in the frontier areas of the northeast, northwest, southwest, and in hill regions, allowed land to be tilled once a year and the harvest of a single crop. Inferior soils, infrequent rainfall, and scarcity of organic fertilizer limited the area that farmers could plant, and restricted crop yields as well. Farmers reclaimed land to help earn a living. The low productivity of the land and the high cost of transport to market prevented commerce and handicraft from developing. Family farms in the single cropping zone produced only a small marketable surplus.

The second cropping system, located throughout the northern provinces and the northern portions of the central provinces, permitted three crops every two years. Winter wheat was sown in September or October and harvested in April or May along with the planting and harvesting of traditional annual summer crops. Crop yields were higher because of heavy manuring, light plowing, and intensive weeding, with some irrigation when conditions permitted. The higher crop yields made possible a larger marketable surplus, increased specialization and trade, and there was a higher population density.

The third cropping system extended through the central provinces eastward to the sea and then southward. It allowed two harvests during the year, except upon hilly land and inferior soils with poor drainage. These provinces produced rice, various coarse grains, and industrial crops in a cropping sequence made possible by heavy manuring, considerable irrigation, favorable climate and soils, and close attention to weeding and plant care. These areas supported a high population density through a large marketable surplus, flourishing commerce, and widespread handicraft industry.

Farm income and household earnings were positively correlated with the cropping index. Buck's farm management study of 2,866 farms in seven provinces surveyed between 1921 and 1924 shows that farm and household earnings were higher in the east-central areas than to the north.[8] Although Buck's findings do not carefully relate regional income differences to the type of cropping system and the amount of marketed surplus, the ability of farmers to cultivate their land intensively was the crucial factor determining available surplus for sale or trade.

Buck's survey of family farms in north and east-central China covered an area where crop-sharing tenancy was practiced. He found that there was no "clear-cut distinction in size of the farm between owners, part owners, and tenants." Further, the size of tenant and owner family farms did not greatly differ. Tenant family farms were only slightly smaller than owner or part-owner holdings. Buck found that the labor earnings of owner operators were less than that of tenants, less for part owners compared to tenants, and less for owners compared to part owners. Tenant farms also obtained slightly higher yields than did owners and part owners.

Buck then estimated the rate of return that landlords obtained from their capital stock by subtracting landlord expenses from receipts and then dividing by the total capital value of that stock to obtain a rate of return of 8.5 percent. The return to capital was roughly the same for tenant and part-owner farms. Buck found no difference between those two categories and the landlord's interest received on investment. Other farm surveys show that the character of family farm behavior for tenants and owners also varied only slightly and resembled the findings of Buck. It seems that tenant farmers managed their land intensively, perhaps even slightly more efficiently than did part owners and owners.

## Fair-Share Rent

Is there any difference in the capabilities of tenant and owner farms to acquire farming technology? Buck and other researchers of this period never addressed this question because modern agricultural technology had just become available. To answer this question we must focus upon the motivation and financial status of farmers. We can presume that all households, irrespective of wealth, certainly wished to earn more income. If convinced that risk was low and the rate of return greater than that obtained from traditional uses of farm capital, farmers would be quite likely to adopt modern technology.

Financial capability was another matter. Buck argued that many tenants probably paid a higher than "fair-share" rent to landlords. He calculated a tenant's fair-share rent according to the proportion of receipts the landlord obtained from investment in land and the tenant's use of his labor. The rate of return the landlord should receive for his capital and the return the tenant should obtain from his labor were always determined by bargaining. If neither party had excessive economic power the final rent terms should have been equivalent to the fair-share rent. Buck tried to estimate this fair-share rent, and findings led him to believe that tenant rents were usually 20 percent higher than what they should have been. Land and labor markets throughout the countryside appear to have been highly competitive. Land rents and rural wages fluctuated according to seasonal supply and demand. The number of landowners with land to lease and tenants seeking land to rent were usually so numerous that no single party could ever influence the general terms of rent agreed upon. Yet, it is possible that considerable economic power, enough to set rents above a competitive fair-share rent, sometimes accumulated in the hands of landowners. Buck favored a modest reduction in land rents. Such a program would have given tenant farmers a financial opportunity to modernize their farms and even become bona fide property owners. Buck did not, however, favor programs of radical land redistribution. What rural China really needed, however, was modern inputs that households could afford to buy. Rent reduction or land reform alone would not have modernized agriculture, but neither would modern farming inputs have extended land ownership to more households. A successful agricultural policy to expand tenant property rights to land and make available modern inputs to farmers would have helped to modernize Chinese agriculture and ensure social stability in the countryside.

## Conclusion

The Chinese rural order had a high rate of land tenancy. However, the complex land tenure system provided the means for households without land to acquire it. The main factor that prevented households from acquiring property rights was that population growth always exceeded the expansion of cultivated land. Even so, from the late seventeenth to the early twentieth century, the land tenure system provided farmland and some land rights for many people. China's complex land tenure system did not obstruct the growth of farm production or prevent farmers from acquiring land rights. Rent reductions probably would have enabled more tenant farmers to farm their land efficiently and to acquire land. Low labor and land productivity was still rooted in the backwardness of farming technology, not the land tenure system. China needed an agricultural revolution, but only modern technology could have initiated that.

## Notes

1. Ramon H. Myers, "Land Distribution in Revolutionary China: 1890–1937," *The Chung Chi Journal,* vol. 8, no. 2 (May 1969), p. 65.

2. Tōa kenkyūjo, *Keizai ni kan suru Shina kankō chōsa hōkokusho: toku ni Hoku-Shi ni okeru kosaku seido* (Report of Investigations on Chinese Old Customs Related to the Economy: The Land Tenure System in North China) (Tokyo: Tōa Kenkyūjo, 1943), pp. 49–51. The discussion on the five types of land tenure systems is derived from this remarkable survey and compilation of investigation reports of Chinese rural land tenure customs.

3. *Ibid.,* p. 66. Landlords invested in their tenants even in north China; see p. 100. In the north and northeast another variant existed. In this system landlords instructed their tenants as to which crops to plant and tenants also performed menial tasks for the landlords for a predetermined wage. Such tasks usually involved working around the landlord's house or farm.

4. *Ibid.,* p. 97. "The crop-sharing system for payment in kind was more prevalent in years following upon very poor harvests. If harvests had been very good, tenant-landowner contracts then reverted to money payments."

5. Tsi-tsi-har is a city in Heilongjiang province and Suiyuan is a former province, which became part of Neimonggol in 1955.

6. Tudi Weiyuanhui (Land Commission), *Quanguo tudi diaocha baogao gangyao* (Draft Report of the Land Survey for China) (Nanking, 1937), preface, p. 2.

7. Two studies confirm this assertion rather convincingly. See Ramon H. Myers, *The Chinese Peasant Economy: The Agricultural Development of Hopei and Shungtung Provinces, 1890–1949* (Cambridge: Harvard University Press, 1970) for north China. For Jiangsu province in east-central China, see David Faure, "The Rural Economy

of Kiangsu Province 1870–1911," *The Journal of the Institute of Chinese Studies of the Chinese University of Hong Kong,* vol. 9, no. 2 (1978), pp. 365–469.

8. John Lossing Buck, *Chinese Farm Economy* (Chicago: The University of Chicago Press, 1930), ch. 3.

### Readings

Buck, John Lossing. *Land Utilization in China.* Chicago: University of Chicago Press, 1937. Still remains the classic study of Chinese rural society and economy. This three-volume set includes one volume of text, one of maps, and one of statistics. The statistics volume is particularly useful, containing a large amount of data on family farm management by land tenure classification.

Hou, Chia-chu. "The Structure and Determinants of Tenure Systems in Modern China: 1900–1940," in Chi-mung Hou and Tzong-shian Yu (eds.), *Modern Chinese Economic History.* Taiwan: The Institute of Economics, 1979, pp. 163–191.

Lippit, Victor D. *Land Reform and Economic Development in China.* White Plains, N.Y.: International Arts and Sciences Press, Inc., 1974. Tries to measure the "economic surplus" produced in China during the 1930s.

Myers, Ramon H. "Theory of Modern China's Agrarian Problem." *The Chung Chi Journal,* vol. 6, no. 2, May 1967, pp. 210–219. Part of the very large literature in Chinese, Japanese, and Western languages about China's agrarian crises during the interwar years that discusses whether the land tenure system retarded agricultural and economic development. Classifies theorists arguing that unequal land distribution caused China's agrarian problem as the "distributionists," and the remaining theorists as "eclectics." "Eclectics" argued that many factors accounted for low agricultural productivity and the influence of land tenure was minor.

————. "Socioeconomic Relationships in North China Villages During the Ch'ing and Republican Periods." *Modern China,* vol. 6, no. 3, July 1980, pp. 243–266.

Nicholls, William H. "An 'Agricultural Surplus' as a Factor in Economic Development." *The Journal of Political Economy,* vol. 71, no. 1, February 1963, pp. 1–29. The best theoretical statement showing how different land tenure systems might have influenced the size and allocation of the "agricultural surplus," which in turn influences economic development. This essay also treats land tenure systems in rural economies with high and low land-population ratios.

Riskin, Carl. "Surplus and Stagnation in Modern China," in Dwight H. Perkins (ed.), *China's Modern Economy in Historical Perspective.* Stanford, Calif.: Stanford University Press, 1975, pp. 49–54. Tries to measure the "economic surplus" produced by China during the 1930s.

# 4
# Natural Resources and Factor Endowments

*Rhoads Murphey*

We are hampered in any analysis of Chinese agriculture by an acute shortage of reliable data. The State Statistical Bureau has acknowledged that at present it has no exact figures for total cultivated area, output for individual crops, or potential for new cultivated land, let alone detailed information on regional and local soils or climate and water resources, all of which are essential in determining mineral fertilizer resources, needs for and current levels of inputs of water and fertilizer, and so on. We do know, however, that China is not well endowed with agricultural potential. By Western standards, as much as a quarter or even a third of China's cultivated land is marginal. The generally monsoonal character of the Chinese climate (Figure 4.1) is responsible for recurrent drought and flood. The shortage of level land forces farmers to use hillsides wherever possible. Finally, natural soil fertility levels are low in many areas, especially south of the Yangtze River.

## Land and Agriculture

Topographically, China can be divided more usefully between east and west than between north and south. West of the Yangtze gorges, along a line between Loyang in the north and Guilin in the south, there are almost no significant breaks in the jumble of mountains that cover west China, merging into the great Tibetan massif in western Sichuan, Yunnan, and Gansu (Figure 4.2). (The Red Basin of Sichuan is a qualified exception, where slopes are less severe and extensive areas are productively cultivated.) River valleys, flood plains, and deltas have built extensive level areas east of this line. Eastern China is better watered than the west, which merges into semiarid or desert conditions (Figure 4.3). East-west distinctions are also responsible for the pronounced clustering of a mainly

FIGURE 4.1. CLIMATIC REGIONS

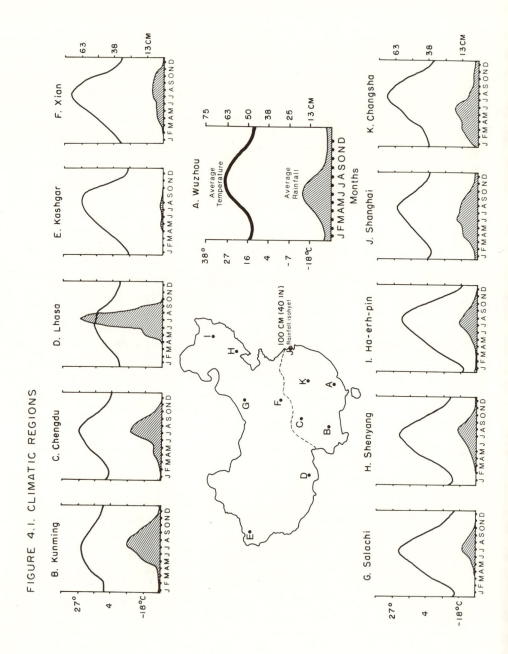

FIGURE 4.2. LAND FORMS

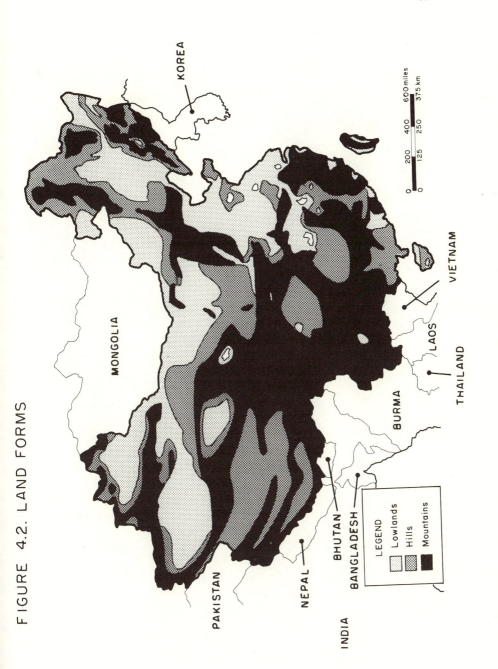

52

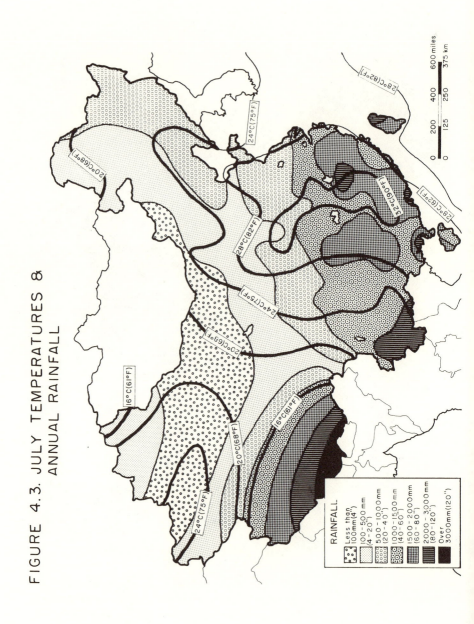

FIGURE 4.3. JULY TEMPERATURES &
ANNUAL RAINFALL

28°C(82°F)

24°C(75°F)

20°C(68°F)

28°C(82°F)

32°C(90°F)

28°C(82°F)

28°C(82°F)

24°C(75°F)

20°C(68°F)

16°C(61°F)

9°C(61°F)

20°C(68°F)

24°C(75°F)

RAINFALL

Less than
100mm(4")
100-500mm
(4-20")
500-1000mm
(20-40")
1000-1500mm
(40-60")
1500-2000mm
(60-80")
2000-3000mm
(80-120")
Over
3000mm(120")

600 miles

400

375 km

200

125   250

0

0

agricultural population in the east. Agricultural occupation of most of west China is still relatively recent and spotty (again except for the Sichuan Basin), and productivity per hectare averages far less than in the east.

The total land area of China is about 9.6 million square kilometers, or slightly larger than the United States including Alaska. About half of this area is occupied by Xizang (Tibet), Xinjiang, Qinghai, and Neimonggol (Inner Mongolia), largely nonagricultural provinces that are thinly populated. Except for Neimonggol, where the proportion of cultivated land is somewhat higher, we may ignore these areas in a discussion of agriculture. At one time there were ambitious plans for extending cultivated lands in Xinjiang, but it has become clear that the limited water resources may be unable to sustain even the present cultivated area.

Only a little over 11 percent of China's total area is cultivated. Estimates of China's total cultivated area vary from 100 million hectares (commonly cited in Chinese official publications during the past two or three years) to 107 million hectares (Food and Agriculture Organization) to 130 million hectares (other U.N. sources). Clearly, China is land poor in comparison with most other countries, especially on a per capita basis. Assuming the 1980 population to be approximately one billion, the per capita share of cultivated land would be about 0.10 hectares. Only Japan and South Korea have a lower per capita share of cultivated land. In assessing China's land endowment, one must allow for the relatively high proportion of cultivated land which is to varying degrees marginal. Much of this land would be ignored in other agricultural systems because it produces low yields at high input costs. In general, nearly all land that can possibly be cultivated is farmed if it can be of any net benefit. Most increases in agricultural output must come from the existing cultivated areas, although some reclamation of coastal wetlands may be possible at heavy and perhaps uneconomic expense.

In contrast to cultivated land, there remain some areas where a careful expansion of permanent tree crops would be rational. Tree crops — mainly fruits and nuts — have been given some attention, especially as marketing facilities have improved. However, although cash yield can be relatively high, there are pressures in China to maximize total caloric output per hectare. Tea and silk (in the form of mulberry) are long-standing tree and bush crops and continue to make good use of marginal slope land.

Other nonfood crops, primarily cotton and tobacco, must share existing cultivated land area together with grains, tubers, vegetables, sugarcane and sugar beets, soybeans, oil seeds, and peanuts. Cotton demands high soil fertility levels and is sensitive to water imbalance. Yields have apparently risen substantially since the 1950s through a combination of more fertilizer, better water management, and more productive crop strains. Total area sown to cotton seems to have remained relatively constant despite chronic cotton shortages caused by increased demand. This is a clear indication of the priority given to food crops. Soybean hectarage has apparently declined sharply since the 1950s so that China is now a net importer.

Significant possibilities for the extension of controlled grazing and thus for increases in animal products may exist. Although animal husbandry is a less efficient form of land use, grazing animals can utilize marginal land areas that could not support field agriculture. Nomadic herding has traditionally been important in Xinjiang, Neimonggol, and Heilongjiang, but it produced negligible surpluses. There is scope for herd improvement through upgrading the quality of animals by selective breeding, through provision of supplementary winter fodder (traditionally there were heavy stock losses in winter), and through increased attention to disease prevention.

The shortage of grazing land within China proper, and the large amounts of submarginal agricultural land in the steppe regions along the northern and western borders of the country, make it pressing that productive uses for these areas be found. Much marginal land that has been cultivated should be returned to grassland. This may be especially true for parts of Neimonggol and western Manchuria. Cultivation has been extended into submarginal steppe regions, often with inadequate irrigation. Wind erosion can also be severe, especially in Neimonggol, and the fragile nature of native loess and chestnut soils makes them especially vulnerable to the kind of destruction familiar in the dust bowls in the United States in the 1930s and 1950s.

## Climate

Next to the shortage of workable land, climate is the greatest constraint on China's agriculture (Figures 4.1 and 4.4). The chief problems are water balance and moisture deficiency. Less than a quarter of the cultivated land receives enough precipitation on a consistent basis from year to year to ensure stable yields. At the other extreme, about a quarter of the land is subject to periodic flooding, damage from excessive rainfall (associated especially with typhoons in the coastal and near-coastal southeast), or inadequate drainage. Irrigation of semiarid areas involves clear risks of soil deterioration through the buildup of salts or alkalines, and possible waterlogging. Soils with more than minimal levels of salts or alkalines are, in effect, poisoned for agriculture.

China's climate is broadly monsoonal, which means that approximately 80 percent of the rainfall comes in the four warmest months. This rainfall coincides with the height of the growing season and hence with greatest

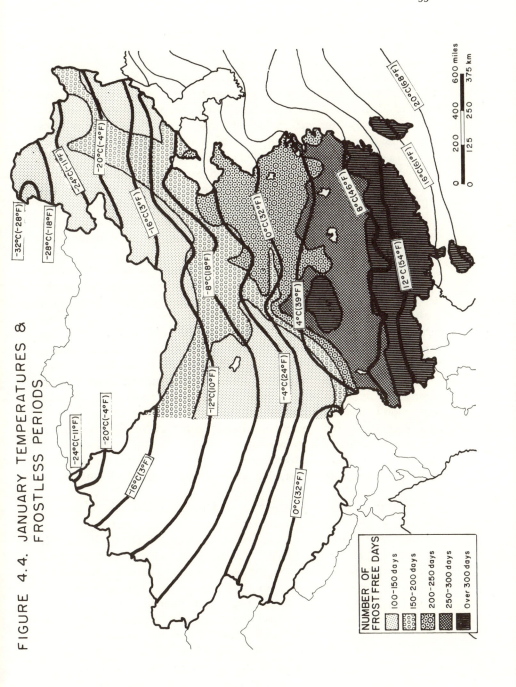

FIGURE 4.4. JANUARY TEMPERATURES & FROSTLESS PERIODS

-32°C(-28°F)

-28°C(-18°F)

-24°C(-11°F)

-20°C(-4°F)

-24°C(-11°F)

-20°C(-4°F)

-16°C(3°F)

-16°C(3°F)

-12°C(10°F)

-8°C(18°F)

-4°C(24°F)

0°C(32°F)

0°C(32°F)

4°C(39°F)

8°C(46°F)

12°C(54°F)

16°C(61°F)

20°C(68°F)

NUMBER OF
FROST FREE DAYS

100-150 days
150-200 days
200-250 days
250-300 days
Over 300 days

0    200    400    600 miles

0    125    250    375 km

*55*

water demands. However, the monsoonal climate also has a high annual precipitation variability, both in total amount and in seasonal or even weekly incidence. Variability is greatest where average annual rainfall is least, especially in areas north of the Yangtze valley where about one year in three is marked by a drought (of varying severity) in parts of at least one province. This may result from a small total precipitation for the year, or more commonly from maldistribution, where spring and summer rains come too late or too early or are too widely spaced. Soils dry out and crops die or are stunted, even when rainfall totals for the year may be statistically adequate. Rain may also be violent and excessive, causing destructive floods, and yet still leave a large part of the growing season overly dry. The 100-cm isohyet (line of 100 cm annual rainfall), which coincides roughly with the line of the Huai River and the Xinling Range farther west, makes a convenient division between the dry, variable north and the humid south (Figures 4.1 and 4.3).

The North China Plain and eastern Manchuria have an annual precipitation average of about 50 cm, which is barely adequate for the needs of most field crops. In addition, few years closely conform to the statistical average, and frequently rainfall is inadequately distributed throughout the growing season. Some sense of the marginality of even this agriculturally prime sector may be derived from looking at its U.S. analog, the Great Plains. Rainfall averages and evaporation rates for the North China Plain are much the same as for western North and South Dakota, Nebraska, Kansas, eastern Colorado, Utah, and Montana. Until recently, population in north China could only be supported by agriculture in good rainfall years. In other years there were disastrous deficits, as a result of drought or flooding. The heaviest floods occur in the Yellow River valley, but intense rainfall concentrated in a short period, a pattern characteristic of the monsoonal system, may damage or destroy crops over a much wider area.

Beyond the plains, in most of Shanxi, Shaanxi, Gansu, and in western Manchuria, rainfall averages drop sharply and annual variability rises accordingly. Periodic drought years may get 12 cm or less of rain. In general, the farther from the sea, which is the origin of the moisture-bearing air masses of the summer monsoon, the less the average annual rainfall and the greater the variability. Mountains north and west of the plain help to disrupt air flows of marine origin, and deplete their moisture.

South China as a whole receives a more equitable distribution of rainfall than the north. However, monsoonal rainfall can also be fickle and may, especially in the Yangtze valley area, leave large areas without adequate moisture in some years. One of the south's greatest advantages is not merely higher annual rainfall averages, but lesser yearly and seasonal variability, plus an annual distribution pattern that (for reasons not entirely clear meteorologically) in most years provides adequate moisture every month. As a corollary, annual sunshine totals are less for the south, with its frequent rain-bearing cloud cover, than for the north. Southern winters are usually mild enough, especially south of the Yangtze valley, to permit winter cropping, with adequate winter rainfall to leave the soil moist for spring planting. Nevertheless, supplemental irrigation (or drainage) is needed periodically, especially for rice, which is the south's dominant crop. Except for the parts of Yunnan located on the fringes of the monsoonal system, which suffer from semiaridity in some years, there are generally ample reserves of water from both surface streams and wells for irrigation.

The length of the growing season, which is the period between killing frosts, is also an important factor (Figure 4.4). The north has a short growing season and is generally limited to a single yearly crop, unlike central and south China, which can produce two or three crops yearly. Southern Manchuria has a growing season of less than 200 frost-free days, and the North China Plain only a little over 200 days. This means that crops lost by drought, flood, and late frosts cannot be replanted. The Yangtze valley in central China has about 250 frost-free days. As one moves southward the frost-free period increases until a frost-free day maximum of 365 days is reached just north of Canton. Favorable temperatures increase yields and are conducive to double and triple cropping sequences in the south. Although the number of cloud-free days is greater in the north than in the south, excessive sunlight, especially in areas prone to drought, may desiccate crops.

### Irrigation

The agricultural need for water in most of north China is very high, and often exceeds the capacities of traditional shallow wells or small local irrigation systems. In addition, excessive dependence on irrigation magnifies the risk of salinization, alkalinization, or waterlogging of the surface layers. Total irrigated area in China has more than doubled since 1949, and approximately half of the total cultivated area is officially reported to be irrigated. In north China only about 15 percent of cultivated land was irrigated in the 1930s. Since 1949 more than 23 million new and deeper tubewells have been constructed. Tubewells (nearly all with power-driven pumps) are responsible for most of the expansion in irrigated area in north China, although the series of dams along the Yellow River and other rivers adds significantly to the supply of water for agriculture.

Dams on the slow-moving rivers of north China have aggravated problems caused by heavy silt loads. Silt from the easily eroded loess soil banks quickly fills reservoirs and clogs distribution systems. Settlement basins, many of which have been built, provide a short-run solution. The Chinese were distressed to find that their projections for the life span of settlement basins and reservoirs behind many of the Yellow River dams completed in the 1960s were far too high. Many filled with silt in three to five years, disrupting plans for both irrigation and power production. The more permanent cure—reforestation in the river watersheds—is long run, expensive, and difficult to maintain in a climate marginal for trees. Many of the trees planted for reforestation purposes on slopes in north China between 1955 and 1970 died from lack of water, which is especially hard to transport to hillside plantings. Peasant needs for wood, primarily as fuel, have also resulted in destructive inroads on reforested areas. This is the same process that progressively denuded north China of its original sparse tree cover.

There has been periodic discussion of a scheme to divert water northward from the Yangtze, via the Grand Canal, directly into the Yellow River (whose average annual flow is only about 5 percent of the flow of the Yangtze) and a connecting grid of reservoirs and canals to help support agriculture on the North China Plain. This might be technically feasible and could possibly help to reduce occasional flooding problems in the lower Yangtze, but it would be enormously expensive. This scheme might become more viable if groundwater levels become depleted by the recent expansion of tubewells in north China.

What the official totals of "irrigated" land do not tell us is the extent to which irrigation is actually available. An area supplied by shallow wells may be described as "irrigated," but may get insufficient water toward the end of even a moderate drought. Increased demands on groundwater from new and deeper wells may draw down reserves faster than they can be recharged, as has happened in many areas elsewhere. For areas supplied from reservoirs fed by rivers, total flow varies widely from year to year or season to season and rapid siltation may weaken or destroy the entire system within a few years. In most of the north, agriculture must have perennial irrigation in large and reliable amounts. Water availability must not vary with gross swings in rainfall amount and must provide all of a crop's demands during hot summer droughts. Nearly all of China's potential for increasing agricultural output lies in the combination of more irrigation, more fertilization, and higher yielding varieties. Of these, water is clearly the most critical and the most limited. It is also the factor that is least amenable to increase.

## Soils and Topography

Most of north China east of Xinjiang and south of Neimonggol is covered with deep deposits of wind-laid alluvium called *loess*. Loess is naturally highly fertile, drains well, and, like most alluvium, is easily worked. Loess soils are soft and friable and, in the absence of adequate vegetative cover, are subject to excessive erosion. Dust storms in north China are frequent and all northern rivers carry exceptionally heavy silt loads. Between the desert soils of northwestern China and the loess areas is a variable belt of chernozem and chestnut soils that are also highly fertile, particularly in Neimonggol.

As one moves southward from the 100 cm isohyet (Figure 4.1), leaching increases. Heavy rainfall and warm temperatures in the south exacerbate leaching of soluble and oxidizable nutrients in the soil. This not only results in low fertility, but also leaves soils with a compacted structure, which prevents adequate aeration. Leaching is also a problem on the sloping land that covers most of south China. Maintenance or increase of yields depends on heavy fertilizer applications.

In contrast, alluvial soils of river valleys, lake basins, and deltas are naturally very fertile. These areas are reasonably level and are the depositories of the rich runoff and silt from surrounding slopes. Population density in these areas is very high and land is exceptionally productive. Unfortunately, such areas constitute only a small fraction of the total land of the south.

On a regional basis, soil quality varies. The soils of Sichuan are reasonably productive while those of the Yangtze River valley and flood plain are highly productive. South of the Yangtze valley, soils are increasingly leached and acid. Soil fertility continues to decrease southward. Compaction and "iron pan," the result of leaching, are also occasional problems. The only naturally productive soils are isolated pockets of river or lake alluvium. Small intermontane basins also have fertile soils, although soil quality is more the result of prolonged human activity and improvement than of natural origins. Nevertheless, the alluvial and basin soils exposed to heavy rainfall and high temperatures require heavy fertilization to remain productive.

The chief problem for agriculture in south China is an acute shortage of level land (Figure 4.2). Level land area has been progressively increased in nearly all valleys, basins, and deltas through terracing around the margins. As population pressure rose, terracing was pushed up onto slopes that in many areas were probably too steep to repay the enormous costs involved. In addition to soils becoming less productive as slope increases, there are associated problems with irrigation water and its distribution, and increased difficulties with cultivation, harvesting, and transport of materials. There are no reliable figures on the amount of terraced cultivated land in the south, but it is estimated that perhaps as much as two-fifths of it occupies moderate-to-steep slopes.

## Fertilization

Soil structure and fertility change with crop growth. Soil fertility was traditionally maintained with heavy applications of organic materials — primarily nightsoil, but also animal manures, crop residues, ashes, mud (dredged from streams, lakes and canals), and old straw roofs and house floors. As population pressure mounted through time, competing demands, especially for fuel, diverted increasing amounts of organic material to other uses. However, more nightsoil was produced as the population rose and this probably helped yields to continue a slow rise, although some of this rise might be attributed to growing labor intensity.

The search for fuel led to increasing denudation of hillsides, where even brush and grass were overcut and slopes were dangerously exposed to erosion. Renewed increases in agricultural output could come only from technological inputs: new sources of water and its storage and distribution, new methods for enhancing soil fertility (and at the same time lessening pressures on natural vegetation in order to check erosion), and increased agricultural research and development. Of the three, fertilizer is perhaps the easiest and quickest method to increase agricultural output.

Almost no chemical fertilizer producing capacity was inherited in 1949, and even by 1957 total output was less than one million tonnes. In 1966 domestic output probably exceeded 10 million tonnes for the first time, but by 1975, with production probably close to 30 million tonnes (plus about 7 million tonnes of imports), the average per-hectare application of organic *plus* chemical fertilizers was estimated as being less than one-quarter of that applied in Japan. These are rough estimates, and it is even more difficult to measure the nutrient content of Chinese fertilizers. Organic fertilizers vary widely in nutrient content, as do chemical fertilizers. From about 1966, great emphasis was placed on chemical fertilizer production in small rural plants. Nutrient content differed from plant to plant (although it was uniformly lower than for more modern large-scale plants). Nitrogen content was frequently unstable, adding to nutrient loss. In addition to quality problems, small rural plants appear to have a high unit cost of production.

By 1972 half of China's chemical fertilizer output was coming from small plants. However, potential capacity was well below China's needs. Therefore, it was decided in the early 1970s to import, and then to develop domestically, a number of large-scale, high technology, chemical fertilizer plants. The first of these came on stream in 1975, and each year since, these plants have accounted for a rising proportion of total chemical fertilizer output.

There is still a large potential for further farm output increases from additional fertilization. This potential can be realized only if China can produce (or import) considerably more chemical fertilizers. The use of additional fertilizer depends on water supply, which may be even more deficient. Increased use of chemical fertilizers can kill plants or stunt growth unless water is also increased.

Chemical fertilizers provide about one-third of China's fertilizer needs by nutrient weight. China is not well supplied with deposits of mineral fertilizers. There are some resources of phosphate rock, mainly in the remote southwest, and a few small deposits of potash in equally remote areas. High extraction and transport costs and small reserves make it unlikely that indigenous phosphorus and potash resources will make a significant contribution to fertilizer availability.

## Research

Significantly improved crop strains were developed at the local level in the traditional agricultural system. In general, however, modern agricultural research and development have lagged behind what has been accomplished elsewhere. This problem is dealt with in greater detail in Chapter 7. Achieving the yield potential of improved crop varieties depends on adequate supplies of both water and fertilizer. In the absence of these inputs, modern varieties are frequently less tolerant of drought and low soil fertility than traditional varieties.

China has a wide range of soils, climates, day lengths, and other local factors. An equally wide range of crop varieties optimally suited to differing regional and local conditions must be developed. This work needs to be done not only for rice, wheat, and maize, but also for sorghum, millet, potatoes, rye, oats, buckwheat, and so on. Research is also critical in upgrading the breeding and care of animals, poultry, and pond-reared fish so as to maximize output from marginal land. Finally, research and development can also reduce crop losses from insect pests and plant diseases through biological controls, pesticides, and herbicides. Agriculture is also dependent on a growing industrial capacity to produce cement and steel for dams and tubewells, pumps, fertilizer, and pesticides. Because of China's extremely unfavorable man-land ratio, a heavy investment in research to develop new technology will be necessary to maintain the growth of output.

## Conclusion

In conclusion, it must be reiterated that China is not well endowed with agricultural resources. There is too little cultivable land, and much of it is marginal and suffers from recurrent droughts, floods, poor soil, and cold. Most potentially cultivable land is already being worked, and the scope for bringing new land under cultivation is limited. In coming years increases in output will be attained mainly through additional use of water and organic and inorganic fertilizers, other modern agricultural inputs, and improved crop strains. China has a long tradition of rational use of water and organic manure, as well as intensive farming practices such as rotation of crops and intercropping. In recent years serious efforts have been made to increase the availability of water, chemical fertilizers, and better seeds. However, irrigation of semiarid areas, as in other parts of the world, has increased the risk of soil deterioration through the buildup of salts, alkalines, and water logging. It is possible, therefore, that the net gains from irrigation may not be as much as is often expected, and that irrigation may be at best a short-term solution to moisture deficiencies. Since all of the easier and cheaper sources have been tapped, it is almost certain that further additions to irrigated hectarage can be brought about only at steeply rising costs.

The challenge is to make this traditionally productive agricultural system increase output through the injection of new technology, without any significant additions to cultivated land. The record so far is encouraging, in that total output has probably doubled in thirty years. However, the population has probably also doubled in the same time span. It is hoped that modern inputs plus a sturdy traditional base will enable Chinese agriculture to achieve another doubling of output. At the same time, population growth should slow. This will help China to break out of the bind that now constricts its overall development.

## Readings

Most book-length studies of Chinese agriculture are now long out of date  or deal with an earlier period. Periodical literature, by its nature, also dates rapidly. Studies of China's physical geography and resource base have been sparse since the revolution. To keep abreast of the rapid changes now taking place in China's agriculture and in studies of its resource base requires continuous attention to a wide range of periodicals and reports as well as to the Chinese press. A few more recent or older standard studies are listed below as a convenient guide to the general problem.

Buck, J. L. *Land Utilization in China.* Nanjing: University of Nanjing, 1937. Still the best statistically based study of pre-Communist agriculture and land use, and hence a basic book.

Chao, Kang. *Agricultural Production in Communist China, 1949–1965.* Madison: University of Wisconsin Press, 1970. A quantitative analysis plus a more general account of the process of socialist transformation.

Dawson, Owen. *Communist China's Agriculture.* New York: Praeger, 1970. A survey of agricultural resources, potential development programs, and estimates of progress as of the late 1960s.

Greer, Charles. *Water Management in the Yellow River Basin of China.* Austin: University of Texas Press, 1979. The physical problem, and progress to date.

Kuo, T. C. *Agriculture in the People's Republic of China: Technical Transformation and Structural Change.* New York: Praeger, 1976. Planning and execution of the development of mechanization, fertilization, water control, improved strains, research, and extension services.

Liu, J. C. *China's Fertilizer Economy.* Chicago: University of Chicago Press, 1970. A detailed technical study of the growth of chemical fertilizer production, but before the import of the new large plants.

Myers, Ramon. *The Chinese Peasant Economy: Agricultural Development in Hopei and Shantung, 1890-1949.* Cambridge, Mass.: Harvard University Press, 1970. A detailed look at a supposedly deteriorating situation. The book nevertheless suggests high productivity and resilience.

Perkins, Dwight. *Agricultural Development in China, 1368-1968.* Chicago: Aldine, 1969. An account of the spread of new crops and more intensive methods accompanying and supporting the great increases in China's population during this period.

Richardson, S. D. *Forestry in Communist China.* London: Johns Hopkins University Press, 1966. By a New Zealand government forester, based on a tour in 1963. This is a specialist's account and is inadequately related to the wider context.

U.S., Congress, Joint Economic Committee. *China: A Reassessment of the Economy.* Washington, D.C., 1975. This is a multi-author volume that includes two useful chapters on agriculture summarizing problems and development as of 1974.

Whyte, R. O. *Rural Nutrition in China.* New York: Oxford University Press, 1972. A careful study that makes the most of very limited data.

Zaichikov, V. T., et al. *The Physical Geography of China.* Washington, D.C.: Joint Publications Research Service, 1965 (JPRS 32,119). Translation of a Russian original based on work in the 1950s; detail on climate, soils, hydrography, vegetation, groundwater, and mineral resources.

# 5
# Agriculture in Communist Development Strategy

*Robert F. Dernberger*

For the past three decades China has been under communist leadership.[1] Thus, an analysis of the role of agriculture in communist development strategy will serve as a useful introduction to more particularistic studies of the agricultural economy of China since 1949. Throughout this chapter the role of agricultural development in China will be compared to that in other communist nations. There is an extensive literature on the subject, especially for the Soviet Union.

In the Soviet Union the agricultural sector served as a resource base to be "exploited" in the service of development strategies. Planners attempted to gain control over and extract a maximum level of surplus from agricultural production for the needs of planned growth in the industrial, urban, and foreign trade sectors of the economy.[2] The collectivization of agricultural production and the sale of agricultural surplus (by means of set quotas) to the state at below-market prices are major features of the "Soviet model" of economic development.

In the 1950s the Chinese enthusiastically adopted many aspects of the Soviet model of economic development. A recent study by Benjamin Ward shows that the economic institutions and strategy developed in China over the past three decades have repeated the major features of the traditional Soviet model.[3] Ward argues that adaptions the Chinese made to the typical Soviet pattern can be viewed only as minor variations. Following this thesis, as the title of this chapter implies, an examination of the role of agriculture in China's development strategy could be expected to reveal considerable similarities to its role in the development strategies of communist countries in general.[4]

This conclusion, however, would lead us to downgrade the significance of Chinese variations. After the Great Leap Forward, the break with the

Soviet Union, and later the Cultural Revolution, some students of China's economic development began to question the assumption that China was an Asian example of the Soviet model. They argued for the existence of a new and unique Chinese or Maoist model of economic development. Moreover, any analysis of the role of agriculture in China's development strategy must take as its initial hypothesis the assumption that the Chinese treatment of the agricultural sector is considerably different from that of other communist countries. As subsequent chapters in the book will reveal, the distinctive agricultural development experience of China is the consequence of differences in both historical antecedents and policy objectives under communist rule.

Until 1949, small-scale, self-sufficient, household farming had been typical of Chinese agricultural production for at least eight centuries. Although three-fourths of the population was engaged in agricultural production, a substantial amount of land was concentrated in the hands of a fairly small minority, with most households owning some land and renting additional small parcels of hectarage. Both absentee landlords and landless peasants accounted for less than 10 percent of the total rural population. Relying on extensive use of irrigation, organic fertilizer, and multiple cropping, Chinese farming was more similar to "garden" farming than to specialized monocropping. By 1949, however, population growth was overcrowding China's arable land. The ratio of farmers to cultivated area increased to a level that far exceeded that found in other communist countries.

The objectives of the Chinese Communist Party differed substantially from those of other communist parties because of divergent historical backgrounds and social settings. We can attribute the popular appeal of the Chinese Communist Party to the emphasis party policy placed on the peasants. Perkins found that the Chinese Communist Revolution "put the people in command," i.e., the objectives pursued and economic policies implemented were consistent with the fundamental long-run interests of the majority of China's peasant households.[5] According to Perkins, this unique feature of Chinese communism is an important explanation for not only Chinese modifications of the typical Soviet development model, but also the extent to which the modifications have been successful. These distinctive features lead Ward to identify China's experience as exemplary of the Soviet model within the context of a "humane agrarian regime."[6] Due to significant differences in inherited physical constraints and the political and social orientation of the new leadership, it was unlikely that the role of agriculture in the development strategy of the Chinese communists after 1949 would closely replicate the treatment of agriculture in development programs of other communist countries. In this chapter we look at how the Chinese communists' treatment of the agricultural sector represents the policies of a "humane agrarian regime."

Economic policies and institutional changes implemented in China over the past three decades do not provide a consistent pattern that can be interpreted as *the* Chinese model for economic development. The priority assigned to agriculture has varied during the succession of development strategies that have been adopted since 1949. These development strategies and their effects on agriculture reflect changes in economic conditions induced by policy implementation or exogenous shocks.[7] Factional politics and economic conditions have also helped alter the balance of power among policymakers. Attempts to determine the extent to which agriculture was "exploited" in China's development strategy must take into consideration the political and economic changes that led to the implementation of new economic policies.[8]

## The Chinese Version of the Soviet Model

In 1949 the Chinese communists gained control over the economy of the world's most populous nation. Approximately four-fifths of the Chinese labor force were peasants, and agricultural production accounted for only a somewhat smaller share of the national income.[9] Per capita annual rural income was less than $100, placing China among the poorest countries in the world. Major objectives of the new government were rapid economic development and transformation of China into a modern industrial power. In the initial stages of industrialization, success depended upon the ability to mobilize and extract a surplus from the dominant agricultural sector for investment and capital accumulation in the "underdeveloped," nonagricultural sectors. Efficient transfer of agricultural surplus is an essential determinant of success in the process of economic development in any large agrarian country.

Many students of China's pre-1949 economy argued that despite the relatively low level of per capita output, China's traditional agriculture achieved yields that provided a considerable potential surplus. This surplus could have been used for the modernization of China's economy.[10] It was claimed that the surplus was lost to the landlord class and the government bureaucracy who "wasted" it in nonproductive expenditures. Therefore, these scholars believed that producers in the agricultural sector were already being exploited prior to 1949. According to this "distributionist" interpretation, the problem facing the nation in 1949 was one of gaining control over that share of agricultural production already being extracted by the traditional "exploiters" of the peasant — the landlords and the government. Even if this were the case, this surplus could only have provided a short-term escape from the inevitable need for even greater surpluses to fuel economic development. If agricultural production failed to grow fast enough to meet these needs, increases could only come from an intensification of the exploitation of the agricultural sector. As other chapters in this volume make clear, achieving a rapid rate of growth in agricultural production to meet the demands of the nonagricultural sectors has proved to be a problem.

Clearly, the Chinese communists did not adopt traditional communist models for agriculture when they first came to power. As soon as they liberated an area they kept their promises to the peasants and carried out a program of land reform. By the end of 1952 all rented land (about 40 percent of China's cultivated area) had been redistributed to poor and landless peasants. Private household farming and the traditional market system were retained. Private farming and marketing created an incentive for increasing agricultural production and allowed the central authorities to obtain some additional surplus through market purchases. However, crucial constraints prevented the peasants from expanding production quickly enough to meet burgeoning urban and industrial needs.

Production problems limited the potential growth of output. After the land reform program the peasants still had an average of only one hectare per household, and many peasant households held less land. Furthermore, the land owned by each family was scattered around the village in which the peasants lived. Finally, the land reform resulted in the elimination of the landlord-gentry class who had traditionally acted as a credit source, and the state did not create new credit facilities to meet this critical need. Many poor peasants still operated farms too small to be self-sustaining over time and the process of renting and selling land could be expected to lead to the same patterns of inequitable land ownership and tenancy that initially had provided support for the communist movement.

These problems were compounded by a heavy reliance on irrigation, organic fertilizer, and multiple cropping — all labor-intensive activities. Private households working small plots could not take advantage of the "economies of scale" present in these sources for higher yields.[11] Constraints on the production side of private household farming seriously threatened not only the regime's economic objective of achieving a rapid rate of increase in production, but also the long-run viability of achieving a more equitable distribution of land ownership and income.

An important priority in China's economic program was the rapid development of a heavy industrial base, including energy, metallurgy, and machine-building industries, which was dependent on the ability of the central authority to secure a large surplus from the agricultural sector. This surplus was needed for: (1) the urban labor force (raw and processed agricultural products accounted for approximately two-thirds of the consumption expenditures of urban workers in 1955); (2) export commodites to earn foreign exchange to pay for imports of capital goods needed for industry (three-fourths of China's export commodites were raw and processed agricultural products in the 1950s); (3) inputs for the production of consumer goods for the urban and rural labor force (over three-fourths of the material inputs in light industry consisted of raw and processed agricultural products in the 1950s); and (4) stocks to meet needs during periods of shortage. Because growth in these areas increased at a significantly greater rate than did agricultural production, the situation created an excess demand for an agricultural surplus. There was also a need to modify traditional cropping patterns to provide the specific product mix required to meet the demands of the nonagricultural sector. To obtain the necessary surplus through market mechanisms, the central authorities would have found it necessary to pay higher prices to the peasant. Whether or not higher prices would have obtained the desired level and composition of agricultural surplus would have depended on the peasants' reaction to these price incentives and their ability to increase output.

Difficulties the peasant may have had in increasing production have been mentioned above, but the problems involved in motivating self-sufficient households to sell an increased share of their output were equally important. We can assume, although not all observers of China's agriculture in the 1950s would agree, that the peasants' mentality and motivations were such that they were willing to bear the greater risks associated with more capital-intensive farming in exchange for a larger money income to be used for purchasing consumer goods to improve living standards and agricultural inputs to help increase farm yields. Conversely, investment in increased production of consumer goods would have contravened the leadership's decision to increase investment in the production of heavy industrial products. Market-oriented attempts to acquire an agricultural surplus would have led to inflationary price rises for agricultural products and consumer goods.

A stable price level was another major objective of China's economic development program. Prior to 1949, rampant inflation had seriously eroded support for the Nationalist government. It is unlikely that peasants would not have realized the inflationary consequences of sharply higher market prices. In addition, the use of markets for securing agricultural surplus would certainly have recreated the income inequality that the Chinese communists had promised their poorer peasant supporters to eliminate.

In light of this situation the Chinese leadership chose to adopt the traditional Soviet model. In this model the role of agriculture can be characterized by: (1) the collectivization of production; (2) increases of agricultural production through mobilization of collectives' resources, including labor, with limited direct investment provided by the state; (3) the acquisition of the necessary agricultural surplus to meet the needs of the nonagricultural sectors through agricultural taxes and contract purchases by the state procurement agencies at below market prices; and (4) the realization of the desired level and commodity mix of agricultural products by means of hectarage plans (by crop), yield targets, and predetermined quotas for delivery to the state. Despite inefficiencies and negative effects on peasant incentives, this system has remained the basis for obtaining agricultural surpluses in the Soviet Union and other communist countries, including China.[12] However, the Chinese modified the Soviet model of agricultural development so as to lessen exploitation of the peasants. Adaptions involved alterations in the structure and sequential adoption of institutional changes.

Agricultural taxes provide a major source of revenue for the state. When the Chinese communists first came to power, they introduced a progressive tax on agricultural land. Cultivated land was classified according to yields under normal conditions and taxes were paid in kind as a share of normal (not actual) yields. Tax rates were set relatively low, were fixed for a period of years, and progressively declined with lower land quality. In 1952, for example, the tax rates on good, average, and poor land were 23, 21, and 15 percent, respectively. On a regional basis, while the rates could be and were adjusted upward during especially good agricultural harvests, they were also lowered in cases of abnormally poor harvests. Although the agricultural tax accounted for about 15 percent of the state's total budget revenue in 1952, it made up only about 7.5 percent of the total net value of agricultural output. Despite problems encountered in securing an agricultural surplus the Chinese communists have not raised agricultural taxes, but, conversely, have reduced rates, so that at the end of the 1970s taxes were reported to be less than 7 percent of total production.

In 1953 the Chinese introduced compulsory purchase quotas, a primary factor in the traditional Soviet model of agriculture. Under this system the peasant receives partial compensation for goods delivered to the state to meet quotas. Before the death of Stalin the taxation aspect of this system was used extensively in the Soviet Union. The peasant was often paid less than three-fourths of the market price for state deliveries. As administered by the Chinese, however, the principal objective seems to have been to acquire agricultural commodities at *stable* prices only. In principle at least, quota contracts were to be "negotiated" between local agents of the state and producer or production units, with the quota adjusted to fit local conditions. The prices of these deliveries were quite close to retail market prices.[13]

In addition to compulsory state deliveries, collectivization of agricultural production, and the creation of central planning in the mid-1950s, the state set quotas for hectarage to be planted by crop. Cropping quotas were reported to cover more than three-fourths of China's cultivated area. As with quotas for sales to the state, cropping quotas were also supposed to be worked out in consultation with the peasants. However, Chinese communist leaders have admitted that agricultural surpluses were obtained through administrative directives issued by local authorities. These directives insured fulfillment of state crop and sale quotas and deprived the peasant of any effective bargaining power.

Prices for most agricultural items were set by the state. This maintained low and stable prices for "necessities" (raw and processed agricultural products). Agricultural products — including grains, cotton, and oils — were strictly rationed to consumers.

The extent to which the extraction of surplus from the agricultural sector represents "exploitation" ultimately depends on the rate of growth of agricultural output and the contribution of the state and nonagricultural sectors to that growth. Whether or not the collectivization of agriculture has aided agricultural growth in the socialist countries is a subject of considerable debate. There can be little doubt that the Chinese communists regarded the collectivization of agriculture as a long-run objective when they came to power in 1949. They initially believed that the period of transition from private to collectivized farming would take at least fifteen years. Mao Zedong and his left-wing followers argued that continued reliance on private household farming would only foster the reemergence and consolidation of "capitalist" values and behavior, while collectivized agriculture would mobilize the poor peasants and "unleash" the productive powers of socialist agriculture. As a result the Chinese peasants were organized into collectives in the mid-1950s.[14]

The collectives were expected to mobilize the land and labor under their control, to raise capital for communal investments, to increase labor efforts, and to allocate current inputs to alleviate existing bottlenecks in production. Thus collectives were supposed to increase agricultural output relying only on traditional inputs, such as increased organic fertilizer usage, multiple cropping, interplanting, or expansion of irrigation systems. The state did not provide investment allocations or large-scale loans. Less than 10 percent of the state's investment funds were earmarked for large-scale irrigation projects. The collectives were successful in mobilizing the peasants' labor power by increasing the labor force participation rate and the number of work days contributed by each worker. In other words, because the peasants did not receive an increase in real income commensurate with the increase in their labor efforts, the collectivization of agricultural production resulted in their exploitation.

Communist land redistribution still left the majority of peasants with land parcels too scattered and small to allow efficient use of family labor. Elementary Agricultural Producers Cooperatives, which pooled land, labor, and capital in units of twenty to twenty-five households, were designed to cope with the problem. These groups were frequently formed along preexisting kinship ties at the village level and thus were rapidly accepted by the peasants. Membership was voluntary and workers received income based on land, capital, and labor contributions. All households retained private plots for their own use. The pace at which collectivization was being carried out between 1953 and 1955 indicates the extent to which the Chinese communist leaders hoped to obtain the voluntary cooperation of the peasant households. In 1953 less than one-half of one percent of the peasant households were members of an Elementary Agricultural Producer's Cooperative; by the end of 1955 their share had increased to only 14 percent. Official policy called for a continuation of this relatively slow pace. As mentioned earlier, Mao and his left-wing followers desired a much more rapid transition to socialized agriculture. Due to pressure from the left wing of the party the pace of collectivization was speeded up in 1956, resulting in the introduction of larger units of production and in different methods of income distribution.

Although the rapid and significant changes in the institutional organization of farming in China in 1956 were unlikely to have been unaccompanied by some force and coercion, the case can still be made that poor peasants were provided with concrete incentives for joining the new Advanced Agricultural Cooperatives. Income distribution was to be based solely on labor performed, with the owners of land and capital losing both their property rights and any share of the collectives' income on the basis of those assets. Furthermore, while the larger units of production increased the benefits of income redistribution for poor members, individual households continued to work in small groups. Except for large-scale projects, which required the mobilization of the collectives' entire labor force, farm work was done by brigades of about twenty-five households, or even smaller teams of about seven households. Finally, Mao argued that 90 percent of the members of these new units would receive higher incomes. The available evidence indicates that this target was kept, even at the expense of failing to meet the quotas for sales to the state and a resulting reduction of the state's stock of agricultural products in 1956 (a poor agricultural year).[15]

In 1958, during the Great Leap Forward, all of China's peasants became part of the large-scale institutional organizations called communes. Communes averaged about 5,000 households each and controlled decision making in almost every sector of rural life. Communes mobilized labor for large-scale irrigation projects, farmland reconstruction, agricultural production, and the creation of small-scale rural industries. Income was redistributed according to personal need and the work was accomplished by individual work groups. When the commune movement ended in a serious agricultural crisis in 1959, Peng Dehuai, a leading party official, openly criticized Mao and his left-wing followers for the agricultural policies they were pursuing, claiming that not only were they counterproductive to the growth of agricultural output, but were also threatening the peasants with starvation. Although Peng was purged from the party for directly challenging Mao's policies, he was partly successful in his efforts. Mao was elevated to a largely honorary post and the right wing of the party took responsibility for managing the crisis.

Although the commune system was retained, in fact much of the labor allocation and income distribution decision-making power was transferred from the commune down to the lower level production team. Private plots and rural trade fairs were also reinstated. Planners made increased efforts to consult peasants before drawing up hectarage and sale quotas. This helped prevent recurrences of some of the gross errors made in the agricultural sector by overzealous cadres and planning groups during the Great Leap Forward.

Left-wingers continued to attack the right-wing policies of individual and task-specific material incentives, private plots, rural trade fairs, and the team as the primary unit for accounting and decision making. From the mid-1960s (the onset of the Cultural Revolution) to the mid-1970s (the death of Mao and overthrow of the Gang of Four), these attacks were successful in eliminating or at least reducing the implementation of these right-wing policies in large areas of China. The Chinese version of the Soviet model, however, continues to be the basic organizational and functional format for agriculture's role in the Chinese communist strategy of economic development. The current Chinese version can be summarized as follows:

1. The commune system of collectivized agriculture, with the team as the basic unit of decision making and income distribution. Commune households are given private plots and can sell the products of their sideline activities in rural trade fairs.
2. The reliance on the commune organization to mobilize its own resources, with limited direct investment by the state, as a means of increasing agricultural production rapidly enough to provide for increases in both the peasants' standard of living and in the

agricultural surpluses required to meet the needs of the nonagricultural sectors.

3. The extraction of the desired level and product mix from the agricultural sector by means of agricultural taxes, planned quotas for sales to the procurement agencies of the state, and planned hectarage quotas covering a major share of the cultivated area of the collectives.

We have seen that Chinese modifications of the Soviet agricultural development strategy attempted to serve the interests of the peasant majority as well as the planned economic development program. This strategy at least partially failed, due not only to the haste with which the radical element of the Chinese Communist Party tried to attain advanced stages of socialism, but also to inability to achieve a rapid growth of agricultural output. We may conclude that although the Chinese tried to ameliorate the degree to which agriculture was exploited for the sake of industrialization, the adoption of the Soviet model led to results similar to those found in most other communist countries.

## The "Agriculture First" Policy

Although the institutional organizations pioneered in the 1950s remained in place, in 1962 Zhou Enlai announced a new strategy to be known as the "agriculture first" policy. This policy provides a good basis for arguing that the Chinese communists were concerned with the welfare of the masses. By the early 1960s, the Chinese realized that to acquire an adequate supply of agricultural products for state use and to improve the standard of living of the peasants the state would have to contribute concrete resources, not just launch campaigns or propose institutional changes. Although the "agriculture first" policy did not call for an increase in direct state investment in agriculture, it altered priorities for growth *within* industries. State investments to industries that supplied inputs to agriculture, such as chemical fertilizer and agricultural machinery industries, were to receive increased state funding. In addition, a program of rural small-scale industrialization—the five small industries—was launched to help the crucial rural industries of cement, coal, iron and steel, chemical fertilizer, and agricultural machinery to rapidly develop. These small-scale industries relied exclusively on local labor, materials, and technology, and were to help alleviate critical transport bottlenecks caused by China's primitive transportation network.[16]

Other economic policies implemented in the years following the Great

Leap Forward included programs which diverted crucial resources from urban to rural areas. Urban medical, educational, technical, and administrative personnel were "sent down" to the countryside to "serve the
people" and to help create and expand rural medical and educational
facilities. Many graduates of urban middle schools (high schools) were
assigned to work on communes or on state farms and, although their
knowledge of farming was limited, they did supply labor power and, more
importantly, bookkeeping and other technical skills. Thus, in dramatic
contrast with the development strategy in most other developing countries,
China's large rural population enjoys a much greater access to medical and
educational services than their level of per capita income would indicate. In
addition, the collectives have had access to considerable technical assistance
from the modern sector.

It is argued by some Western observers that the state pricing policy has
been of greatest material benefit to the peasants. Although prices paid by
state procurement agencies for quota sales increased slightly between the
mid-1950s and mid-1970s, significant reductions in the prices of
agricultural inputs such as chemical fertilizer and agricultural machinery
shifted the balance of trade in the peasants' favor. These changes in the
terms of trade may have contributed to increases in income in rural areas,
although by international standards inputs are still expensive.

## Post-Mao Policies

The death of Mao Zedong in September 1976 was quickly followed by
the overthrow of major left-wing leaders. The post-Mao leadership has
assigned much of the blame for the present plight of the peasants to the
more radical economic policies of their predecessors. While those radical
policies certainly exacerbated the problem, the post-Mao leadership's
discussion of current economic problems makes clear that the present low
standard of living of China's peasants is the result of the basic strategy of
economic development relied upon since the collectivization of agriculture
in the mid-1950s.

The state's investment allocation priorities have been reordered in favor
of industries producing agricultural inputs. In addition, the share of investment in the consumer goods industries was increased to provide greater
supplies of these commodities for the peasants. Equally important, the
state's direct investment in the agricultural sector has increased from less
than 10 to almost 20 percent of the state's total investment in the economy.

Within the commune system, the team's role as the basic decision-
making and accounting unit is reaffirmed once again, and the peasants
have been promised that higher authorities will stop requisitioning the

team's resources without fair compensation. Planned crop hectarage and quota sales to the state continue in force so as to guarantee the "needs of the state," but the determination of these quotas by means of negotiations with local units is being asserted. In drawing up these plans, specialization in production to better fit local conditions is encouraged. It is no longer a policy that everyone must produce grain for the sake of self-sufficiency. The production teams are now urged to subcontract work and output quotas to small groups of households. Inefficient and wasteful rural small-scale industries are being closed, while individual households are encouraged to utilize their private plots and to develop sideline activities to supplement income from the collective. Rural trade fairs for private commercial transactions of these products are permitted, and price controls on many nonessential commodities and services have been removed.

The Chinese admit that the increase in purchased inputs per unit of output, and the relatively stable purchase price of quota sales to the state, meant that over time there was a reduction in the income per unit of output sold. By the mid-1970s, when the average value of agricultural labor was included, the peasants were losing money growing the basic grains and cotton. This explains why it was necessary to force the crop hectarage plans and quotas for sales to the state upon the peasants. To remedy this situation, the average price for quota sales to the state has been increased by 20 percent and the price for above-quota sales has been increased by 50 percent.[17]

In the brief period since 1979, when these new policies were introduced, they have contributed to a rapid growth of agricultural output as well as increases in the peasants' income. On the other hand, as the other chapters in this volume indicate, China's agricultural development still faces many obstacles and the peasants' standard of living remains very low.

## Notes

1. During the Cold War era following World War II, the terms communism and communist gained widespread use as labels for the political ideology of those who were Marxists and for the governments that were aligned with the Soviet Union. Marx, of course, made a clear distinction between socialism and communism. According to his definition the present "communist" countries are really "socialist" countries. Having noted this distinction, however, and with apologies to those who prefer the "rectification of terms" for the purpose of avoiding the political biases these terms acquired during the Cold War, I will use the widely accepted and understood label "communist" in this chapter.

2. One of the leading controversies over the last decade among noncommunist students of Soviet-style collectivized agriculture has been whether or not the state

could have acquired the same agricultural surplus by means of market prices — that is, stimulated higher levels of production and voluntary sales to the state through the creation of material incentives for the peasant producers. In the two countries of East Europe (Yugoslavia and Poland) that have offered the peasant a real choice, the peasants have chosen private, household farming over collective organizations by a wide majority.

3. Benjamin Ward, "The Chinese Approach to Economic Development," in Robert F. Dernberger, ed., *The Chinese Experience in Comparative Perspective* (Cambridge, Mass.: Harvard University Press, 1980).

4. Among the available analyses of China's agricultural development experience, this assumption and/or conclusion is most evident in the work of Anthony Tang. See, for example, Anthony Tang, "Policy and Performance in Agriculture," in Alexander Eckstein, Walter Galenson, and Ta-chung Liu, eds., *Economic Trends in Communist China* (Chicago: Aldine, 1968).

5. Dwight H. Perkins, "The Central Features of China's Economic Development," in Robert F. Dernberger, ed., *The Chinese Experience.*

6. Ward, "The Chinese Approach to Economic Development."

7. For an attempt to analyze the interaction of these exogenous shocks and economic policies as a major explanation of the cyclical behavior of China's economy since 1949, see Alexander Eckstein, "Economic Fluctuations in Communist China's Domestic Development," in Ping-ti Ho and Tang Tsou, eds., *China in Crisis,* vol. 1, book 2 (Chicago: University of Chicago Press, 1968), pp. 691–729.

8. My use of the term "exploited" refers to its more traditional Marxian definition: the extraction of a share of a producer's output without the return of an equivalent value of commodities. Most taxes can be narrowly defined as exploitative, and the peasants in most countries are being exploited for the sake of economic development. The proper way to assess the extent to which the agricultural sector was exploited by China's post-1949 leaders in their economic development strategies would be to present and analyze quantitative data for the resulting resource and commodity flows between agriculture and the rest of the economy. Unfortunately, the necessary empirical evidence for the latter approach is not available. However, in this chapter reference will be made to the quantitative evidence that is available.

9. Western estimates indicate that the agricultural labor force accounted for over 80 percent of the total labor force in 1953. Recent reports in the Chinese press refer to agriculture as having contributed 70 percent of the total material output of agriculture and industry in 1949.

10. See Carl Riskin, "Surplus and Stagnation in Modern China," in Dwight H. Perkins, ed., *China's Modern Economy in Historical Perspective* (Stanford, Calif.: Stanford University Press, 1975), pp. 49–84.

11. The collective mobilization of labor for creating and maintaining projects which collect, store, and distribute water offer results beyond the means of household or team projects. With multiple cropping, as long as the ratio of land to labor within households varied, pooling in a collective created opportunities for coordination of multiple-cropping activities. Thus while statistical analyses of mono-cropping agriculture indicate the existence of decreasing or constant returns

to scale (see P. K. Berkhan, "Size, Productivity, and Returns of Scale: An Analysis of Farm-Level Data in Indian Agriculture," *Journal of Political Economy,* vol. 81 [November/December 1973], pp. 1370–1386), statistical analyses of Chinese agriculture indicate the existence of economies of scale (see D. L. Chinn, "Land Utilization and Productivity in Prewar Chinese Agriculture: Preconditions for Collectivization," *American Journal of Agricultural Economics,* vol. 59, no. 3 (August 1977) pp. 559–564.

12. As will be discussed later in this chapter, many reforms of China's economic system have been advocated following the death of Mao in 1976. The discussion of these reforms in the Chinese press have been highly publicized in the West, with special emphasis given to the more revolutionary extremes being either experimented with or merely advocated as "suggestions." Thus readers of this chapter may challenge the argument that the basic set of institutions described here are still in effect today. Reforms in China's economic system are obviously taking place, but my reading of the Chinese press and discussions with Chinese involved in the debates over economic reform clearly indicate that the institutional framework described here is not only still in force, but is likely to remain in force in the foreseeable future.

13. This is the implicit argument and conclusion in Dwight Perkins's detailed analysis of the prices and quotas involved in the Chinese systems of advanced purchase contracts. See Dwight Perkins, *Market Control and Planning in Communist China* (Cambridge: Harvard University Press, 1968).

14. Only those aspects of the collectivization of Chinese agriculture that are relevant to the assessment of the role of agriculture in the Chinese communists' development strategy are discussed here. A more detailed analysis of the collectivization of Chinese agriculture is presented in Chapter 6.

15. See David Ladd Denny, "Rural Policies and the Distribution of Agricultural Products in China," unpublished Ph.D. dissertation, Department of Economics, University of Michigan, 1971.

16. See Chapter 9 for an expanded discussion of the "five small industries."

17. The 50 percent higher price for above-quota sales implies a 50 percent increase above the new quota prices. To prevent the peasants from meeting the quota commodities at the 50 percent premium price, the above-quota deliveries are paid for at a price 50 percent above the weighted average price paid for whatever commodities were first sold to the state in fulfillment of the quota. (My thanks to Steven Butler, Visiting Associate Professor, Cornell University, for this information.)

## Readings

Buchanan, Keith. *The Transformation of the Chinese Earth; Aspects of the Evolution of the Chinese Earth from Earliest Times to Mao Tse-tung.* New York: Praeger, 1970.

Burki, Shahid Javed. *A Study of Chinese Communes, 1965.* Cambridge, Mass.: East Asian Research Center, Harvard University, 1969.

Schran, Peter. *The Development of Chinese Agriculture, 1950–1959.* Urbana: University of Illinois Press, 1969. Study of the process of transition from private to collectivized farming in the early 1950s and its impact on input supplies, outputs and productivity, peasant incomes and income distribution.

Tang, Anthony. *Agriculture in China's Economic Development* (forthcoming). A collection of published articles on China's agriculture written by Tang over a period of several years. These have been brought up to date and were published in a single volume by the Center for Chinese Studies, Unviersity of Michigan, in early 1982.

Tang, Anthony, and Bruce Stone. *Food Production in the People's Republic of China.* Research Report No. 15, International Food Policy Research Institute, May 1980. An analysis of quantitative estimates for the changes in inputs and outputs between the early 1950s and mid 1970s and a projection of the demand for agricultural products in 1985. Contains an evaluation of the changes in inputs necessary to achieve the required supply of agricultural products in that year.

U.S., Congress, Joint Economic Committee. *Chinese Economy Post-Mao.* Washington, D.C., 1978. An updating of the Joint Economic Committee's tri-annual collection of multiauthor papers on China's economy. The 1978 volume includes three papers specifically devoted to China's agriculture: production, grain trade, and agricultural technology. (The volume in this series that appeared in the fall of 1981, *China Under the Four Modernizations,* also included three articles on Chinese agriculture.)

# 6
# Rural Institutions in China

*Benedict Stavis*

A distinctive aspect of China's rural development strategy is the tripartite commune system (commune, brigade, team) that formed a base for the communist restructuring of rural social institutions. New rural institutions were created to serve three primary purposes. First, they were designed to strengthen socialism and increase equality in the countryside. This has meant collective ownership of most means of production, as well as controls over the remaining private sector. The second goal was to provide incentives for rural development. By facilitating growth in agricultural productivity and promoting social services, rural life has been more secure and pleasant. Finally, the institutions were to provide capital, commodities, and labor for the development of China's industrial sector. To attain this end, government control over trade, finance, and personnel was implemented.

Of course, these goals are not entirely consistent, and in China, as everywhere, there is disagreement over the priority attached to each goal, as well as over the best way to attain each goal. Through time, perceptions and expectations change. Thus, there has been ongoing debate in China over the structure of rural institutions.

Each goal — equality, growth, and industrialization — has required strengthening the power of the state. Autonomous sources of leadership, which might have competed with the state, have been weakened or dissolved. The inevitable result of this process has been to strengthen the bureaucracy. By the mid-1970s the middle levels of the bureaucracy were frequently acting arbitrarily, inefficiently, and selfishly. A major challenge of institutional reform in the 1980s will be to establish controls over the bureaucracy.

The first two sections of this chapter describe the function of rural family and village institutions. They reveal important continuities with, as well as changes from, the past. The remainder of the chapter focuses on the evolution of the collective system, its contribution to the economic and social growth of China, and its inherent problems.

## The Family

Although the role and structure of the family in Chinese society has changed over the decades, it is still the most important rural institution. Prior to 1949 the family had a crucial economic role because it owned farmland. All decisions relating to production, including farm management, hiring of labor, consumption, and marketing were based on the family unit. The family had a significant legal role because the head of the household was held responsible for taxes and the behavior of household members. Hierarchical family relations were reinforced by intrafamilial economic dependency. After brothers married and had children, psychological and social tensions within the family required a division of the old family, including property, and the creation of new families. However, only males could legally inherit family property. Family structure provided important social stability. Old people were supported by their grown children. At the death of the oldest male in the family unit, the serious task of worshipping ancestral spirits was continued by sons. Having a male heir to pay respect to the ancestors of the family was critical, and a son could be adopted if necessary to perform this function.

Before 1949, family size and structure in China were related to economic status. Wealthy families could afford to support many dependents, but poor families could barely feed a few children. Sons were preferred to daughters, and in depressed areas occasional female infanticide occurred. Daughters were considered a partial burden because they consumed food but could not perform heavy farm labor and, in the Chinese social context, were not capable of carrying on the family name and worshipping family ancestors. Bride prices, to the extent they existed, did not compensate for these disadvantages. Marriages were arranged, often in infancy, largely with the goal of creating alliances between families. After marriage, and sometimes before, a daughter would enter her husband's family. Her labor and children would help her new family. Tension between wives and mothers-in-law was commonplace. Since 1949, marriages have begun to be self-arranged by the participants. Concubinage is outlawed and monogamy is rigidly enforced.

Since 1949, the role of the family has changed in important ways but the family still remains a crucial rural institution both economically and socially. The family no longer owns farmland or hires labor, and cash income and grain allotments are computed on the basis of individual labor and needs. However, income accrues to a family account controlled by the head of the household and is distributed within the household. Garden plots are sometimes assigned to the family on the basis of family size. The family works this land and eats or sells its produce (vegetables, hogs, etc.). In addition, the family can engage in handicrafts — such as basket weaving — and gathering — firewood, wild animals, etc. — as long as it does not hire labor.

Religious beliefs are dissolving, and a male heir is no longer needed to worship ancestors. However, children are needed to provide old-age security, particularly in rural areas, and sons are still preferred. This desire for male offspring interferes with birth-control policies. The government has tried to reduce the population problem by encouraging newly married couples to live with the wife's family when there are no sons. In some areas rural collective institutions are obligated to care for the elderly who have no other means of support. Some localities (e.g., Shanghai) are establishing a regular pension system for retired farmers. So far these new institutions have made only shallow inroads into traditional expectations.

In addition, a family's total income is determined largely by its labor power. The income per capita is determined by the ratio of producers to consumers within the family. This naturally changes with a family's life cycle as children grow up and as adults become elderly. A family with many children is poor, but, as the children begin to work, family income increases. A wife and children may help provide labor and management for gardening and animal husbandry activities and sometimes the size of the private plot is adjusted to take into account larger families. Thus, there are many direct economic advantages to a large family. In addition, in the past in some regions, children were entitled to a full adult food ration, which exceeded the child's food requirements and therefore provided additional grain for the family to eat or sell.

Family planning and birth control have been official government policies since the early 1970s. These campaigns have increased in intensity throughout the past decade. At first, family planning was voluntary. The government provided birth control information and materials. Next, villages were encouraged to make plans for births, and social pressure was mobilized to reduce the number of births. These programs may have been partially effective, but were not judged adequate, particularly with the post–land-reform baby boom entering marriageable age. In 1979, the government commenced an intense campaign to encourage families to have only one child and certainly no more than two. Financial rewards to one-child families were given out. Punishments, including reduced wages, were threatened for large families. In some cases, grain rations were not increased for additional children. Social pressure is mobilized for abortion, and local bureaucrats undoubtedly have been tempted to use coercion to sterilize people with large families.

Rural families generally own their houses, and, in theory, can buy, sell, and rent the house. Buying a house is expensive (compared with rural cash income), and accumulating the funds to purchase a house is a major element in the financial plans of married couples starting families. In recent years, as population has grown and pressure on land has intensified, some villages have constructed new row housing, which is rented to villagers. This saves farmland and in many cases brings residents closer together. This gives people better access to services and removes the interference of scattered farmsteads for farm management. Unfortunately, dense housing patterns are not well suited to private farming, livestock, and gardening activities.

There are a few rural residents who do not share in the normal family life. Sometimes sons of former landlords inherit the guilt of their fathers and village girls are reluctant to marry them for fear that their own children will also inherit this guilt. In addition, in the late 1960s and 1970s, urban high school graduates were sent to live in the countryside. Generally they lived in groups and did not marry, hoping eventually to return to the cities.

Changes in family structure have generally been in conformity with government policy. The government officially opposes traditional values and superstitions and supports women's equality, the reduction of exploitation within the family, and increased female participation in the labor force. Conversely, the government endorses the family unit and the social and economic security it gives. Many local officials have very traditional family lives (including many children) and this undermines some of the propaganda to change family values.

Only for a brief period in 1958 was there a direct attack on the traditional family structure. In an effort to mobilize female labor for tending field crops, the collectivization of some household functions was advocated. This included collective dining, child care, sewing, and other activities. For a wide range of social and technical reasons, this effort failed.

## Village Organization

Village level organization also reflects a complex combination of old and new patterns. Many of the preexisting village organizations have been used to form the foundations for new organizations. The names, leaderships, and functions are new, but some of the patterns of village level interaction have been retained.

Before 1949, China had a wide range of local social institutions to meet different needs. Some institutions were essentially egalitarian, while others were more hierarchical. Informal, voluntary groupings included friends and neighbors exchanging labor and sharing tools and draft animals. Crop-watching societies to protect ripe crops from thievery were fairly widespread. Funeral and credit societies also existed. These egalitarian and voluntary organizations were strongest in regions characterized by widespread peasant ownership of land rather than tenancy.

Another pattern of organization was determined by lineage. Male children were automatically in the lineage of their fathers; females joined the lineage of their husbands. In some regions the lineage was an important and powerful institution that owned land and buildings, including temples and ancestral halls. Land might be rented out and the income used to support ritual needs, maintain a temple (and its staff), or support a school, which would help train bright members of the lineage to take examinations for the bureaucracy. In some cases lineage land was controlled by a small group of elders who treated this property virtually as private property. The power of lineages differed widely from place to place. In some villages, all families were members of the same lineage, which could be a strong institution, particularly where it owned a large portion of the surrounding land. In other places a village would have several lineages, and village politics would be characterized by rivalry between them. Sometimes lineages were organized on a large scale, covering hundreds of villages. By and large, lineage organizations were strong in south China, particularly in stable and isolated communities such as in Guangdong, and weak in north China because floods, drought, and famine caused more internal migration, and families tended to scatter more.

The village itself was yet another social unit. Village elders might arbitrate disputes within families or over land and water rights. A voluntary militia might be organized at the village level for some degree of protection from bandits and warlords. The state administrative system also organized villagers into small groups that shared responsibility for organizing police work and tax collection. Village (and lineage) leadership typically came from people who were wealthy or literate.

On a slightly larger scale, market villages provided special opportunities for social exchange. People from all social levels participated in the market, but in different ways according to wealth and power. Most parts of China had periodic rotating markets, a pattern widespread throughout rural areas of the world. Market day might be every fifth day, and thousands of people would come from a radius of 5–10 kilometers to buy and sell the hundreds of special products rural people grow, make, and use. The marketplace was a center not only for economic exchange, but also for social exchange. Marriage brokers arranged marriages, and teahouses provided meeting places for gentry to arrange rural public works. Temples and religious festivals were also based in the market town.

Local government was fairly well established at the county level. The magistrate, posted by the central government, was a key figure. Major functions of the magistrate and his aides included tax collection, law and order, justice, and military recruitment. Extensive land and population records were maintained for tax purposes. In many regions local officials had to organize corvée labor to build and maintain water conservancy projects and undertake road work. County government had hierarchical local branches — the district (qu) and below that the township (xiang), as well as village level organizations. County officials generally had to work closely with local village and lineage leaders to mobilize labor, catch criminals, and collect taxes.

## Land Reform

After the founding of the PRC in 1949 village institutions were modified. The crucial first step in building new rural institutions was the destruction of old ones. The rural elite, which drew power from land ownership and political access, was the primary target for land reform. Land reform was carried out in 1947–1948 in north China. After the communist government was established, land reform was undertaken in the rest of the country in 1950–1952. Land was taken without compensation from absentee landords, local landlords, clans, and some rich peasants  and given to tenants and small farmers. Altogether, about 4 percent of the population lost land, and 60 percent gained. About 43 percent of the cultivated land area changed hands.[1]

Land reform was very effective in destroying the economic and social power of the rural elite. Land was not redistributed through calm administrative procedures. Rather, meetings were held in villages to determine people's economic class and to denounce landlords. In some villages these meetings were violent. In the Chinese culture, this loss of face was devastating. Landlords or other elite were beaten, humiliated to suicide, and sometimes executed. In the emotion-charged environment of village meetings, excesses were frequent. At least one-half to one million were killed and another two million imprisoned.[2] Although this was a low percentage of China's vast rural population, it meant that perhaps every five or ten landlord families experienced one fatality — a frequent enough occurrence to bring deep fear to the landlord families. Of course, in some places, landlords organized their forces and struck back militarily, but in the face of the unified Red Army, supplemented by communist-organized local guerrilla and militia units, military resistance was futile.

Clan leaders lost all financial power when lineage lands were seized and redistributed to peasants. Lineage temples were taken over and used as sites for local administration, granaries, etc. The lineage as a set of family relations was not destroyed, but the lineage as a powerful economic and political organization was ended.

In view of these policies, the rural elite had few choices — to adopt a low profile in the village, working only on their own land, or to migrate to the cities. In some cases the old leadership tried to join the new revolutionary institutions, hoping their business skills would be indispensable to the new order. In other cases, they sought to protect themselves through traditional alliances, such as giving their daughters in marriage to the new communist leadership.

The same revolutionary processes that eliminated the old leadership as a social class also created a new rural leadership. Often new leaders were from poor families — tenants or even landless laborers. As activists in the land-reform campaign they assumed positions of power. At a broader level, the process of land reform gave peasants a new psychology. They now had the power and capacity to alter village relationships and had "turned over a new body" and "stood up."[3]

Women played an important role in the land-reform process. At public meetings they were often key witnesses. When land was redistributed, women and men received equal shares, and female infants had the same rights as male infants. These precedents had a deep impact on both men's and women's perception of the woman's role in the village. At roughly the same time as land reform was carried out, the communist government passed a marriage law that specified the rights of women to free, self-selected marriage, to divorce, and to property ownership. Of course, these events did not suddenly change the social position of women. Indeed, there had been changes throughout the previous decades, symbolized by the laws against footbinding and its gradual disappearance, but after the early 1950s many old customs still remained. Nevertheless, land reform and the marriage law made the 1950 period a watershed for the woman's role in the village.

Although land reform was revolutionary, it included certain conservative features. Land reform was directed primarily at the small number of absentee landlords and not at the large number of rich peasants who lived in the villages and rented out small pieces of land. The Communist party wanted to be sure that rich peasants would remain neutral in the land-reform struggle and refrained from criticizing this group as heavily as the absentee landlords. From an economic point of view, the rich peasants had a crucial role. They managed substantial amounts of land and produced a large share of China's food. If they were directly attacked they might have refused to sow or harvest, and might have slaughtered their farm animals. Production would have sagged and food shortages would have resulted. In addition, the rich peasants had surplus grain and might consider selling it to meet urban consumption. Finally, the Korean War made China eager to reduce domestic disorder. For these reasons the Chinese government carried out land reform, but simultaneously strengthened what they called the "rich peasant economy."

Some traditional rural institutions of leadership were destroyed, but voluntary, communal peasant organizations were invigorated. Indeed, destruction of the rural elite made it possible for old patterns of social organization to be utilized without fear of recurrent gentry power. Gradually, a new set of rural institutions was created, culminating in the commune system, which has gone through many phases and is still evolving.

To some extent Chinese leaders emulated institutional models developed in the Soviet Union. However, the Chinese leadership was well informed about the human death toll, animal slaughter, and general agricultural depression that accompanied collectivization in the Soviet Union. They also knew that continued high extractions from the rural sector in the Soviet Union had further depressed the countryside. The Chinese tried to learn from Soviet mistakes and avoid comparable problems.

## The Growth of the People's Commune System

After land redistribution, farmland was still privately owned, but the government prohibited sales of land, hiring of labor, and loaning of money. However, farm families still faced differing producer/consumer ratios, peak labor demands, and credit needs. These problems were to be solved by the formation of cooperatives. The first stage of cooperative organization was the Mutual Aid Team (MAT). Small groups of neighboring farm families were urged to work together, to exchange labor voluntarily and purchase simple farm tools or draft animals together. Rural self-help organizations like the Mutual Aid Teams were already prevalent in many areas prior to 1949, so their acceptance was widespread. Under government pressure these voluntary groups were formalized and became year-round organizations instead of seasonal. By 1954, 68 million rural households (58 percent of the rural population) were in 10 million Mutual Aid Teams.[4]

In 1955 the communist leadership merged MATs into larger Agricultural Producer's Cooperatives (APC). Each cooperative averaged 27 families.[5] It was suggested that a larger group could manage tiny, scattered parcels of land better and would be able to mobilize more labor for water conservation work. Joining these cooperatives was purely voluntary and some farmers "went it alone." After joining an APC the farmer retained title to the original parcel of land. He could (and occasionally did) withdraw from the cooperative, but a wide range of financial incentives and social pressures made this difficult. Farmers were not compensated for land, but were repaid for recent investments in land improvement.

Remuneration to cooperative members was for capital contributions (land, animals, and tools) and labor during the year. A variable percentage (under 50 percent) of the profit of the APC was distributed as a dividend according to capital shares. The remainder was distributed according to labor. A system of work points was developed for this purpose. In general, each farm job was given a certain number of points. Difficult jobs, such as carrying water and transplanting, were worth 10 points per day. Easy jobs, such as tending animals, were worth 5–6 points per day. Each year the total number of points accumulated was divided into the total profit to compute the earnings per point. Individual wages were derived by multiplying the total number of points an individual had accumulated times the computed value per point. In this system a person's labor wages were determined by the number of days he worked, which jobs he did, and the total profitability of the cooperative. This system of computing income for labor has remained basically intact since the mid-1950s.

Rich peasants were largely unscathed by land reform, and maintained agricultural and trading skills and positions of social leadership. If allowed to join the cooperatives, they could have easily assumed formal positions of leadership and perhaps even used the resources of the cooperative to reestablish or consolidate their prior position. For this reason the model regulations for cooperatives published in 1956 stated that former rich peasants and landlords would not be allowed to join for several years. In addition they would be banned from positions of leadership for a specified period of time.

By 1956 the Communist party was again urging reorganization of the countryside by amalgamating existing cooperatives into a new form of cooperative, the Higher Level Agricultural Producers Cooperative (HAPC). The new cooperatives showed two differences from the old. First, they were much larger. By 1957, 630,000 old cooperatives had been reorganized into 680,000 new ones, and the number of participating families jumped from 17 million to 118 million. Each new HAPC averaged around 165 families. Often, the old cooperative or MAT retained its organizational structure and became a work team within the HAPC. The other critical difference was that the HAPC no longer acknowledged private ownership of land. Under this system the dividend distributed according to property share was eliminated. All remuneration was based on labor points accrued through the work point system. Because everyone was working the land jointly, equal payment according to labor seemed fair.

Scarcely had the HAPCs been established when they were amalgamated into people's communes. By the end of 1958, 27,000 communes were set up, each one averaging 4,600 families. As with earlier reorganizations, the lower-order institutions were retained as component parts. The HAPCs became brigades, and the former lower-level APCs retained their status as teams.

Before communes were established, government responsibilities included the traditional ones of police, population registration, military recruitment, judicial settlements, and some provision for health, education, and welfare services. Government administration provided political leadership for land reform and cooperativization campaigns, handled arrangements for distributing agricultural inputs, and procured crops for government and urban needs. As the agricultural cooperatives grew in scale and the functions of government turned more toward issues of economic organization, confusion often arose over the division between government and cooperative. When communes were established they merged all these functions, becoming a unit of both local government administration and economic cooperation.

Because the commune was a unit of local administration, commune leaders were appointed by the county government from a pool of professional administrators. In theory, brigades elected their own leaders, but in practice their nominations were arranged by the Communist party, with many "suggestions" from higher levels. Production team leaders were elected in what appears to have been open processes. However, higher levels could force the removal of team leaders who contravened national policy.

When first set up, the commune owned all assets, and labor teams were treated like troops. Teams were sent to work in one field or another much as soldiers are sent to take one hill or another. This made no sense in agriculture as it denied the responsibility, continuity, and localized knowledge needed for good farm management. Communes also experimented with a free supply system in which people received what they "needed," regardless of how much work they did. This was a literal enactment of the communist principle of distribution, to each according to his needs. Many rural areas set up public kitchens and dining halls and people could eat as much as they needed or wanted. Consumption rose steeply and reserves were quickly exhausted. Later, shortages occurred and work incentives were undermined. People saw little reason to work if their food was provided regardless of effort expended. In addition, private plots were absorbed into collective fields and the traditional periodic markets were closed.

During this period (1958–1960) excessive commune size, military labor allocation, poor incentives, and abolishment of the private sector combined with an inappropriate technology policy for disastrous results. Seeds were planted too close together for the available fertility; irrigation channels were dug without drainage; labor was mobilized and exhausted with deep planting; varieties and cropping patterns were popularized without testing for local suitability; and labor was withdrawn from agriculture to make low quality iron in inefficient backyard furnaces. Catastrophic weather, which brought both floods and drought, accentuated these problems. Faced with falling production, China's farm economy entered a deep depression. Grain production sometimes fell below survival requirements, and health conditions deteriorated. Under these stresses the collective system disintegrated to some extent and people farmed whatever land they could.

In 1961 and 1962 there was a major reorganization of the commune structure. Size was one of the primary factors restructured. Large communes were divided into smaller ones and the total number of communes was raised to 74,000, averaging 1,000 families each. An apparent reason for this reduction in size was to make commune size coincide with the traditional marketing village. In this form, the commune was built upon preexisting patterns of economic and social interactions.

By 1961 the principle of property ownership was reestablished, 5–10 percent of the cultivatable land was reserved for private plots, and markets were reopened to enable individuals to sell and exchange their produce. Specific properties and assets were assigned semipermanently to the commune, brigade, and team. Farmland and draft animals were assigned to the team level, comprised of 20–40 families.

Communist party documents promulgated in 1961–1962 specified that the basic rural system should remain stable for thirty years.[6] There was, however, some reorganization in the late 1960s in which the number of communes was reduced to around 50,000. In 1974 it was estimated that communes averaged 3,000–4,000 families each. There were a total of about 750,000 brigades (15 per commune) averaging about 200 families each, and about five million production teams (7 per brigade) averaging 30 families each.[7]

There has been continued debate about the details of commune organization. One important issue concerns the method of determining work points. Points can be associated with a specific job, such as plowing, or alternatively may be allocated for a certain amount of work, e.g., plowing or harvesting a specific field, regardless of time. Production teams have shifted back and forth, and sometimes have used both systems depending on the season. An additional system was proposed by Dazhai brigade in the late 1960s. One of its features was that work points were determined by self-appraisal at a public meeting.

Another issue has been the extent to which distribution of food should be related to work. People generally receive a certain percentage of their grain rations automatically. The remainder is distributed according to work done. Sometimes 70 percent of food rations come automatically. Such a program may have reduced incentives to work. It should be noted that regardless of the system, a monetary charge is associated with food. The value of food is deducted from work point earnings. Families needing more food than their work point earnings are called "overdrawn households." They are routinely granted loans to be repaid in later years when the ratio of producer to consumer becomes more favorable.

The precise limits of commune responsibility have been another important issue. Some communes control tractor and experiment stations, schools, and hospitals. Some own factories, providing profits for further investment. In some periods, such as 1961–1966 and after 1978, however, the political and economic power of the commune was constrained. At these times, many economic and social activities were controlled and funded by departments of the county government. It was argued by government officials that the commune lacked the technical proficiency, economic scale, and personnel system to develop effectively these activities. The battle for control of local resources reflected the divergent interests of party and government institutions.

The existence of collective institutions at several levels has meant that there are organizational structures that provide leadership, labor, and funds for development activities of virtually any scale. Through these institutions, agricultural innovations can be tested with minimal risk to individuals. Issues of collective concern, such as investment and consumption, are subject to public scrutiny. Social pressures are mobilized to keep down current consumption and its related "revolution of rising expectations," as well as to lower the birth rate.

Collective institutions do have disadvantages. They have often been difficult to manage. In the early years of commune development few leaders were prepared to manage the rural economy on such a large scale, and people with accounting skills were scarce. Even after a decade or two, these problems remain. Also, just as the risks of innovation are spread over many people, so are the benefits. No individual can gain significant profit by production of a new commodity or entry into a new market.

Local problems stem from the fact that commune leadership has been primarily appointed by, and is responsible to, the political hierarchy. In general, local social and economic realities and pressures have had little influence on local leaders. Of course, there have been numerous exceptions to this pattern, especially when local communities were united and strongly motivated, or when local leaders had strong personalities. But, by and large, local administrators have been willing to enforce policies that restrained regional specialization, emphasis on cash crops, and development of the private sector.

The state has discouraged local or regional control over agricultural decision making to simultaneously strengthen state control over production and to increase local self-sufficiency. Regions were encouraged to be self-sufficient in grain to reduce the need for the state to supply commodity grain to localities. Cash crops specialization was discouraged to avoid local grain shortages and possible oversupply and resulting price instability. In addition, there were ideological and political reasons to restrict the private sector — otherwise private accumulation of wealth could lead to challenges to the collective economy and the dominance of the state.

Although the commune system is the major social and economic organization in rural China, there are a few other modes of organization that should be noted. In non-Han, national minority areas, the commune system may exist in name and form, but the substance of organization may be substantially different. This would apply particularly to scattered mountain peoples in southwest China, to Xizang (Tibet), and to animal-herding peoples of Neimonggol and Central Asia.

The state farm system covers 5 percent of China's cultivated area and employs 4.8 million people. State farms are concentrated primarily in the frontier areas of Heilongjiang and Xinjiang. On a state farm the national government owns the land directly and therefore owns all the produce of the land. The workers on the farm receive a fixed salary just as factory workers do. Frequently, state farms are highly capitalized, and specialize in commodity production of grain or cash crops. There is no indication that the Chinese intend to expand the role of state farms in the manner of the Soviet Union, where state farms account for roughly half of the farmland and farm workers. However, because of their high level of capitalization and technology, state farms may play an expanded role in spreading new technology and serve as focal points in developing processing, storage, and marketing systems.

## Rural-Urban Linkages

The central government exercises tight control over all linkages between the rural and urban-industrial economies. The central government has almost a full monopoly over markets for major crops, including grain, cotton, sugar, and oil crops. Vegetable, dairy, and livestock purchases for urban areas are handled by public marketing companies (supply and marketing cooperatives) in the cities. Private marketing of some crops — especially vegetables — is important, but these markets are influenced by government actions.

Similarly, the distribution of modern agricultural inputs — fertilizers, machinery, fuel, electricity, hybrid seeds, and credit — is handled by various state agencies. This gives the state substantial power in determining the pattern of diffusion of new technology.

Moreover, the state exercises substantial control over internal migration and assignment of skilled personnel. Generally speaking, rural residents cannot move to cities on a permanent basis. They may become temporary contract laborers in factories, but their families remain in the villages, and their food and income are channeled through their production team. Similar constraints block migration to other rural areas where wage rates might be higher.

The state also exercises substantial control over the assignment of urban people to rural areas. This includes health and education professionals as well as agricultural specialists. Although the state has been relatively successful in assuring that trained specialists spend some time in rural areas, during periods of confusion, technicians sometimes return to the cities. The return of urban youth to urban areas has been fairly common.

## Rural Institutions in the 1980s

In the late 1970s China reviewed rural policies and institutions. New policies were issued at the third plenum of the Eleventh Central Committee meeting in December, 1978. The policies were adopted by the Eleventh Party Congress in September 1979 and subsequently published.[8]

In a broad sense the new policies downplay the role of the commune level institution. Price, tax, and market incentives are to be used to guide rural development, rather than asking commune cadres to pressure teams to adopt specific programs. A wide range of technical services are to be organized directly under the government or by semiautonomous public corporations controlled by legal mechanisms, strict economic accounting, and market pressures.

A key element of the new strategy is that of price incentives. To improve rural income, quota procurement prices for grain and other crops have been raised 20–30 percent, and above-quota prices even more. Rural investment and loans are being increased, and rural taxes are being reduced. In late 1979 price controls were removed on sideline and handicraft products. Most prices are to be set by the interaction of supply and demand, although grain, cotton, and other basic commodity prices continue to be set by the government. It is difficult to predict the impact of these changes. Ostensibly changes were made to allow prices to rise, but it is likely that as production of some sideline commodities increases, prices will eventually be depressed. Preliminary market surveys in China already show some falling prices.

Diversification is being encouraged, and teams that emphasize nonfood crops will be allowed easier access to commodity grain. The mountainous, semiarid areas will emphasize livestock production, with special attention given to ruminants such as sheep, goats, and cattle. Marginal areas are also being encouraged to stress forestry production. In addition the private sector is being allowed to expand substantially.

Important changes are being made in the institutional system of the team, brigade, and commune. The right of the team to determine its own field management is being reaffirmed so that cadres cannot force teams to adopt inappropriate cropping systems. In many places teams are being broken down into smaller work groups, and division of land to individual households is being allowed in some regions of China (mainly sparsely populated and minority regions). Teams are encouraged to see that wages and grain rations are allocated according to labor in order to maximize work incentives. The number of communes may have been increased in winter 1980/1981, reflecting division into smaller units.

Even if current policy stresses more self-determination by local forces, the government is not withdrawing from rural management. On the contrary, government power has been strengthened in some ways. The government is requiring adoption of work incentives where villages prefer egalitarian distribution patterns. Furthermore, although localities are given more freedom in field management, planning still exists and localities will have to fulfill plans for specific crops, notably grain and cotton. The government is studying the ecological needs of various crops and is developing an agricultural zoning plan to maximize yields. Preliminary zoning work has been done in several provinces. There inevitably will be tension between the contradictory policies of agricultural zoning and self-determination.

The government is using its police power more directly. New forestry and fishery laws were passed in 1979 to protect collective resources from unregulated exploitation. The government is also developing strong incentives for drastically reduced population growth. Families are to be rewarded if they have only one child and penalized if they have more than two.

The government is considering fundamentally different rural institutions for the future. There has been some discussion about separating the economic and political functions presently merged in the commune. If this plan is carried out, the local political administration would assume more responsibility for government services, but would have less influence over economic activities. The commune, presumably, would have a narrower set of responsibilities, centered on marketing, input supply, and credit, as do farmers' cooperatives elsewhere.

Another experiment involves what is called an agricultural-industrial-commercial joint enterprise. These are units which grow, process, and market crops. The inspiration for this system may have come from Yugoslavia, but to some extent it is similar to vertical integration in capitalist systems. In China, state farms may be a crucial part of the agricultural-industrial-commercial farm, as they have access to processing equipment and trucks. This new system will engender far more integration between state and collective farms. So far this system is being tested on an experimental basis with 40 complexes in 26 provinces. Examples include the dairy industry in Tianjin and diary and poultry enterprises in Hangzhou.

Another institutional innovation being tested is the "youth farm," in which a farm is established as a branch of a factory or urban center. In this way, wages, living conditions, and social services can be subsidized by the urban economy and are comparable to urban levels. This system is being tested as a way of finding employment for urban youth in rural areas without a loss in living standard. These youth farms will specialize in highly profitable cash crops and will be linked to the agricultural-industrial-commercial farm. Models of such farms are Xingdan in Hunan and Benxi in Liaoning.

Although recent major reforms in rural institutions have some advantages, there are risks also. Some reforms involve increased demands on the state to supply grain and to subsidize agriculture financially. Such resources have to come from somewhere, and claimants to state resources from other sectors are reluctant to take a decreased share of state aid. The ideological and political implications of allowing an increased private sector are difficult to foretell. The potential chaos of unregulated marketing of agricultural produce is another issue. Thus the future of the announced reforms must be considered controversial and uncertain.

These reforms reflect the philosophy that the collective system is inherently sound and that past problems were caused by the extraordinary and peculiar events of the succession crisis and the rise of the "Gang of Four." It is suggested that adjustments could guard against repetition of mistakes in the future. An alternative view is that the weakness in the rural institutions reflect inherent problems in collective agriculture. This view emphasizes that collective leadership is more responsive to higher political levels than to local needs, and therefore mistakes and problems are endemic. According to this view, the solution is a fundamental restructuring of the rural institutions by substantially dissolving the collective system. During 1981 this viewpoint began to prevail, and the responsibility system was widely adopted. In this approach, individual households and small groups of households are assigned land and contracted with the state to meet production and marketing quotas. It is still too early to say how widely this system has been implemented and what ramifications for the collective institutions will be.

## Conclusions

Looking at the past three decades, China's rural institutions have performed reasonably well in terms of the government's objectives. The institutions have greatly equalized economic and social status in rural areas. However, regional differences are substantial, and differences between families remain unavoidable. The urban-industrial sector has received food and industrial crops without being swamped by migrants from the countryside, and the Communist party's political primacy has not been seriously challenged.

From the point of view of improving people's livelihoods, change has been modest in percentage terms, but very important in terms of assuring personal and family security. Gone are the days when over half the adults would experience three or more famines in their lifetimes. Food supplies, although not greater in total per capita terms than in the 1950s, have probably been distributed more evenly and more securely. Access to social services, including health care and education, has improved.

China's rural institutions have been especially successful in applying resources to overall economic development. Vast amounts of labor have been mobilized to change China's rural landscape. This has increased food security and crop yields. Agriculture has received some central investment funds, but the bulk of rural investment has come from local funds. The central government has concentrated on industrial development.

Although the rural institutions have had their successes, they have also had their problems. A middle-management layer has emerged that is not adequately controlled by either participatory local institutions or higher levels of administration. It has become embroiled in factional politics and has been technically unsophisticated. Incentives for good management and entrepreneurship have been weak. This has served as a serious drag on agricultural production in some areas. Popular political participation has been constrained, and this has dampened popular enthusiasm in the past decades. The next few years will test whether problems can be resolved while the basic advantages are retained.

## Notes

1. John Wong, *Land Reform in the People's Republic of China* (New York: Praeger, 1973), p. 160.

2. Benedict Stavis, *The Politics of Agricultural Mechanization in China* (Ithaca, N.Y.: Cornell University Press, 1978), pp. 25–30.

3. William Hinton, *Fanshen* (New York: Random, 1966).

4. Susan Horsey, "Mutual Aid Teams, 1949-1955: The Beginning of Socialist Transformation in China's Countryside," M.A. thesis, Columbia University, 1970, p. 30.

5. Nai-ruenn Chen, *Chinese Economic Statistics* (Chicago: Aldine, 1967), pp. 370–371.

6. CCP Central Committee, "Regulations on the Work of the Rural People's Communes," revised draft, September 1962, in *Documents of Chinese Communist Party Central Committee, September 1965–April 1969,* vol. 1 (Hong Kong: Union Research Institute, 1971), p. 695-726.

7. Frederick Crook, "The Commune System in the People's Republic of China, 1963-1974," in *China: A Reassessment of the Economy* (Washington, D.C.: U.S. Joint Economic Committee, 1975), p. 366–410.

8. CCP Central Committee, "Regulations on the Work in the Rural People's Communes," draft for trial use, December 22, 1978, *Issues and Studies,* vol. 15, no. 8 (August 1979), pp. 100–112, and vol. 15, no. 9 (September 1979), pp. 104–115. See also CCP Central Committee, "Decisions of the Central Committee of the Communist Party of China on Some Questions Concerning the Acceleration of Agricultural Development," Third Plenary Session draft, January 1979, *Issues and Studies,* vol.15, no. 7 (July 1979), pp. 102–119, and vol. 15, no. 8 (August 1979), pp. 91–99.

## Readings

Burki, Shahid Javed. *A Study of Chinese Communes, 1965.* Cambridge, Mass.: Harvard University Press, 1969.

CCP Eleventh Party Congress. "Decision on Certain Problems of the Facilitation of Agricultural Development." In *Renmin ribao,* October 6, 1979, and *Bejing Review,* vol. 12, March 24, 1980, and, vol. 13, April 1, 1980.

Stavis, Benedict. "The Standard of Living in Rural China, 1978" (forthcoming).

Wiens, Chu Mi. "The Origins of Modern Chinese Landlordism." Taipei: Lianjing Shuji, 1976.

_____. "Lord and Peasant: The Sixteenth to the Eighteenth Century." *Modern China,* vol. 6, no. 1, pp. 3–40.

# 7

# Technological Change

*Thomas B. Wiens*

Chinese agriculture today is so unmechanized, so akin to gardening, that "technological development" seems a misnomer—surely there has been little change from traditional practice? But then, as one notices a hand tiller here, an electrified irrigation pump there; as one notes the application of chemical fertilizers (by hand), or remarks on the uniformly impressive condition of standing crops, one might concede that there are some elements of "modern farming" visible in the scene.

In fact, the statistical litany suggests rapid modernization. Chemical fertilizer (nutrient) production has grown for over two decades at an average rate of 16 percent per year, and today an average of over 89 kilograms per hectare of chemical nutrient is applied. Over the same period, the hectarage plowed at least once a year by tractor has grown from 1.6 percent to 46 percent of the total. The power supply of irrigation and drainage equipment has increased from 0.56 million horsepower in 1957 to 64 million today, and the percentage of land that is irrigated rose from 31 percent to 46.6 percent. At the same time, the average annual increase in grain output over 26 years is 2.5 percent, safely above the population growth rate, despite a decrease in the area cultivated. Is this not a reflection of rapid technological progress, and, having recited the statistics, need we say more?

Actually this is not what economists normally mean by technological progress. These statistics detail increases in "inputs" (albeit modern inputs) and "outputs," whereas "technology" (along with "management") is defined as a set of practices that determine the quantitative and qualitative relationship between inputs and outputs. The distinction may be muddy in practice, but it is clear-cut in theory. If, for an entire region or country, all inputs change by a certain proportion and outputs change by a different proportion, then there must have been a change in technology and/or management—other things, such as weather, being equal. If some inputs increase by a certain proportion, but others, such as cultivated area, cannot, then the law of diminishing returns would generally imply that output would increase by a lesser proportion. But technological improvements can overrule or ameliorate the law of diminishing returns, and have done so in countries that are cited as agricultural success stories.

Because the rate of increase of modern inputs in Chinese agriculture has far exceeded the growth rate of its total product, could we conclude that there has been no technological progress, according to the above definition? For three reasons, we cannot. First, it is difficult to know what the quantitative impact of the law of diminishing returns should be in light of fixed or declining cultivated area. Perhaps the growth of total product would have been smaller still in the absence of technological progress. Second, technological change is often required merely to permit an increase in inputs. China could not have extended its irrigated land without changes in the sources of water, and means of drawing and applying it. Nor could the multiple-cropping rate have increased from 141 percent to 151 percent without the development of early maturing varieties, which make it possible to squeeze more crops into limited frost-free periods. Finally, modern inputs—chemical fertilizer, pump irrigation, and tractors—supplement or substitute for traditional inputs—organic fertilizers, canal irrigation, and draft animals.

At the same time the growth rate of modern inputs exceeds that of total inputs by a wide margin. The 1957–1978 trends in output value and major inputs, both traditional and modern, are shown in Table 7.1. If each input is weighted according to an estimate of its relative marginal productivity in 1957, then it appears that total inputs have grown less rapidly than total output, the difference perhaps being due to improvements in technology (and/or management). However, the results of this kind of exercise are very sensitive to the choice of weights, and should not be taken too seriously.

When the communists came to power in 1949, they inherited an agricultural technology that was relatively advanced, and perhaps as far advanced in some areas as was conceivable in an economy that lacked a modern scientific and industrial base. It was advanced in the sense that most arable land was under continuous cultivation using labor-intensive techniques and exploiting available sources of organic fertilizer and water, so as to produce yields higher than were found in most other premodern agricultures. Although weaknesses in this technology were easily identified, they were not so easily remedied.

In critically assessing the Chinese program for agro-technological development in the early years of the People's Republic, one can easily ignore the fact that at the time there were no relevant external models and little readily transferable technology. Certainly U.S. and West European agriculture were recognizable success stories, but the factor endowments

Table 7.1   Index of Growth in Agricultural Output, Inputs, and Factor
Productivity

|  | Factor<br>(weight) | 1978<br>(1957=100) |
|---|---|---|
| 1. | Labor (35%) | 150.0 |
| 2. | Land   (36%) | 109.9 |
|  | Sown (23%) | 96.1 |
|  | Irrigated (13%) | 134.3 |
| 3. | Capital   (9%) | 124.0 |
|  | Tractor services (0.04%) | 2,505.0 |
|  | Draft animal services (8.96%) | 113.0 |
| 4. | Current inputs   (20%) | 177.0 |
|  | Seed   (4%) | 144.2 |
|  | Chemical fertilizer (0.6%) | 2,381.0 |
|  | Organic fertilizer   (15.0%) | 140.4 |
|  | Pesticides, etc.   (0.4%) | 357.7 |
| 5. | Total inputs | 145.7 |
| 6. | Gross value of agricultural output | 172.9 |
| 7. | Productivity index | 119.0 |

Sources:

1.   Growth based on reported 47% increase in agricultural labor force between
1957 and 1977, and an assumed 1.8% growth of agricultural labor force in
in 1977-1978.  Weights based on estimates of agricultural production functions for the 1930s.
2.   Growth based on most recent Chinese statistics.  Weights based on 1957
proportion of hectarage irrigated and an assumed 25% higher productivity
for irrigated hectarage.  Overall weight for land is a residual, but is
also consistent with pre-1949 rental shares of gross agricultural product
value.
3.   Tractor plowed area used as a proxy for tractor services; stock of large
animals for draft animals services.  Relative weights based on 1957 estimates of plowing rates per draft animal and per 15 horsepower standard
tractor and 25% higher yield for tractor plowed land.  Overall weight of
9% for capital services drawn from earlier work by Anthony Tang, "Policy
and Performance in Agriculture," Eckstein, Galenson and Liu, eds., Economic
Trends in Communist China (Chicago: Aldine, 1968), p.483, Table 7.
4.   Overall weight and several components based on value of material inputs as
a proportion of gross value of agricultural product in 1957; relative weights
of chemical and organic fertilizers based on rough estimates of proportion of
total nutrients in 1957 (considering only large animals, hogs, nightsoil,
green manure, and bean cakes as sources of organic nutrient).  Growth rate
for organic fertilizer is the author's (conservative) estimate.
5.   Linear-weighted sum of input growth indices.

6.   Computed from average annual growth rate of gross value of agricultural
product in 1949-1978 of 4.3%, adjusted by estimated growth in 1949-1957
(based on 1957 definition of this measure).

7.   Computed from average annual "productivity growth" of 0.83%, the difference
between the average annual growth rates of inputs and output.

were very different, and in any case China had first to create an industrial base. The cases of successful growth in labor-intensive agriculture—as in Japan, Taiwan, and South Korea—only became noticeable as such in the 1960s, and a "Green Revolution" technology applicable to other less developed countries (LDCs) was also a late-1960s development.

Although there were no outstanding external models, there were many preliminary tasks to complete, such as the restoration of Chinese agricultural technology and production. The water conservancy system, for instance, was suffering from a century or more of neglect as well as war damage. Pure strains of the best existing seed varieties had not been maintained, and it was important to restore these and enlarge the area utilizing them. Whether the basis of modern farming was to be mechanization or chemicalization, a larger heavy industrial base had to be constructed. To facilitate the purchase of new seeds, chemicals, and equipment, the agricultural sector had to be reorganized to permit a higher savings rate and more productive investment pattern. Finally, the agricultural research and extension infrastructure needed to be reorganized and enlarged. These measures, which were accomplished during the 1949–1957 period, laid the foundation for subsequent development.

Although crop varieties existing in 1949 were not necessarily the best yielding under all conditions, they had benefited from continuous farmer selection. The characteristics of these crop varieties reflected the importance of risk avoidance to farmers whose living levels were never much above the margin of subsistence. Yield potential was often sacrificed for adaptability or hardiness, which could insure at least some yield even under adverse environmental conditions. The use of additional fertilizers was largely unsuccessful because vegetative growth increased but grain yields did not. Tall and overburdened stalks tended to lodge (fall over) in response to heavy fertilizer use.

In 1949, seed breeders were under party pressure to achieve rapid high-yield breakthroughs. The development of new seeds, from initial crosses through seed multiplication and distribution, historically required 12–13 years, and could not be speeded up without causing problems. The breeders initially were forced to rely on a combination of farmer selection, Republican-period experiment station products, and imported varieties. Attention was concentrated on wheat, rice, cotton, and beans. Two varieties of wheat, one of rice, and one of cotton each were sown on more than 3 million hectares by the end of the decade. Of these, one wheat variety was from Italy and the cotton variety was from the United States. In the spring wheat area, severe devastation from rust in the early 1950s was overcome through the introduction of resistant varieties, nearly doubling average yields. In the cotton-producing areas, there were two major changes in varieties, the first increasing yields by about 15 percent and staple length by 2–4 millimeters, and the second adding between 10 and 30 percent to yields with a further increase in staple length in some areas. Overall, it was claimed that by 1957, 55 percent of food-grain areas and 94 percent of cotton areas were sown with improved seeds. These changes occurred in parallel with the movement to organize producer's cooperatives, and by 1956 the number of agricultural experiment and demonstration stations had reached the level of about one per 8,000 households. In retrospect, however, the most important breakthrough occurred at the beginning of the breeding effort in the 1960s with the development and distribution of dwarf, high-yield rice strains and hybrid corn.

A number of problems were noted during this period, which were to plague the breeding program for many years. First was the general difficulty of borrowing, whether from abroad or from the best seeds of a particular locality. Locally selected varieties of wheat proved to have limited scope for application elsewhere because of ecological sensitivity. A variety of rape imported from Japan, which has many useful characteristics and was widely planted after 1955, ripened two weeks later than the variety it replaced, requiring extensive fertilization and contributing to a tight labor situation that caused a yield decrease in the next crop (rice). Therefore, after a few years, the peasants returned to the old variety of rape. Imported Japanese rice varieties proved better suited to cooler temperatures than to the warm climate of most of south China, and required more fertilizer than Chinese peasants could readily provide. High-yielding Mexican tropical wheat required too much sunlight to be suitable for China's northerly wheat region. In short, there was a need for a wide menu of new types adaptable to specific Chinese conditions.

The breeding and extension program itself had notable weaknesses. Too much attention was given to high-yielding varieties (HYVs), which required unusually favorable conditions, and not enough attention was given to varieties that performed well under poor conditions such as drought. Excessive enthusiasm of local cadres sometimes led to replacement of well-adapted local varieties with unsuitable "superior" varieties from other areas, especially when the failure of improvements (such as deep plowing and greater fertilizer use) to lead to major yield increases was blamed on local seed varieties. Another consequence was a tendency toward varietal uniformity, at the expense of the hardiness and adaptability built into local varieties over centuries of selection pressure. There also remained a serious problem of deterioration due to cross-pollination with other crops and hasty distribution before genetic characteristics had been stabilized. A proper seed multiplication system was never established, and the peasants continued to set aside seed from their own production despite varietal mixing at harvest time.

Mechanical innovation was handicapped by the lack of a machine building industry capable of supplying power equipment to the peasantry, and by a lack of refined fuels or a rural electric supply. Consequently, the state concentrated on successively restoring the stock of traditional implements, making improvements in their design, and finally the introduction of semi-modern, but still animal-powered, equipment.

The early Chinese plow, like its counterpart in other societies, was light, small, simply constructed, and inexpensive, owing to a minimum use of metal. But it required considerable human and animal energy, plowed to an average depth of only 10–12 cm, and did not turn over the soil well. Improved plows were introduced in large numbers and were characterized by an enlarged share and moldboard, the addition of a guide wheel (for dry-field plows), and sometimes an iron beam, adjustable share, or double handle. In general, these plows reduced effort, turned over the soil better, and permitted deeper and more even plowing depths. On the other hand, they required more metal and thus were more costly. By plowing to depths of 15–17 cm, fertilizer and moisture absorption capacity of root structures was increased, fulfilling one precondition of a seed-fertilizer revolution.

Other mechanical innovations included the introduction of man-powered carts with bicycle wheels and lightened frames, improvements in the efficiency of the power transmission of traditional irrigation devices (for example, through use of pedal-powered chain drives), and multifunctional cultivation implements with rotary parts but minimal use of metal.

One innovation seriously misfired. In 1956–1957, when the cooperativization movement was energized, the state attempted to promote large-scale adoption of the double-wheel, double-share (DWDS) plow. In truth, Chinese industry at the time could produce nothing more sophisticated in quantity. These were animal-powered, all-metal implements, of Soviet and Polish design, and eight to nineteen times more costly than traditional plows. They were supposed to permit greater and more even plowing depth, as well as much greater speed, but in fact the depth, although more even, was no greater than that of the improved traditional plow, and greater speed was offset by the need for at least two draft animals rather than one. The greater weight and durability offered advantages in working difficult or unbroken soils, and, following successive price reductions, they achieved a measure of acceptance, at least in the North China Plain, with adequate numbers of draft animals.

However, the government blundered by overproducing this plow and then promoting it for use in paddy cultivation in south China. Rice-growing peasants reacted negatively to the plow, inventories piled up, and many that were sold were later returned unused. The government's error was not the last dramatic instance of political imperatives causing leaders to ignore limitations exposed by experimental or field testing and to exaggerate the efficacy of the innovation. The DWDS plow did not work well in mountainous areas, terraced or muddy (marshy) fields, or in areas where draft animals were scarce. These conditions eliminated some 55 percent of cultivated land in Zhejiang, for example. Even in areas where the DWDS plow was useful, animals and plowmen had to be retrained, paddy fields restructured, and the plow rebuilt by the purchasers. The labor shortages due to expansion of multiple cropping and fertilizer collection became so serious as to demand extraordinary labor and time-saving efforts during the crop turnover period. Even then, the gains in yields over those derived from plowing with traditional implements averaged only about 5 percent, and the advantages in labor savings over the improved traditional paddy plow were trivial. Unfortunately, these limitations were not publicized except in the appraisal following the rejection of the DWDS plow.

Mention should be made of the effect of Soviet aid on Chinese agricultural science in the 1950s. This was a rather dismal period in Soviet agriscience. The greatest impact was made by the "peasant scientist" Lysenko and his two idols, Michirin and V. R. Williams, a favored Soviet soil specialist, who argued that mineral chemicals were useless until proper soil structure had been built up through grassland rotations. Lysenko was sent to China shortly after the founding of the PRC, and there introduced Michirinian doctrines and other officially favored theories to the receptive ears of the Chinese political elite. Lysenkian doctrine was immediately used to attack theoretical and laboratory research and to promote work inspired by advanced peasant practices. Chinese agricultural scientists in 1953–1954 were "sent down" to the countryside to work with the peasants to solve practical production problems. Michirinian doctrine, with its claim that environmental influences were heritable, found official favor as the only "scientific" foundation for biology because it raised the promise of rapid and controllable evolutionary change and seemed to accord well with the theory of dialectical materialism. The theories of Williams were introduced to Mao, who read and publicly quoted his works with approval.

As one result of this influence, the problem of "degeneration" of potatoes, which afflicted large areas in China with unfortunate consequences for yields, was interpreted as a result of environmental influences, rather than of viral origin. Although Chinese scientists experimentally confirmed the viral origin theory in 1960, these results apparently were not published until 1979, and a virus-free breeding program was set up only on a small scale in the mid-1970s. As a result, in the two decades between 1957 and 1978, the hectarage in potatoes fell to one-half of the previous levels.

Similarly, the Lysenkian belief in the lack of intraspecies competition and the advantages of numbers when one species was in competition with another—for example, crops against weeds—was readily accepted by Maoists. They appreciated the analogy between the "collectivist nature" of plants and the process of communalization. Dense plantings became a popular expression of this theory. This idea, and that of the efficacy of deep plowing, were soon to be enshrined in Mao's "Eight-Character Charter" for agrotechnical reform.

However, the Maoists were not yet the dominant force in agricultural science, and the 1950s saw considerable conventional research, which may have contributed to the sustained advances in agricultural production following the 1959–1961 decline. The achievements, some of which reached fruition during 1958–1959, included the following improvements:

1. Cultural practices. Large amounts of data were collected and subjected to analysis focusing on cultural practices responsible for high yields. Problems in switching to double-cropped rice, to *Japonica* varieties, and to continuous cropping rather than rotation were addressed. A variety of methods for earlier cultivation of rice seedlings were developed, none of which were to prove practical.

2. Plant protection. Chemical seed treatments were developed that proved fairly effective in controlling the spread of wheat smut and mildew. The traditionally serious locust and aphid problems were brought under control. Chemical pesticides were introduced.

3. Soil and fertilizer. A nationwide soil survey was carried out (but using a Soviet classification scheme of more interest to geologists than agronomists). Considerable work was done on the problems of improving or transforming various types of low-yield soils. Improved methods of composting and means of generating and collecting methane were developed and publicized.

4. Animal husbandry and veterinary science. The hybridization program created China's first fine-wool sheep breed. Artificial insemination was introduced. Effective vaccines were developed or produced for swine influenza, hoof-and-mouth disease, bovine tuberculosis, and sheep pox. Experimentation with acupuncture as an animal treatment was begun.

## The Great Leap Forward, 1958-1961

The period of the Great Leap Foward saw the ascendancy of Maoist ideas and policies in the agro-technical field as well as in other spheres. These included the famous Eight-Character Charter, which Mao enunciated in late 1958, as a concentrated expression of the technical measures that the peasantry was supposed to adopt. The measures were:

1. Increased irrigation
2. Increased fertilization
3. Soil improvement and deep plowing
4. Popularization of good strains
5. Dense planting
6. Innovation of farm tools
7. Pest control
8. Improved field management

The list appears innocuous enough at first glance, but it begs the real questions: "when?", "where?", and "how?" To these, the cadres in effect replied, "now," "everywhere," and "with whatever resources you have and whatever methods have been reported successful elsewhere." Moreover, the radicals refused to accept the "bourgeois law of diminishing returns" and were convinced that the objections or warnings of the "experts" were a product of conservatism, if not class hostility. The creativity of the masses was deemed sufficiently boundless as to overcome all existing constraints. Due to the pressure on lower-level cadres to report successes, there was no shortage of "evidence" to throw in the face of the experts, and few experts had the courage, or opportunity, to challenge the absurd claims that appeared in print. In fact, a good proportion of the agricultural experts were "sent down" to the countryside to "learn from the masses."

The problem was also this: If the ingredients of the Eight-Character Charter were really efficacious, why had the peasants, in their wisdom, not already accomplished them in their many centuries of farming experience? There were no novel ingredients in the prescription — the state could not offer any new resources, such as tractors or chemical fertilizers, and there were no significant new innovations, such as "miracle seeds." Basically, the prescription called for more intensive use of labor while ignoring the opportunity costs and the human desire for rest. Peasant opinion was not requested; peasants were simply instructed to accept the charter with enthusiasm. Only when this process had gone much too far did the top leadership add some essential qualifications to the charter:

All of the eight measures must be carried out simultaneously. It is
necessary, however, to adopt different measures in accordance with the local
characteristics of agricultural production such as climatic conditions and
under no circumstances must an overall measure be enforced. Also, it is
necessary, in carrying out the "Eight-Character Charter," to follow the mass
line by frequently consulting the opinions of the peasants as to how the
charter can fit in with the concrete conditions of the local areas and how its
content can be further enriched.[1]

Unfortunately, the warning came after the damage had already been
done. The dense planting campaign provides the best illustration.
Although its origins may be traced to Lysenkian doctrines, Chinese experiments did establish that, in conjunction with deep plowing and increased fertilizer use, high plant density raised yields, and there was a
marginal response to nitrogen. But the political leaders did not foresee any
limits to this effect. The traditional rice planting density in Guangdong, for
example, was less than 1.5 million seedlings per hectare, similar to traditional standards elsewhere in Asia. With the enunciation of the Eight-
Character Charter, peasants were persuaded to increase density to 6–7.5
million seedlings per hectare, and even higher in some localities. In 1959,
the Guangdong Provincial Committee called for a further increase to 12–15
million seedlings per hectare. The net effect was severe economic loss.
Although yields did improve with density up to a point, the increase was
almost cancelled by the additional seed requirements. Moreover, land had
to be reserved for seedbeds at the expense of both the preceding and current
crops, and added labor and fertilizer were required at a time of year when
labor supplies were least available. Also, tools had to be redesigned to fit the
narrower row spacing.

The implementation of the charter also went awry in the sphere of irrigation. Coordinated water conservancy planning was cast aside as the party
exploited mass enthusiasm to expand irrigation through thousands of
small-scale facilities. With inadequate supplies of both concrete and
engineers, earth and stone and local designs were substituted, creating a
long-term hazard that today is a source of national concern. The greatest
effort was in the North China Plain, where groundwater levels during the
rainy season were close to the surface. Massive irrigation raised the
groundwater levels  and caused land to turn alkaline, ultimately forcing a
prohibition of irrigation in the affected areas.

With Soviet advice, Chinese engineers had expected to eliminate the
problem of silting in the Yellow River, thereby making possible a large irrigation scheme in its basin. It was believed that, in the short run, the silt
could be bottled up in the San Men Dam and that afforestation in the

northwest loess areas would complete the solution. The dam was finished in short order, but the effects on silt content downstream were minimal because scouring of banks and beds below the dam allowed the river to pick up large quantities of silt again. Irrigation works, constructed on the lower reaches of the river in the expectation that the silting problem would be solved, rapidly became clogged with silt. The continued buildup in the river beds, canals, and irrigation channels added to the severity of the flooding in 1959–1961. The afforestation campaign also was unsuccessful, even in the long run, perhaps because of the underpopulation of the northwest and the lack of concern there for a program from which the greatest benefits would accrue elsewhere.

Implementation of other aspects of the charter were less damaging, although often wasteful of labor. Under pressure to implement the reforms, local cadres pushed the peasants in whatever direction they could. The hours expended collecting "fertilizers" with little nutrient value, substituting humans for exhausted and undernourished plow animals, or hand-picking insects off field crops increased political merit if not crop yields.

The call for innovation of farm tools produced interesting results. A large number of simple designs or modifications of traditional models were submitted. These were mostly animal- or human-powered implements, made almost entirely of wood, and usually substituted somewhat more efficient means of power transmission or replaced single-function with multifunction capabilities. It is difficult to say how many were really successful, and none had the impact of the improved plows or rubber-tired carts introduced earlier. The best publicized was the invention of a (human-powered) rice transplanter by a Hunan peasant youth. However, the transplanters approved for widespread production in 1960 were experiment station products with their own special problems.

If the Great Leap Forward had few other virtues, it was at least highly educational. For the first time, large numbers of agricultural scientists and technicians were out on the "front lines," rather than in the laboratories. Responding to the calls for technological models, there were many studies of the biological bases of high-yield, high water, and fertilizer-use technology. The techniques studied were often suitable for experimental plots or yield competitions, but not for efficient production use. More useful were the studies aimed at understanding where the application of the Eight-Character Charter was erring. Experiments with improvements on existing peasant practices, such as interplanting techniques, also produced a potentially yield-raising body of knowledge, which was later implemented. The plant breeding work, which was to open so many new doors, continued. A consensus emerged that a multidisciplinary systems approach, focusing on the total readjustment of the farm production system and giving special attention to the problems of low-yield areas, should be the primary focus for the overall research program. In short, by the end of the Great Leap, the level of technical agricultural knowledge was vastly improved.

## Recent Technology, 1962–1977

Because of the massive crop failures in the last years of the Great Leap, the radical influence on agricultural and agro-technical policy waned, and the Chinese Communist Party formally revised its priorities to "put agriculture first." Chinese sources suggest that the changes were largely cosmetic. The higher priority accorded to agriculture certainly did not mean that it would have first claim on state investment, which continued to be directed overwhelmingly to industry. Nevertheless, crop and animal purchase prices were raised and industrial input prices lowered, improving the peasants' terms of trade, and perhaps even eliminating the negative balance of resource flow between agriculture and other sectors. Indirect investment in agriculture — that is, investment in factories that produce agricultural inputs and importation of agricultural chemicals — was certainly stepped up. And, at least for a time, both policy and practice swung toward use of persuasion and demonstration rather than commandism as the basis for agricultural extension work.

Government policy sought two objectives. In the short run, the aim was to stabilize yields in areas with high-yield potential, so as to provide a measure of security against the impact of varying natural conditions. High-yield areas were accorded priority in the supply of agricultural chemicals, machinery, and investment funds. In the long run, the goal was to induce low-yield areas to overcome their environmental constraints and to "bootstrap" themselves out of poverty. During the Cultural Revolution the focus was on low yield areas, which struggled to overcome impossible environmental odds. This led to a more egalitarian distribution policy for industrial inputs and state funds.

The long-awaited breakthrough in seed development finally occurred in 1964, as the Chinese began full-scale distribution of dwarf rice varieties with high-yield potential. The initial crossing of a dwarf variety with an improved conventional variety had occurred in 1956, after rice breeders had realized that they had been pursuing the wrong breeding objectives. They knew that the key to increasing fertilizer response was to strengthen the stalk of the plant to enable it to bear the burden of more and heavier tassels of grain, but their first response had been to select strains with tall and strong stalks. However, after observing the lodging resistance of a glutinous dwarf Champa rice variety from Guangxi and the practice followed by some farmers of deliberate stunting through fertilizer and water control, the breeders became convinced that exceptionally short stalks should be the key breeding objective.

The varieties that resulted from this and later crossings offered yields that were well above those of existing varieties, whether planted as an early or second crop. The yields were roughly equivalent to those of IR8, the dwarf variety developed in the Philippines (and released two years after China's dwarfs), which launched the Green Revolution elsewhere in Asia. The Chinese varieties had one significant advantage — their growing period was up to two weeks shorter. Therefore they not only could be fit into existing multiple-cropping systems, but also were a significant benefit in areas where two crops of rice were environmentally feasible, but not economically advantageous with existing varieties. Over the next 15 years, dwarf paddy rice varieties spread to over 80 percent of China's rice-sown area.

At about the same time, new hybrid maize varieties were released, which were rapidly accepted because of their yield advantages over existing summer crops. During this period, soybeans were not favored over other grains in terms of either price or quota fulfillment, despite their nutritional superiority. The higher yields of the new maize varieties thus contributed to a decline in soybean hectarage and production. The high maize yields also facilitated the growth of a new cropping system in the North China Plain. Winter wheat was planted with very wide row spacings, and maize was interplanted a few weeks before the wheat harvest, providing the extra growing period required to complete a fall harvest safely. Presumably the positive yield effects caused by greater light exposure for the wheat in combination with the extra crop of maize more than compensated for the reduced plant density of the wheat crop. However, the hybrid maize varieties introduced in the early 1960s lacked sufficient disease resistance, and their popularity waned when this became painfully apparent in the late 1960s.

Whether one speaks of dwarf rice, hybrid corn and sorghum, improved cotton varieties, or other crops, there was suddenly something worth promoting. In order to multiply the seeds as rapidly as possible, and to prevent the deterioration of improved seeds through varietal mixing and/or cross-pollination, a program was launched in 1963–1965 to establish a coordinated seed replication system. The system was structured so that pure line breeding, selection, and maintenance were carried out at the national level. County-level work concentrated on selection for adaptability and improvement of varietal characteristics. Within communes, seed multiplication and replication was treated as a specialized activity on fields set aside for that purpose. Where crops were geographically concentrated, special brigades concentrated on seed raising only; and for hybrids, special farms were set up for seed production.

The economic significance of this program deserves recognition. Successful multiple cropping, as well as attainment of maximum yield potential, require uniform maturation and varietal purity. This could not be achieved so long as peasants set aside seed as part of their normal harvest (seed purity may have averaged as low as 75 percent in the late 1950s). During the Cultural Revolution this seed distribution system was named the "four-level research network."

By 1965, the Chinese machine-building industry was capable of providing significant support for agricultural modernization. Fuel and electric power became increasingly available in the villages by that time, as well. Chinese agricultural engineers had been searching for a replacement for the traditional paddy plow, and in the late 1950s took a close look at the Japanese power tiller, or "walking tractor," as the Chinese called it. Even though they conceded that with this machine, labor productivity in plowing was tripled, quality of work was much higher, and the time utilization rate was high regardless of the area of field to be worked, they initially rejected it because the depth of cultivation with the power tiller was less than with the improved paddy plow (only 12 cm on average), and this did not accord with the "deep plowing" prescription of the Eight-Character Charter. In the 1960s improved varieties made increased multiple cropping desirable, and the time/labor bottleneck was of greater concern than plowing depth. The power tiller was seen as the solution, and factories began producing them in large numbers.

Whether this judgment was correct is moot; power tillers are more often seen pulling carts than plowing the fields, even at plowing time. Perhaps the transport burden was the real bottleneck—moving bulky manures, seeds, seedlings, harvested crops, etc. consumes more labor power than plowing. Certainly cheap and light transport vehicles should have been mass produced with the same zeal as the power tillers, which are not efficient sources of motive power for transport.

Another constraint tackled by the machine-building industry was that of irrigation water. Areas with access to water sources were easily served by growing electrification and increased supplies of diesel, kerosene, or electric pumps. The area of greatest potential for improvement was the North China Plain, where surface-flow irrigation systems were ruled out by the groundwater problem until drainage could be greatly improved. Well irrigation was relatively safe, since it replaced only what it removed from the groundwater. But water supplies at shallow depths in the north were subject to drastic seasonal fluctuations, and therefore were unreliable when most needed. Three breakthroughs occurred in the late 1960s that overcame this problem: (1) it was discovered that extensive underground water resources existed throughout most of the North China Plain at depths of 30 meters or more; (2) a cheap well-drilling technique evolved, which used a steel bit but local materials (concrete, bamboo, rattan, etc.) and human labor power; and (3) Chinese industry became capable of mass-producing submersible pumps with the efficiency necessary to move meaningful quantities of water from such depths. Until that time, the North China Plain had been left out of the seed-fertilizer revolution for want of water, but in less than a decade over a million tubewells were dug and equipped. The wheat-maize inter-cropping system became viable, and the long-term growth rates of both wheat and maize yields came to greatly exceed those of paddy rice. Maize moved into second place behind rice in national total hectarage and production.

Three other types of machines were introduced in quantity in the mid-1960s and deserve some comment. The first was the hydropowered pump, which was designed to solve the irrigation problems of the mountainous areas of the south, where low volume, fast-moving streams were a potential source of both power and water. The 1965 models required a water head of 1 meter or better, and were rated at 10 to 30 percent efficiency. Later, small hydroturbines were introduced for electric power generation in the same environmental context.

The paddy rice transplanter, invented in 1958, went through a variety of engineering improvements, yet even today is used on only 1 percent of paddy land, although large numbers of such machines sit idle on communes. There are several reasons for this. Most transplanters handle only one variety of seedling (e.g., short or long) at one planting density, whereas rice varieties and densities are continually changing. The transplanters generally work better with short seedlings, but the main transplanting bottleneck is with late rice under triple cropping, where seedlings are typically over-mature with long root structures. To be used in transplanters, seedlings must be specially and carefully grown. Use of transplanters incurs cash costs for fuel and repairs, which many teams would rather minimize. Quality of manufacture, training of users and maintenance personnel, and availability of service facilities are all weak. Finally, most teams with transplanters believe that their use results in damage to seedlings and lower crop yields.

The Japanese appear to have made mechanical transplanting a viable proposition by using seedlings, grown in specially constructed flats, that are transplanted with soil attached. The Chinese have not been able to borrow this technology because seedlings for late rice cannot be grown in this way without significant yield losses. Also, with double-crop rice, planting density is higher than allowed by the mechanism on which the Japanese machines are based.

The remaining major mechanical innovation — the mechanically powered fodder shredder — played a major role in a complex process, involving the interaction of crop and animal agriculture. Improved crop varieties required more fertilizer than the large amounts already applied, yet chemical fertilizer supplies were still inadequate. Pig manure was the best alternative source, but pig numbers were limited by the availability of feed supplies. Fallow paddy rice land provided one additional feed source. As double-cropped rice grew in popularity, more of this land became available, because double-cropped rice permitted a fallow period during the winter, whereas in a rice–winter wheat system, wheat occupied the land in the winter season. Green manure crops planted on this land in the winter seasons were mechanically shredded, combined with small amounts of grain, fermented, and fed to pigs. Because the numbers of draft animals were not growing nearly as fast as grain production, supplementary concentrate was also diverted to the pigs. Aside from the additional meat production, pig manure thus helped sustain an intensified cropping system. Judging by the rapid growth of pig numbers and the tripling of green manure hectarage, this was a successful program, and one that required only one industrial input — the fodder shredder.

Most of this long list of successful innovations was first implemented in the years 1963–1965. The exception is probably the tubewell sinking program, which accelerated in the late 1960s. These technological changes seem to be reflected in the unusually rapid growth rate for grain of 4.6 percent per annum in 1962–1967. To be sure, a portion of this should be attributed to recovery from the crop failures at the end of the Great Leap period, but data suggest that while some provinces did not fully recover until a later date (including those in the North China Plain), others advanced well beyond their previous peak levels (primarily in the south). Government policy exacerbated varying regional growth rates. Not only were the new innovations more applicable to southern conditions, but policy for distribution of industrial inputs favored areas considered to have high-yield potential. Toward the end of the 1960s and into the 1970s, northern growth rates improved markedly because of the technical transformation wrought by the availability of water from tubewells. Obviously the process was not uniform, as the conditions affecting the rate of absorption of higher-yielding technologies varied from area to area, and could be transformed radically through a major irrigation project or the addition of local chemical fertilizer plants.

How, then, did the Cultural Revolution affect how regions absorbed new technologies? Undoubtedly the disruption of research and education slowed the flow of important research results and delayed the solutions of major problems. Limited communication with the outside world contributed to slower improvement of machine designs. Still, Chinese agricultural scientists were generally better protected from political damage than their colleagues in other disciplines, due to the priority and practicality of their research. They were not so isolated from the outside that they could not obtain new releases of seed from the international centers.

Local research and experimentation done under the radical influence facilitated adoption or adaptation of the best of existing alternatives. Against this must be weighed the damage done, first, by suppression of incentives and, second, by a resumption of technological commandism on the part of political cadres. A notable example of the latter was the insistence of certain provincial leaders that double-cropped rice be grown where it was environmentally or economically tenuous—that is, in general, immediately north or south of the Yangtze River. In marginal areas, this system imposed serious pressure on time, labor, and input supplies. Although fairly high yields often resulted over the year as a whole, the yields of each crop, especially those of barley or wheat and late rice, were low, and equal or better aggregate yields could often have been obtained from a winter wheat–rice system at lower input and labor cost.

## Technological Developments After 1977

Since the fall of the "Gang of Four" in 1976, there has been a rapid reversion in agricultural policies back to the course charted in the 1962–1965 period. Theoretically far-reaching decision-making powers and financial incentives have been restored to the production team. Decreases in the relative prices of agricultural inputs and a subsequent rise in the prices of agricultural outputs have improved rural incomes. Agricultural scientists have returned to their laboratories, universities, and institutes to engage in research, and the government has significantly increased the proportion of its budget devoted to agricultural investment. The long-run effects on the development and promulgation of new technology will be positive, except perhaps in one respect. Persuasion, loans, and incentives are now the favored methods for diffusing new technology, as opposed to commandism. If this policy remains, the rate of adoption may be slow, but fewer mistakes resulting from commandism may occur. In the short run, China must rely on innovations already introduced or hastily borrowed from abroad. Enough was accomplished in the early 1970s to give some cause for optimism.

One interesting breakthrough has been the introduction of $F_1$ hybrid rice. Rice and wheat, unlike maize and sorghum, are self-pollinating plants. To create a hybrid, breeders must emasculate the female parent and hand-pollinate, a procedure complicated by low pollen viability. The process is quite labor intensive and yields of seeds are low; thus, the process would not appear to be commercially promising. Moreover, for commercial seed production, one must find a genotype that is male sterile (a very rare genetic characteristic), cross it with "maintainer lines" to produce offspring with male sterility but other desirable characteristics, and then cross again with "restorer lines" to produce seeds with normal self-fertilizing powers.

Chinese scientists discovered a male-sterile variety (a cross between domestic and wild rice) in 1970, and this began a high priority breeding program. The program received heavy political backing almost immediately, probably for three reasons: (1) success would represent a scientific achievement of world importance, and might provide the technical basis for increased rice yields lacking since the spread of dwarf varieties; (2) Maoist-Marxist theory provided an explanation for heterosis (hybrid vigor) in terms of the theory of the "unity of opposites," whereas "bourgeois science" had as yet no accepted explanation, and demonstration of heterosis in rice could buttress claims that Mao thought was the proper basis for "true science"; and (3) the research was carried out in Hunan Province where Hua Guofeng had worked for many years. Hua himself quickly backed the research and turned Hunan into the testing ground for the new variety. In 1974 there were only 16 kilograms of male-sterile seed in the entire province; in 1977 more than 1 million hectares were planted to the new variety.

The hybrid varieties have been heavily promoted since 1977, and are already credited with adding 3.5 million tonnes to annual production of rice. Although the very low yields of seed production fields would seem to impose a prohibitive cost, this problem is almost completely offset by reduced seed requirements due to the low plant density necessary in hybrid rice fields. However, most hybrid varieties require a longer growing season and have forced reduction in cropping intensity in some areas. Perhaps due to such problems in integrating this variety into the existing cropping system, the introduction of hybrid rice has already met with some farmer resistance and tested the willingness of the authorities to permit local decision making on choice of crops or technique.

In the last few years the Chinese have developed and released excellent strains of wheat and maize, incorporating the best foreign germ plasm. The potential yield increases in these crops, due to adoption of new strains in conjunction with improved water supply and other inputs, appear to be high. In the tuber crops, recognition of the viral origins of degeneration points the way to abandonment of local self-sufficiency in production of seed potatoes and the development of disease-free production bases as a short-run solution with high payoff. An alternative, which would not eliminate viroid problems but could greatly increase the economic value of the crop, is production of potatoes from true seed. The Chinese are already well in advance of the rest of the world in demonstrating the practicality of this technique.

A major problem continues to be the low yields in areas where environmental conditions are not suitable for adoption of HYV strains of food grains. However, the Chinese are well advanced in research on distant crossing, which can combine the drought tolerance and hardiness of certain coarse grains with the higher yield potentials of the fine grains. Triticale—wheat × rye—or sorghum × sugarcane are examples where Chinese researchers have improved varieties at the release stage. This work has benefited from the Chinese obsession with heterosis as a source of yield potential. This research is also facilitated by the vast labor power that the Chinese can use to help conduct and evaluate the thousands of crosses that may be needed to obtain positive results from distant hybridization work. Finally, Chinese technique in anther culture is well advanced, and widely practiced at almost all levels of the "four-level experimental network." By cutting out the years required to stabilize a cross, China can proceed quickly to the evaluation and distribution stage.

Perhaps the one exception to a generally bright potential for breeding breakthroughs in the near future is the soybean work, which, as elsewhere in the world, has had little success. China's stagnant soybean production has been due, at least partly, to a refusal to price the crop in relation to its nutritional advantages. This has recently been partly remedied by giving soybeans a grain-equivalent rating of two in quota fulfillment.

The spread of HYVs has been generally limited by the rate of development of irrigation. Growth has slowed recently simply because the rate of increased exploitation of underground water sources in north China could not be maintained indefinitely without a drastic drop in the water table. However, neither the short- nor the long-run outlook for extended irrigation is as bleak as some have maintained. First, there is considerable potential for improved utilization of existing facilities, which, as in other LDCs, are currently exploited at well below designed capacity. It is estimated that 8 million hectares (16 percent of existing irrigated hectarage) can be brought under irrigation merely by completing ancillary facilities of existing projects.

However, much of China's crop area is mountainous or extensively cultivated due to limited water sources, and these areas have often not benefited from either surface or tubewell irrigation. China has recently begun to promote sprinkler irrigation for such areas, because it saves water, labor, and the land absorbed by canals, ditches, and furrows in surface-flow systems. As experience in the western United States has demonstrated, this technology can transform barren areas into thriving production bases, albeit at a relatively high capital cost per hectare.

Finally, in the long run, there is the proposed project to divert Yangtze River water over 500 kilometers to the north. Work was scheduled to begin during the current Ten Year Plan period (i.e., before 1985), but planners were unable to agree on the scale of the project. Some suggested a simple extension of current pumping and storage capacities of the Grand Canal System. This option was less costly, but delivered only limited amounts of water to the Hebei-Shandong areas. Others favored a more expensive and ambitious project that would distribute water from the San Xia project (currently under construction) on the middle reaches of the Yangtze via the Danjiangkou Reservoir and a newly built canal through Henan and Hebei. Because cost, engineering, and drainage all pose unresolved problems, it now seems that this project has been tabled indefinitely.

Although the Chinese have emphasized tractor production in the past, the extent of mechanization varies tremendously by process — 46 percent of cultivated hectarage is supposedly tractor plowed at least once a year, but only 10 percent of sowing, 2–3 percent of harvesting, and 1 percent of transplanting are mechanized. At the National Conference on "Learning from Dazhai" in 1975, Hua Guofeng called for 70 percent mechanization of all major farm processes by 1980 and 85 percent mechanization by 1985, and it seemed that a major drive was on to rectify the imbalance. However, the targets were absurdly high and in 1979 were quietly abandoned as more realistic views prevailed.

The thrust for mechanization came from recognition of the gap in labor productivity, not only between Chinese and Western agriculture, but also between Chinese agriculture and industry. However, the dilemma was that by closing the gap through rapid mechanization, massive rural underemployment would result. This was clearly indicated by an experiment in which a production team of twenty farm workers fully equipped with John Deere machinery, herbicides, and sprinkler irrigation replaced 300 peasants on the Friendship Farm in northeast China. If full mechanization could displace 93 percent of the labor force in the underpopulated northeast, the consequence would be even more serious for the rest of China.

As a result of the reappraisal, the content of the mechanization program was restricted to full mechanization only in the northeast and in selected underpopulated farm areas. Elsewhere, each province will develop one fully mechanized county near a major urban or industrial center for experimental and demonstration purposes. To absorb the released labor, urban industries have been instructed to develop a Japanese-style subcontracting system whereby simple manufacturing is supplied by small-scale factories attached to suburban communes.

Aside from feeling its way to a mechanization program suitable to an intensive farming system, there is scope for significant improvements in the existing program. In recent years, too much defective machinery was sold, inadequate provisions were made for repairs and spare parts, insufficient accessories were provided for use with tractors, and lack of standardization of parts resulted from small-scale, decentralized production. Much can be learned from foreign experience in management and machinery design, as, for example, with the Japanese version of the rice transplanter. The tendency for tractors to be used for transport more than for plowing should lead to a program to produce small farm trucks. Finally, distribution of machinery according to market demand, instead of an egalitarian rationing program, should help end a situation in which communes with the greatest need for and ability to pay for machinery were unable to obtain it.

In the near future, at least, chemicalization rather than mechanization is the path most likely to contribute to increased productivity in agriculture. This encompasses not only chemical fertilizers, where production capacity will continue to grow at a rapid rate, but also pesticides and herbicides, in which China's production technology is still rather backward. Chinese authorities are already coming to the conclusion that herbicides are a more economical approach to the weed problem than the development of machinery for intertillage. Nevertheless, there is considerable scope for mechanization in animal production, which at present is characterized by the technology of household production even when carried out on a communal scale, and in agriculture in the northeast, where the short growing season puts an exceptional premium on time.

As a whole, many of the elements that distinguished the "Chinese model" of agro-technical development in the past are now or will soon be seen as obstacles to further progress. The general policy of local self-sufficiency, as it affects cropping patterns and production of industrial inputs, has been a mixed blessing in the past, and currently is being criticized. The practices of dense planting and high multiple-cropping rates are changing under the influence of new crop varieties. Intercropping and terracing, which had spread rapidly during the last decade, are now controversial practices because they conflict with mechanization. However, all of these practices have advantages in particular situations or environments, so one should not expect the Chinese countryside to change beyond recognition.

As suggested in this chapter, the "production possibilities frontier" — the potential — of Chinese agriculture has shown a continuous and perhaps accelerating increase since 1949. There seems to be enough currently being accomplished to sustain this source of growth in the near future, although it will always be partially offset by the law of diminishing returns. Actual production, of course, has been affected by weather, agricultural policy, and the availability of modern inputs, as well as the timing of innovations and their diffusion. The impact of weather variations has diminished as the reliability of the irrigation system has improved — a striking instance being the record harvests achieved in 1978 in the more securely irrigated parts of the drought-stricken Yangtze delta (due presumably to high incidence of sunlight during the growing season). The impacts of the timing of innovation and diffusion cannot be precisely measured due to lack of data, but certain relationships with varying regional growth rates during different periods can be perceived. Finally, the effects of changing agricultural policy and its execution, especially price policy, are difficult to assess. The conclusion of this study is that the presence or absence of an appropriate agricultural policy, rather than the amount of productive technology, is likely to be the limiting influence on Chinese agricultural growth in the next decade.

## Notes

1. "Glorious achievements on the agricultural front during the past ten years," *Beijing Renmin Ribao* (People's Daily), Sept. 26, 1959.

## Readings

The sources for this chapter include articles in Chinese newspapers and journals, manuals of agricultural technique, and radio broadcasts translated by the Foreign Broadcast Information Service. The author has also greatly benefited from discussions with and trip reports of agricultural scientists who have visited China, as well as with scientists in the People's Republic of China. Citations of most sources consulted may be found in the author's paper, "On the Evolution of Policy and Capabilities in China's Agricultural Technology," in U.S. Congress, Joint Economic Committee, *Chinese Economy Post-Mao,* Washington, D.C.: U.S. Government Printing Office, 1978. See also Henry J. Groen and James A. Kilpatrick, "Chinese Agricultural Production," in the same volume.

# 8
# Agricultural Employment and Technology

*Thomas G. Rawski*

China's labor force increased by an estimated 148 million persons between 1957 and 1975. Of these, 58 million entered industry and other nonagricultural pursuits. Urban unemployment has declined by approximately 7 million persons during this period. These estimates imply the absorption into agriculture, which includes water conservancy and land improvement projects, of nearly 100 million workers. In addition, considerable growth of mechanization has reduced several components of rural labor demand, thus enlarging the potential problems of labor absorption.

This chapter will show that these potential problems have not materialized. Although China's farm sector succeeded in absorbing an increase of more than 40 percent in its agricultural labor force, there were no significant additions made to cultivated hectarage.[1] Despite the resulting increase in the man-land ratio, which was high to begin with, both the number of workdays per laborer and the value of agricultural output per man-year increased between 1957 and 1975. At the same time, however, diminishing returns are discernible in the declining level of farm output per man-day and in falling total factor productivity in agriculture.

## China's Agricultural System

Several important features of Chinese agriculture should be noted here. For many centuries China's dense population and high man-land ratio have stimulated the development of intensive methods of cultivation. Large inputs of labor, fertilizer, and water were applied to small plots of land. This

This is a condensed and updated version of Chapter 4 of the author's study on *Economic Growth and Employment in China* (New York: Oxford University Press, 1979). Unless otherwise noted, data and estimates are taken from this source.

system of farming, more akin to gardening than to Western techniques of extensive cultivation, supported a sevenfold population increase between 1400 and 1950 with no apparent decline in per capita availability of foodstuffs.[2] By the twentieth century there were few areas in which agricultural reform could bring about sharp increases in output in the absence of chemical fertilizer, machinery, and other modern farm inputs.

Despite its success in supporting a growing populace at constant living standards, traditional Chinese agriculture failed to provide full employment in the countryside. Survey data from the 1930s indicate that seasonal idleness existed in all farming regions, with most regions clustering near the national average of 1.7 idle months per able-bodied rural male.[3] At the same time, the intensity of the farming cycle was restricted by seasonal periods of peak labor demand.

## Collectivization and Supply of Modern Farm Inputs

The success of China's agricultural sector in absorbing large numbers of workers and in raising output to accommodate an unprecedented rate of population growth can be traced to two factors: collectivization and the infusion of industrial products into farm production.

During the extensive and violent land reform of the immediate post-1949 years, 40–50 percent of arable land was confiscated from its owners and redistributed to lower-income farm households. Following this, family farming remained the dominant form of agricultural organization until 1956, when most farm households were grouped into cooperatives in which remuneration was based solely on labor contributions.

In 1958, the rural populace was organized into large-scale collectives called People's Communes. The communes attempted to practice full communism. The consequent rupture of the link between peasant effort and income combined with general disorganization and bad weather to produce a series of disastrous harvests. This prompted a radical decentralization in which the drive to attain full communism was abandoned and control over agricultural production and income distribution was returned to smaller units corresponding roughly to the lower-level cooperatives formed before 1956.[4]

There have been no major reorganizations since the decentralization of the early 1960s. The commune remains the basic unit of local government and administration in rural China. Chinese statements giving the number of communes and of their constituent production brigades and teams yield the following rough estimates of the average size of these units:

| Type of Unit | Number of Units (1978) | Average Size of Units | |
|---|---|---|---|
| | | households | persons |
| Commune | 53,000 | 3,383 | 14,887 |
| Production brigade | 600,000 | 299 | 1,315 |
| Production team | 4,000,000 | 45 | 197 |

In addition to the collective lands cultivated by commune members under the direction of production team leaders, rural households are permitted to maintain small private plots. The size of private plots has varied somewhat with the political climate. Private plots occupied approximately 5 percent of arable farmland during the 1970s and provided about one-fifth of the total income of farm households.[5]

Initial problems encountered by communes were largely responsible for the disastrous harvests of 1959-1961. These problems stemmed from unrealistic ambitions, inexperienced management, and the erosion of incentives associated with egalitarian distribution of income at the commune level. Growth of experience, abandonment of full communism, and the return of control over cultivation and distribution to the team level have overcome most of these difficulties and at the same time allowed the commune system to exploit the advantages of collective agriculture. These advantages include increased central control over rural life, the possibility of mobilizing seasonally idle labor to participate in construction projects, acceleration of the distribution and adoption of new farming techniques, and increased opportunity for diversification and specialization within the farm sector.

The existence of collectives does not ensure that these potential advantages will be exploited. However, following the initial period in which the net impact of collectivization on agricultural performance was strongly negative, the combination of growing managerial experience and sensible economic policies at all levels of government allowed communes to make an increasingly positive contribution to agricultural development.

The second major change that contributed to the development of China's agricultural sector since 1957 is the presence of rapidly increasing supplies of industrial inputs, including power, machinery, building materials, steel, petroleum products, and chemical fertilizer. The rapid growth of industrial inputs can be seen from the following average annual growth rates:

| | |
|---|---|
| Rural power consumption, 1957-1978 | 21 percent |
| Small-scale cement output, 1962-1977 | 23 percent |
| Chemical fertilizer output, 1957-1978 | 22 percent |

| | |
|---|---|
| Stock of irrigation and drainage equipment, 1957–1978 | 25 percent |
| Stock of tractors (horsepower), 1957–1978 | 20 percent |
| Stock of power tillers (horsepower), 1970–1978 | 50 percent |
| Stock of irrigation and drainage equipment, tractors, and power tillers (horsepower per hectare), 1957–1978 | 24 percent |

The addition of growing quantities of chemical fertilizer, much of it manufactured in county-level plants, to traditional organic fertilizers has pushed China into "a class with some of the world's highest users of fertilizers including Japan."[6] Chemical manufacturers also provide the farm sector with large quantities of pesticides and plastic sheeting. Rural construction projects, including annual winter works campaigns, depend on cement, steel, explosives, and other manufactured construction materials.

The expansion of farm machinery production has led to a significant degree of agricultural mechanization. Inventory estimates for three types of farm equipment—irrigation and drainage machinery, tractors, and power tillers—show that these types of equipment alone now furnish substantially greater mechanical power than the 0.69 horsepower per cultivated hectare available to Japanese farmers from all types of machinery in 1955. Despite the evident labor intensity of Chinese farming practices, Chinese agriculture will soon approach Japanese mechanization levels of the early 1960s.

Rural electrification and farm machinery, both of which have spread rapidly through the Chinese countryside since the mid-1960s, illustrate the impact of industrial goods on the farm economy. Perhaps the largest quantitative impact of electrification on rural employment patterns has come from the mechanization of grain processing, which has relieved women of a time-consuming chore. Mechanization of cotton spinning is another innovation that has released large quantities of female household labor.

Irrigation, which absorbed 12–17 percent of farm labor in China's rice growing areas during the 1930s, is also being transformed by electrification and mechanization.[7] Twenty-five million hectares, or roughly one-fourth of China's cultivated area, is now irrigated by electric or diesel pumps.[8] This reduces the demand for human and animal power formerly required by traditional methods of moving water  and creates opportunities for modified cropping systems that require greater quantities of resources but promise a higher output in return.

Transportation is another area in which machines have influenced rural employment patterns. Increased rail, water, highway, and bicycle transport have helped ease labor bottlenecks, but the greatest impact has come from the growing substitution of tractors and power tillers, which

Chinese farmers use primarily as transport vehicles, for carrying poles and man- and animal-drawn carts. Power tillers are manufactured in most provinces and cost approximately 2,000 yuan ($1000).[9] They are powered by 7-12 horsepower diesel engines.

What economic impacts does increased mechanization have on China's farm economy? Mechanization is often expensive relative to the costs of manual labor. High costs imply that mechanization will not be useful unless it leads to an increase in total farm output. High yields achieved under traditional systems of husbandry make it unlikely that substantial output growth will result merely from replacing human or animal labor with machines. In the words of Zhao Ziyang, "the greatest efficiency of mechanization is that it saves manpower; it does not necessarily increase output very much."[10]

Unless the labor released by mechanization is diverted to activities that contribute to further intensification of cultivation or create new income-earning opportunities, mechanization is likely to raise farm costs and reduce employment opportunities. In an economy already troubled by seasonal idleness, introduction of large quantities of machinery might do more harm than good. Problems of this nature have not occurred in China because the farming systems in most regions of the country have been modified to permit mechanization to complement rather than compete with rural labor.

The success of China's farm economy in raising production through the simultaneous absorption of both labor and machinery is best seen by reviewing recent changes in the agricultural sector. These changes are grouped into four categories: intensification of cropping practices, intensification of the cropping cycle, shifts toward labor-intensive farming activities, and rural construction programs.

## Intensification of Cropping Practices

Intensification of cropping practices refers to an increase in the resources applied to each unit of sown hectarage in the absence of changes in the type of crops grown or in the rotation cycle. Chinese publications and visitor accounts indicate that this type of intensification has absorbed considerable quantities of labor. This is illustrated by substantial changes in land preparation, planting, transplanting, and crop management.

The major increase in labor devoted to land preparation has come in the sphere of organic fertilizers. Organic fertilizers, which include human and animal manures, plant wastes, ash, silt-bearing mud, and a variety of other materials, are applied in large quantity. Two American groups touring China in 1975 and 1976 visited communes that applied an annual total of between 5 and 22.5 kilograms of organic fertilizers to each square meter of cultivated land.[11] Despite the growing share of chemical products in the national fertilizer total, Thomas Wiens has shown that organic manures still contributed more than half of the increase in nutrients supplied between 1957 and 1971.[12]

The most significant characteristic of organic fertilizer is the enormous labor input associated with its collection, preparation, and application. One pig produces an annual average of 1,642 kilograms of excreta. Nitrogen retention is substantially increased by mixing the excreta with dirt from the floor of the pigsty and burying it in covered pits to promote fermentation. In this way, one pig can provide up to 20 tons of compost. The number of pigs in China increased from 146 million in 1957 to an estimated 301 million at the end of 1978. During the same period large animal numbers rose from 83 million to 94 million, and the number of sheep increased from 45 to 170 million.[13] Although there is no precise information about the supply growth of other organic fertilizers, there can be no doubt that collection, mixing, storage, transport, and application have absorbed a substantial share of the increased labor input into China's farm economy. One Chinese economist observes: "Under the present condition of having to supply an abundance of organic fertilizer, the amount of manpower and animal power spent in the accumulation, transportation, and application of manure generally takes up between 30 and 40 percent of the total amount of manpower and animal power expended in the whole year."[14]

Chinese farm specialists have advocated close planting since the early 1950s. Results have been mixed. Some areas report large increases in cotton yields following the adoption of close planting, but other regions find that yields are lowered. The contribution of close planting to output growth and labor absorption in other types of cropping is equally uncertain.

Transplanting rice shoots from seed beds into a main field is a well-known feature of traditional Chinese agriculture. This procedure economizes on land by reducing the growing period in the main field, thus allowing an increase in the index of multiple cropping within a fixed growing season. This highly labor intensive practice has been adopted for a growing range of crops—in addition to rice, which is "universally transplanted," and vegetables, which were commonly transplanted before 1949, some regions now transplant wheat, corn, cotton, soybeans, rape, and fiber crops.

The amount of labor devoted to each cropped hectare is considerably greater than in the past. Visitor reports suggest that in advanced farming regions, growing supplies of water and fertilizers have created labor requirements (exclusive of composting) amounting to roughly five times the prewar national average for each unit of land sown to wheat and corn, 2.3

times the prewar average for cotton, and 1.5 times the prewar average for rice. If these figures are compared not with national averages but with figures for regions of peak prewar labor input for each crop, it is clear that the labor requirements for intensive cultivation in the 1970s outstrip even these higher figures for every crop except rice.

To what tasks is this extra labor assigned? Detailed information concerning cotton growing shows that cultivating and pruning (which involve hand care of each individual plant), harvesting, and indirect labor (composting) are responsible for most of the increase in labor time. Scattered references indicate similar changes in the cultivation of grain crops, peanuts, beans, and other crops. The impact of increased labor on yields, however, is not clear.

Growing use of chemical technology also requires a substantial labor input. The Chinese have moved away from DDT, which bred resistance among target species and caused environmental problems, toward "narrower spectrum, less persistent organophosphorus insecticides" that require repeated applications.[15] Chinese sources also stress the desirability of multiple applications of chemical fertilizers in the root zone of growing plants, again indicating high labor requirements.

In summary, intensification of cropping practices—an increase in resources applied per cropped hectare—has absorbed large amounts of labor during the past two decades. The largest sources of labor demand appear to be increased application of organic fertilizers and large increases in labor requirements for transplanting and cultivating cotton, wheat, corn, other grain crops, and, to a lesser extent, rice.

## Intensification of the Cropping Cycle

Intensification of the cropping cycle refers to an increase in the number of crops harvested per unit of cultivated land. Both multiple cropping and intertillage have long histories in China. The national index of multiple cropping (sown area divided by cultivated area) has risen from 1.31 in 1952 to 1.41 in 1957, and to over 1.50 in 1977 or 1978.

Raising the index of multiple cropping requires major increases in farm labor. In rice-growing areas, a shift from one to two annual crops raises labor requirements by 60–70 percent. If farmers attempt to complete rotation cycles where resources or labor cannot meet peak demands, yields will decline.[16] Under these conditions, machines capable of replacing labor devoted to irrigation, harvesting, threshing, transport, plowing, and transplanting can eliminate seasonal labor bottlenecks limiting the spread of multiple cropping.

The rise of the multiple-cropping index, along with increases in the area planted to green manure crops (excluded from Chinese calculations of the multiple-cropping index) indicates modest success in intensifying cropping patterns. New double-cropping areas have emerged north of the Yellow River, and shifts from double- to triple-cropping are reported for the delta regions of Jiangsu and Guangdong.

Intercropping, or simultaneous cultivation of more than one crop in a single field, is common in many regions of China. Although visitors report a wide variety of intercropping patterns, the extent of innovation in this area remains uncertain, as does the treatment of interplanting in Chinese calculations of multiple-cropping indexes. It is worth noting, however, that intercropping raises requirements for both direct and (through fertilizer, water, and so on) indirect labor inputs.

### A Shift Toward Labor Intensive Farming Activities

One way of raising agricultural manpower requirements is to increase the share of highly labor intensive activities in the total farming picture. Available data show that the years since 1957 have witnessed a modest trend in this direction. Between 1957 and 1974 the value of China's agricultural output increased at an average annual rate of about 2.6 percent. Within this total, grain output grew at an average rate of about 2.1 percent, while output from more labor intensive activities, including animal husbandry, vegetables, cotton, tobacco, sugar, silk, and tea, increased at an average rate of about 3.5 percent.

### Rural Construction

Annual campaigns to build water conservancy and land improvement projects during the winter months have become a regular feature of Chinese rural life. They have absorbed vast amounts of manpower during the past 15 years. These campaigns, which encompass major projects coordinated by the central government as well as local projects planned and carried out by communes and brigades, cover a wide range of activities including water encatchment, afforestation, irrigation, flood control, hydroelectric stations, tubewells, and leveling, terracing, and reclamation of arable land.

Available data show the massive scale of China's winter work campaigns, which in recent years have involved over 100 million workers, or 30 percent of the entire rural labor force. As a result of these efforts, irrigated area has risen from 31 percent of cultivated land in 1957 to nearly 50 percent in 1977. With over half of this increase attributable to tubewells, the bulk of the construction work is directed toward improving the utilization of existing water supplies and reducing the vulnerability of crop yields to inadequate or excessive rainfall.[17]

In studying winter works campaigns during 1962–1972, Nickum found that the pattern of seasonal idleness reported by Buck in surveys conducted during the 1930s "corresponds closely to the recent winter-spring water conservancy activities" in which "the average participant . . . is active for 1½ to 2 months."[18] It appears that winter works campaigns have reduced or eliminated traditional slack periods in the farming calendar of a substantial segment of China's rural populace, particularly in the north.

## Overall Results: Supply and Demand for Agricultural Labor

This chapter has surveyed various labor absorption mechanisms that have operated in China's farm economy during the past two decades. In summarizing their overall impact on the balance between supply and demand for rural labor, it is important to point out the interactions among various components of labor demand. The following passage gives some indication of these interrelations:

> Agricultural development, in the Chinese scheme, begins with water management and land improvement. . . . With the provision of timely and adequate supplies of water, it becomes possible to introduce fertilizer-responsive plant varieties together with the fertilizer needed to achieve high yields for these varieties. Effective water management may also make it possible to increase the cropping index . . . and this increase will in turn require more fertilizer as well. All of the above steps raise the demand for rural labor.[19]

Rural industry can provide the tools and construction materials needed for water control and land development projects, which in turn stimulate local demand for pumps, fertilizer, threshers, electricity, and other industrial goods. Increased consumption of industrial products stimulates nonindustrial components of the farming cycle. Assured water supplies raise the returns to labor-intensive construction projects and rising consumption of chemical fertilizers improves not only crop yield, but also the yield and nutrient content of green manures, which provide raw materials for organic fertilizers.

During the past two decades, collectivization and industrialization have modified the framework of China's rural economy. These changes have permitted rural labor as well as land to be utilized with growing intensity. Intensification of cropping practices, increasing adoption of labor-using plant and animal products, and massive farmland construction campaigns

Table 8.1. Supply of, and Demand for, Agricultural Labor, 1957 and 1975

| Category | 1957 | 1975 | |
|---|---|---|---|
| | | Estimate A[a/] | Estimate B[b/] |
| | | (billions of man-days) | |
| 1. Labor supply assuming 275 man-days of work a year | 63.7 | 90.4 | 90.4 |
| 2. Labor demand, total | 36.9 | 89.4 | 67.9 |
|    A. Farm work | 27.4 | 71.2 | 49.7 |
|      (i) Cultivation | n.a. | 49.7 | 33.1 |
|      (ii) Organic manuring | n.a. | 21.5 | 16.6 |
|    B. Subsidiary work | 6.2 | 9.9 | 9.9 |
|    C. Construction | 2.3 | 8.3 | 8.3 |
|      (i) Winter works campaign | n.a. | 5.0 | 5.0 |
|      (ii) Other | n.a. | 3.3 | 3.3 |
|    D. Other | 0.9 | 0.0 | 0.0 |
| 3. Degree of full employment | | | |
|    A. Total labor demand ÷ total supply | 0.58 | 0.99 | 0.75 |
|    B. Annual work days per worker | 159.0 | 272.0 | 207.0 |

Source: Thomas G. Rawski, Economic Growth and Employment in China (New York: Oxford University Press, 1979), p. 115.

n.a.    Not available.
Note:    Column totals may not add because of rounding.

a/   Estimate A - Based on an assumed labor input of 430 man-days for fertilizing and cultivating each sown hectare of land.
b/   Estimate B - Based on an assumed labor input of 300 man-days for fertilizing and cultivating each sown hectare of land.

have contributed to agricultural development by simultaneously raising output and absorbing rural labor. The overall impact of these changes on the rural labor market is summarized in Table 8.1, which presents estimates of the supply of and demand for agricultural labor in 1957 and 1975.

In his study of Chinese agriculture during the 1950s, Schran concluded that the typical agricultural laborer worked only 159 days during 1957.[20] The results shown in Table 8.1 indicate that between 1957 and 1975, China's farm sector not only absorbed an estimated 97.3 million new workers, equivalent to over 40 percent of the 1957 agricultural work force, but also raised the average number of days worked considerably above the levels observed before 1960. Taking all factors into consideration, it seems

Table 8.2.  Labor Productivity in Agriculture, 1957 and 1975

| Category | 1957 | 1975 | |
|---|---|---|---|
| | | Estimate A[a/] | Estimate B[b/] |
| 1. Gross value of agricultural output (billions of 1957 yuan) | 53.700 | 83.907 | 83.907 |
| 2. Labor input | | | |
|     Millions of man-years | 231.5 | 328.8 | 328.8 |
|     Billions of man-days | 36.9 | 89.4 | 67.9 |
| 3. Labor productivity in gross value | | | |
|     Yuan per man-year | 232.0 | 255.2 | 255.2 |
|     Yuan per man-day | 1.46 | 0.94 | 1.24 |

Source:   Thomas G. Rawski, Economic Growth and Employment in China (New York: Oxford University Press, 1979), p. 120.

a/   Estimate A - Based on an assumed labor input of 430 man-days for fertilizing and cultivating each sown hectare of land.
b/   Estimate B - Based on an assumed labor input of 300 man-days for fertilizing and cultivating each sown hectare of land.

most likely that the nationwide average for 1975 is in the vicinity of 250 working days per man-year.

## Overall Results: Productivity Trends in Agriculture

At several points in the foregoing discussion we have suggested that agricultural reforms that absorb labor may fail to increase or perhaps may even reduce total output. What conclusions can be drawn from calculation of partial labor productivity and from more speculative analysis of total factor productivity in Chinese farming?

Estimates shown in Table 8.2 indicate that the gross value of agricultural output per man-year increased by 10 percent between 1957 and 1975. Conversion of these results to a value-added basis would eliminate some, and perhaps most, of this increase. It does appear safe to conclude, however, that the average product of labor in Chinese agriculture did not decrease between 1957 and 1975, even though nearly one hundred million workers were added to the labor force.

When productivity is measured in terms of output value per man-day, the results are equally clear. Output per man-day declined sharply between 1957 and 1975, with the fall ranging from 15 to 36 percent, depending

Table 8.3. Estimated Factor Productivity in Agriculture, 1957 and 1975

| Category | Weights | Growth of Total Inputs 1957 | 1975 |
|---|---|---|---|
| Labor[a/] | 0.55 | 100.0 | 184.0-242.3 |
| Land[b/] | 0.25 | 100.0 | 105.4 |
| Current inputs[c/] | 0.11 | 100.0 | 202.6 |
| Capital[d/] | 0.09 | 100.0 | 680.8 |
| Total input | 1.00 | 100.0 | 211.1-243.2 |
| Gross value of agricultural output | ---- | 100.0 | 156.2 |
| Total factor productivity | ---- | 100.0 | 74.0- 64.2 |

Source: Thomas G. Rawski, Economic Growth and Employment in China (New York: Oxford University Press, 1979), p.120.

a/ Man-days.
b/ Sown hectarage.
c/ Total nutrients provided by organic and chemical fertilizers.
d/ Large animals (weight 0.9) and horsepower of machinery (weight 0.1).

upon which assumptions are chosen with regard to the labor intensity of cultivation and fertilizer preparation. Since man-days provide a much better measure of labor use than man-years, these unambiguous results point to diminishing returns as a serious problem facing Chinese agriculture.

The impact of diminishing returns can be seen in further detail through the highly tentative estimates of overall factor productivity in Chinese agriculture presented in Table 8.3. These calculations distinguish four categories of inputs: land, measured in terms of sown hectarage; labor, measured in terms of man-days; current inputs, measured in terms of total nutrients provided by organic and chemical fertilizers; and capital, measured in terms of large animals (weight 0.9) and in horsepower of tractors, power tillers, and irrigation machinery (weight 0.1). The weights used to aggregate these inputs are those proposed by Tang for calculations covering the period 1952-1965.[21]

The figures in Table 8.3 reveal a distinct downward trend in agricultural factor productivity during the years 1957-1975. If output were measured in terms of value added rather than gross output value, the decline would be slightly steeper than the 1.7 to 2.4 percent annual rate derived here. These results suggest that declining factor productivity has been a regular feature of China's farm economy since 1952.[22] The seeming acceleration of productivity decline since 1965 points to several possible problems including intensification of diminishing returns as farm employment rises and organizational deficiencies in China's system of rural collectives.

## Conclusion

China's success in providing increased employment opportunities for a growing agricultural population raises the question of how this experience is relevant to the problems of other countries whose political, social, and economic systems may differ widely from China's. Several features of China's political economy appear to stand in the way of wholesale application of Chinese methods to problems confronting other developing countries. China's climate, topography, farm technology, and agricultural population are all well suited to the system of intensive farming built up over the centuries and further developed over the past three decades. China's farming technology, especially the wet-rice culture of the south, proved its ability to adjust to large increases in population density centuries before 1949. Recent reforms in cultivation practices consist largely of introducing the technology of wet-rice culture — with its transplanting, irrigation, heavy fertilization, and intensive plant care — into northern and central regions in which irrigation was previously the exception rather than the rule.

Pursuit of intensive farming methods is facilitated by a wide dispersion of literacy and entrepreneurship, by traditions of private and governmental economic organization and social control, and by the presence of a well-developed and widely distributed industrial system capable of responding to shifting patterns of demand originating in the farm sector. These advantages enjoyed by China's economy may not find counterparts elsewhere.

On the other hand, John Mellor's proposed strategy for India's economy illustrates the potential value of Chinese experience in looking at other countries. Although Mellor does not discuss China, his suggestions for an agriculturally based, employment-oriented development policy closely parallel many actual Chinese programs.[23] This shows that despite the unique aspects of China's social, political, and economic arrangements, China's success in enlarging agricultural employment opportunities may offer an instructive example for policymakers in other countries.

A review of China's agricultural labor scene over the past two decades raises the question of whether policies that produced largely favorable outcomes in the past will continue to do so in the future. Projections of labor force growth show that unless nonfarm employment grows more rapidly than the 5 percent rate observed during 1957–1975, China's agricultural sector will be called upon to absorb tens of millions of new workers before the farm labor force reaches a peak sometime after 1990. With output per man-day already falling and labor utilization approaching the full employment level, it is by no means certain that a decline in average farm output per man-year will not accompany further absorption of new workers into agriculture. Raising the price of farm products, as was done in 1979, can forestall a decline in farm income per capita, but unless urban consumers are forced to pay higher prices without compensatory wage increases, such policy changes may lead to increased subsidy payments, reduced investment, slower growth of nonfarm labor demand, a larger influx of labor into the farm sector, and hence a further reduction in farm labor productivity.

Mechanization appears to have created a net demand for extra farm labor between 1957 and 1975, but further development of farm machinery may turn out to reduce rather than increase labor requirements. If chemical fertilizers begin replacing, rather than complementing, organic manures, additional reductions in labor demand are possible.

It is also possible that collective farming, which sacrifices the flexibility and incentive efforts produced in a system of household farming, may be detrimental to the rapid growth of farm output so ardently desired by China's political establishment. The expansion of private plots and encouragement of a "production responsibility system," in which small groups of farmers rent land from their collectives for fixed sums and retain all extra yields for their private use, may soon lead to further erosion of collectivism in Chinese farming.

The searching review of economic strategy and policy now underway in China should come as no surprise to students of economic development and history. In China, as in every country, the passage of time and the evolution of a dynamic economy make it necessary to reevaluate old policies in relation to new economic realities. Old institutions, such as People's Communes, can begin to obstruct rather than encourage progress. The costs of previously successful policies, such as the expansion of small rural manufacturing plants, can come to outweigh their advantages. As a result, the obvious lack of unity and decisiveness in recent policy discussions should be interpreted as a healthy indication that Chinese economists and planners recognize that old solutions, however successful in the past, may not be the best way to confront new generations of economic problems.

### Notes

1. Cultivated area rose from 1.6 to 1.7 billion mou between 1952 and 1957, but declined to 1.5 billion mou in the late 1970s. Nai-ruenn Chen, *Chinese Economic Statistics* (Chicago: Aldine, 1967), pp. 284–285 and *U.S. Joint Publications Research Service* (hereafter JPRS) 73,389 (Washington, D.C., 1979), p. 22 (one mou = 0.0667 hectares). Robert M.E. Tomski of the University of Toronto has discovered reports of declining cultivated hectarage in most provinces outside the northwestern region.

2. Dwight H. Perkins, *Agricultural Development in China, 1368–1968* (Chicago: Aldine, 1969), chs. 1, 9.

3. John L. Buck, *Land Utilization in China* (Nanking: University of Nanking, 1937), p. 294.

4. Audrey Donnithorne, *China's Economic System* (London: Allen and Unwin, 1967). Chapters 2 and 3 provide a detailed account of collectivization.

5. The size and importance of private plots are discussed by Frederick W. Crook, "The Commune System in the People's Republic of China, 1963–1974," in U.S. Congress, Joint Economic Committee, *China: A Reassessment of the Economy* (Washington, D.C.: U.S. Government Printing Office, 1975), pp. 402–405; Shahid Javed Burki, *A Study of Chinese Communes, 1965* (Cambridge: Harvard University East Asian Research Center, 1969), p. 40; William L. Parish and Martin K. Whyte, *Village and Family in Contemporary China* (Chicago: University of Chicago Press, 1978), p. 365; and Christopher Howe, *China's Economy: A Basic Guide* (New York: Basic Books, 1978), p. 49. According to Fox Butterfield, "Chinese Province Tests Profit Incentive in Industry," *New York Times*, January 27, 1980, p. 14, Sichuan province "will raise the amount of privately cultivated land to 15 percent of the total arable area from 7 percent." Other provinces have announced similar changes.

6. Dwight H. Perkins et al., *Rural Small-Scale Industry in the People's Republic of China* (Berkeley: University of California Press, 1977), p. 199.

7. Buck, *Land Utilization*, p. 304.

8. U.S. Foreign Broadcast Information Service, *Daily Report, People's Republic of China* (hereafter FBIS), December 12, 1979, L-9.

9. To provide the reader with a rough notion as to the value in U.S. dollars, we have chosen an exchange rate of 2 yuan to the U.S. dollar. This is approximately the rate that existed until 1976 and falls somewhere between the current official exchange rate of 1.7 yuan to the U.S. dollar and the current trade transaction rate of 2.8 yuan to the U.S. dollar. Chinese currency, as of early 1980, was considered to be overvalued.

10. FBIS, January 9, 1980, Q-1.

11. Perkins et al., *Rural Small-Scale Industry*, Table 8.3; Virgil A. Johnson and Halsey L. Beemer, Jr., eds., *Wheat in the People's Republic of China* (Washington, D.C.: National Academy of Sciences, 1977), p. 163.

12. Thomas B. Wiens, "Agricultural Statistics in the People's Republic of China," in Alexander Eckstein, ed., *Quantitative Measures of China's Economic Output* (Ann Arbor: University of Michigan Press, 1980), p. 92.

13. Animal population data for 1978 are from "Communique on Fulfillment of China's 1978 National Economic Plan," *Beijing Review*, vol. 30, no. 27 (Peking, 1979), p. 38.

14. Yan Ruizhen, "Several Questions on Increasing the Economic Benefits of Fertilizers," *Jingji yanjiu* (Economic Research) 6 (Peking, 1964), translated by U.S. Consulate General, Hong Kong, *Extracts from China Mainland Magazines*, no. 429 (1964), p. 24.

15. Harold Reynolds, "Chinese Insect Control Integrates Old and New," *Chemical and Engineering News*, vol. 54 (March 15, 1976), p. 30.

16. In Songjiang county, Jiangsu, for example, "the total yield of the double cropping surpassed that of the triple cropping. At the same time, the production cost decreased and income increased" following a reduction in multiple cropping (JPRS 73,320 [1979], p. 49). For similar reports see JPRS 73,415 (1979), pp. 6–10 and FBIS, December 12, 1979, 0–6.

17. James E. Nickum, *Hydraulic Engineering and Water Resources in the People's Republic of China* (Stanford, Calif.: U.S.-China Relations Program, 1977), p. 28.

18. James E. Nickum, "A Collective Approach to Water Resources Development: The Chinese Commune System, 1962–1972," Ph.D. dissertation, University of California, Berkeley, 1974, pp. 172, 293.

19. Perkins et al., *Rural Industry*, p. 194.

20. Peter Schran, *The Development of Chinese Agriculture, 1950–1959* (Urbana, University of Illinois Press, 1969), p. 75.

21. Anthony M. Tang, "Input-Output Relations in the Agriculture of Communist China, 1952–1965," in W. A. Douglas Jackson, ed., *Agrarian Politics and Problems in Communist and Non-Communist Countries* (Seattle: University of Washington Press, 1971), p. 287.

22. *Ibid.,* pp. 289, 295.

23. John W. Mellor, *The New Economics of Growth* (Ithaca, N.Y.: Cornell University Press, 1976).

## Readings

Aird, John S. "Population Growth in the People's Republic of China," in U.S. Congress, Joint Economic Committee, *Chinese Economy Post-Mao*. Washington, D.C.: U.S. Government Printing Office, 1979, pp. 439–475. The most recent study by the best informed writer in the difficult field of contemporary Chinese demography.

Emerson, John Philip. *Nonagricultural Employment in Mainland China, 1949–1958.* International Population Statistics Reports, Series P-90, No. 21. Washington, D.C.: U.S. Department of Commerce, 1965. The most thorough and detailed study of China's nonfarm labor force.

Howe, Christopher. *Employment and Economic Growth in Urban China, 1949–1957.* Cambridge, Eng.: Cambridge University Press, 1971. Examines policy and planning as well as quantitative developments on the urban employment scene.

Keesing, Donald B. "Economic Lessons from China." *Journal of Development Economics,* no. 2, 1975, pp. 1–32. Thoughtful observations on the transferability of the Chinese experience by a development economist who is not a China specialist.

King, F. H. *Farmers of Forty Centuries.* Emmaus, Penna.: Organic Gardening Press, n.d. A classic account that provides a detailed picture of traditional Chinese farming practices.

Rawski, Thomas G. *China's Transition to Industrialism.* Ann Arbor: University of Michigan Press, 1980. A study of industrial development that discusses the impact of industrial expansion on agricultural technology and employment.

———. *Economic Growth and Employment in China.* New York: Oxford University Press, 1979. A detailed examination of the labor market implications of Chinese economic growth on which the present essay is based.

# 9

# Rural Industrialization in China

*Christine Pui Wah Wong*

Agricultural growth in China has been fueled by a strong commitment to rural development. The gradual modernization of agriculture has created demands for vast quantities of industrial inputs, which to a large extent have been supplied by rural, small-scale industrial enterprises. These enterprises are complementary to the modernization process, absorbing excess labor released by agricultural mechanization.

First promoted on a large scale under the slogan of "walking on two legs" during the Great Leap Forward, small-scale industries constitute an important part of the rural economy in China today. Over 1.4 million rural enterprises employ nearly 20 million workers. Of particular importance are the "five small industries" (FSIs), consisting of iron and steel, chemical fertilizer, farm machinery, cement, and energy (coal and electricity) industries. These enterprises constitute the core of China's rural industrialization program.

FSI plants generally have a higher technical level and greater capital intensity than other rural industries, although they are extremely small and labor intensive compared to Western counterparts.[1] For example, most of the synthetic ammonia plants (for nitrogenous fertilizer production) built around the world by the Pullman-Kellogg Company have annual capacities of 300,000 tonnes or more. In China, a typical county-run plant has an annual capacity of only 3,000 tonnes. Small Chinese plants employ as many workers as Pullman-Kellogg plants 100 times their size.

In 1977, small plants in the FSIs produced over 40 percent of China's total nitrogenous fertilizer output, over 50 percent of the phosphorus fertilizers, 64 percent of the cement, 33 percent of the hydroelectricity, and almost all of the medium and small farm machines and tools (Table 9.1).

The rural industrialization program grew out of China's commitment to national autonomy, full employment, a rising standard of living, a controlled pattern of urbanization, and a regionally equitable distribution of industrialization. China's problems, such as low per capita income, large

Table 9.1.  Output as a Percentage of National Production, Average Size, and
            Primary Level of Administration for the Five Small Industries

| | Output as percent of industry total | Plant size (output/yr) | Administrative level |
|---|---|---|---|
| Nitrogenous fertilizer (1979) | 55[a] | 4873 tonnes[b] | county |
| Phosphorus fertilizer (1978)[c] | 50+ | 5000 tonnes | county/commune |
| Iron and steel (1978)[d] | 32 | 22,000 tonnes | prefecture |
| Cement (1979)[e] | 67 | 14,000 tonnes | county/commune |
| Hydroelectric (1979)[f] | 12.2 | 70 kilowatts | county/commune/ brigade/team |

[a]  By bulk weight.  New China News Agency (NCNA) 1/14/80, in British Broadcasting
     Corporation, Summary of World Broadcasts, W1078/A/12.
[b]  Ammonia.  NCNA, 11/4/80, in BBC W1110/A/19.
[c]  Estimated.  See C. Wong, "Nutrient Supplies in the PRC: an Assessment of the
     Small-Scale Phosphorus Fertilizer Industry," Current Scene, June–July, 1978.
[d]  Productive capacity.  NCNA 7/12/80, in BBC W1096/A/12.
[e]  NCNA 10/9/80, in BBC W1108/A/16–17.
[f]  Generating capacity.  NCNA 1/4/80, in BBC W1074/A/9.

agrarian population, and low foreign exchange earnings, dictate a development strategy that deviates from that of the West.

The rapid industrialization of Japan and Russia in the early twentieth century has been partially attributed to their advantage as latecomers. They were able to borrow technologies from advanced industrial countries, thus bypassing the time-consuming and expensive intermediate steps of research and development.[2] Paradoxically, as the technology gap between more and less developed countries has widened, advantages accrued from wholesale borrowing have diminished. Advanced technologies have become increasingly inappropriate to the needs of developing countries. New technologies typically originate in affluent industrial countries and tend to utilize labor-saving innovations and greater capital intensity. The low labor absorption of new technologies has caused concern among less developed countries (LDCs) with large populations like China. With a population of nearly one billion and a labor force estimated at over 400 million, China can hardly ignore the adverse implications for employment in choosing modern technologies.[3]

Interindustry linkages, which in the past stimulated technical development during early stages of industrialization, are increasingly weakened in LDCs as the gap between imported technology and the domestic technical level widens. As new technologies are imported it is frequently discovered that the local machine-building sector is unable to provide the appropriate equipment. This necessitates additional imports of machinery. As many studies have noted, this pattern of technical imports provides only minimal stimulus to local industries.[4] In addition, technological imports have a multisectorial impact. Imports to one sector necessitate the use of associated technologies in related sectors. The total cost to LDCs is steeply increased by this phenomenon. For example, in China not only did the choice to import chemical fertilizer technology require construction of transport facilities, power plants, and water systems to aid in manufacture and dispersal, but even unloading and transporting the imported equipment presented enormous difficulties.[5] As a consequence, the People's Republic of China (PRC) considers the completion of modern port facilities as an urgent task under the "four modernizations" program.

Although it is clear that in most cases imported Western technologies are unsuitable for conditions in developing countries, more "appropriate" technologies are difficult to find. Experts emphasize that even though the Intermediate Technology Group and other organizations have claimed success in finding some applicable technologies, ". . . their examples appear to be clustered in a few agricultural activities and small manufacturing activities outside the major production processes of both sectors. In the absence of benefit cost analyses for new intermediate technologies, it must be concluded that for the major processes in mineral transformation, power generation, and the metal and electrical industries—i.e., much of the stuff of modern life—village-level intermediate technologies remain unfulfilled goals."[6] Chinese experiences with the development of the five small industries provide valuable examples, which other less developed countries may follow.

## Genesis of the Small-Scale Industries

The term *five small industries* was first used in 1966 during the First National Conference on Farm Mechanization. A program of rural industrial development was formulated in which the iron and steel, chemical fertilizer, farm machinery, cement, and electricity needs of individual regions were to be provided by local, self-managed, small-scale industries. The FSIs were designed not only to form a core of independent industrial bases, but also to provide substantial linkages among the five industries and with agriculture.

Systematic promotion of the FSIs actually began with the Great Leap Forward when ambitious plans were made to expand output of certain key products using less-advanced technologies. Millions of "backyard furnaces" were erected to produce crude pig iron for steel mills. Farm machinery plants were set up at the county and commune levels to produce a variety of farm machinery. Large numbers of small fertilizer plants were built to manufacture products ranging from ammonium sulfate to processed night-soil. Unfortunately, during the chaotic atmosphere of the Great Leap Forward, little attention was paid to whether production processes were suitable for small-scale, labor-intensive operations. The bulk of these small plants were set up without prior investigation of raw material availability. In some cases, no market could be found for products from newly promoted industries (e.g., phosphorus fertilizers), resulting in wasted capacity.[7]

The failure of the Great Leap Forward and the ensuing economic crisis led to a retreat from all Great Leap programs, including the rural industrialization campaign. The 1961–1965 period was characterized by a more cautious approach to the development of rural industries. By 1963, after gradual economic recovery, the construction of small plants was carefully revived in the chemical fertilizer, farm machinery, and cement industries. Considerable effort went into improving small-scale technologies, developing appropriate blueprint designs, and setting standards for product quality. The Cultural Revolution accelerated the development of rural industries. During the 1968–1975 period large numbers of FSI plants were set up. Technologies developed or perfected during the early 1960s provided the bases for these plants.

Technologies employed in these industries were "intermediate" in the sense that they were adapted from older, less-advanced technologies that were no longer used in the West. For example, the Chinese small nitrogenous fertilizer plants primarily use the partial oxidation method in gas generation. In this process a bed of coal is alternately reacted with steam and air to produce nitrogen and hydrogen gas, the two ingredients needed for ammonia synthesis. This method was used extensively in the 1940s and early 1950s in the advanced industrial countries, where it has since been replaced by a steam-reforming method using naphtha or natural gas as feedstock. A visiting American chemical engineer reported that the equipment used in small Chinese fertilizer plants bears a strong resemblance to that used in the Tennessee Valley Authority fertilizer plant built in the 1940s.[8]

Similarly, most of the small cement plants used a vertical-shaft kiln, the oldest type of kiln used to produce cement. It was replaced in the 1920s in most parts of the industrialized world by the rotary kiln, which uses a continuous process to produce cement of a superior quality and also economizes on fuel consumption. In the production of phosphorus fertilizers, indigenous hydroelectricity and coal are substituted for imported or refined materials, and the plants are characterized by a low degree of mechanization. Furthermore, because FSIs operate on a small scale and use less complex technology than Western counterparts, they can be successfully managed by lower level administrative units in the countryside. Table 9.1 summarizes the scales of operation and levels of administration in the FSIs.

### Rationale for the Choice of Intermediate Technology

The Chinese have never disputed the technical superiority of modern technologies. In the nitrogenous fertilizer industry, a spokesman from the Ministry of Chemical Industry explained that "large plants have a higher degree of mechanization, lower production costs, lower raw material consumption rates and higher labor productivity. But our country's farmland is too broad, our agricultural need for chemical fertilizer is too enormous to be met by the few existing large plants in the shortrun. Therefore we have built many medium and small plants, according to different natural and resource conditions in various places, as a supplement."[9] Thus the development of the FSIs can be seen as part of the "walking on two legs" strategy. Although modern large-scale technologies are widely used in some sectors, acute deficiencies exist in others, particularly in remote rural areas. The Chinese leadership in part chose to encourage development of rural industries to alleviate these problems.

The main advantages of older, less-mechanized technologies are small-scale operations, minimal equipment requirements, and the ability to use lower quality inputs. While using the partial oxidation method for ammonia synthesis, for example, the Chinese reportedly made improvements that have simplified the production equipment and reduced raw material and fuel consumption. More importantly, the older technology uses coal instead of oil products as a feedstock. Given that China is hoping to expand oil output for domestic consumption and export, the opportunity cost of oil must be considerably higher than that of locally mined coal. In the cement industry, the vertical shaft kiln can be built at a fraction of the cost of a rotary kiln. With technical improvements, shaft kiln product quality is said to have risen, and input coefficients are comparable to those of rotary kilns operated in much larger Indian plants. The Chinese point out that these technologies are within the capability of their domestic machine-building sector, they are more labor intensive, and they allow a dispersed geographical distribution of production.

Spatially scattered plants minimize transport and help assure timely supplies by making use of local resources. This stimulates the local economy by generating linkages and raising the technical level of the local work force, thereby creating a market for backward-linked industries and producing inputs for forward-linked industries. Decentralized production tends to preserve the current population distribution, easing pressure on urban areas. Local repair and manufacturing capacities also ensure prompt service for communities. In addition, due to the underdeveloped nature of local transport systems a decentralized production pattern results in a significant savings in transport costs. This applies particularly to industries whose markets are widely scattered.

## Assessment of the Development of FSIs[10]

After over a decade of development, the FSIs have posted a mixed record of performance. Although promoted as a package of basic industries to support agriculture and other rural industries, the FSIs are quite heterogeneous in their production processes and development patterns. Among the more successful are the nitrogenous fertilizer, cement, and hydroelectric industries, where the distributional advantages of small plants are most marked. The changing locations of small nitrogenous fertilizer plants over time reflects the importance awarded to minimizing transport costs. Plants were initially built in the northern and eastern provinces near coking coal supplies. Later, with technical innovations that allowed the use of anthracite and other coals as feedstock, the construction of small plants spread southward to make use of lower quality coals available in those provinces. In the cement industry, press reports emphasize that small plants enjoy a cost advantage over large plants because of the savings in freight costs. Small hydroelectric stations provide electricity to rural areas not linked to state power networks. These stations can be built in a few months with little capital investment  and are a temporary solution to the problem of providing power to remote villages.

Farm machinery production was decentralized in an attempt to make use of machine-building capabilities at all administrative levels, with a division of labor such that scarce engineering skills at the higher levels would not be wasted in making farm machines that can be assigned to lower-level production. The locational rationale for machinery plants lies not so much in the minimization of transport costs, as in the fertilizer, cement, and hydroelectric industries, but instead in the flexibility, timeliness, and responsiveness of small plants in supplying and maintaining local machinery. The attempt was quite successful in expanding output of farm tools, small hand-operated machines such as threshers and insecticide sprayers, small, mechanized, farm-produce processing machines, and others. Small plant output not only helped to eliminate the shortage of farm tools pervasive throughout the 1950s and early 1960s, but also allowed many rural units to achieve mechanization or semimechanization in their nonfield tasks.

Decentralized production of power equipment, such as small diesel engines and walking tractors, was much less successful. Even though their output also grew at rapid rates throughout the Cultural Revolution decade, most of this growth came from a few urban plants. A large number of small rural plants built during this period were never able to produce tractors or diesel engines on a regular basis. Most were operating at scales substantially below their break-even levels, and some failed to pass the trial production stage even after several years of development. Furthermore, the overall

Table 9.2.  Summary Assessment of Industries

| Industry | Performance Appraisal | Complex Technology | State Support | Widespread Availability of Resources | Significant Scale Economies |
|---|---|---|---|---|---|
| Nitrogenous fertilizers | successful | yes | + | yes | + |
| Phosphorus fertilizers | unsuccessful | no | 0 | no | 0 |
| Iron and steel | unsuccessful | yes | + | no | + |
| Farm machinery (I)[a/] | successful | no | + | yes | 0 |
| Farm machinery (II)[b/] | unsuccessful | yes | + | no | + |
| Cement | successful | no | 0 | yes | 0 |
| Hydroelectricity | successful | no | 0 | yes | 0 |

a/  Simple machines and tools: threshers, sprayers, processing machines, etc.
b/  Power equipment: walking tractors, diesel engines.

quality standards of these products deteriorated dramatically, thus undermining one of the main benefits expected from local production. Failure was due to the enormous difficulties in coordinating the supply and assembly of the large number of inputs required.

By 1972 the small-scale iron and steel industry had run into difficulties. Construction of local plants virtually came to a stop. Recent statements in the press reveal that many are operating at substantial losses due to a lack of local raw materials. In Qinghai province, where at least two plants were recently closed, it was reported that because no nearby sources of iron ore existed, supplies had to be hauled from 500 kilometers away. Coking coal was also brought in from other provinces at high cost. Together, these unfavorable conditions resulted in a per-tonne cost of pig iron that was three times the state price. Similarly, because local raw materials are often unsuitable, many small plants in the phosphorus fertilizer industry are producing low quality products that may be useless on much of China's farmland.

Successful development of small plants seems to depend primarily upon the industry's inherent "decentralizability," rather than the amount of state subsidies allocated to it. Decentralizability is determined by the production process, distribution of needed resources, and transportability of the end product.

Table 9.2 summarizes the main characteristics of industries covered in this study. The minimum feasibility condition for decentralized production is widespread availability of resources. Beyond that, simple, straightforward production processes involving few inputs are more easily adopted into the rural environment where managerial and technical skills are relatively scarce and coordination of inputs more difficult.

After over a decade of development, not surprisingly, the FSIs are concentrated in the relatively developed provinces. However, the distribution of plants has improved in recent years. Information exists to show that widening plant distribution is the result of substantial subsidies allocated as "geographic transfer payments." These monies are designed to help less developed areas set up industrial enterprises. Data from the nitrogenous fertilizer industry suggest that central allocations of equipment played a significant role in equalizing the distribution of plants across provinces. Provincial and prefectural governments often provided technical and financial assistance to poorer counties for the construction of small fertilizer plants. Similarly, in the farm machinery industry, support was given to many prefectures to aid in the development of production facilities for walking tractors.

Fostering the growth of a local machine-building sector is a key objective of the rural industrialization program. Machine-building industries capable of producing equipment for small ammonia plants spread rapidly across provinces. Compression chambers and synthesis towers designed to withstand high pressure and high temperature chemical reactions can be manufactured only in workshops equipped with specialized machine tools. These tools were made available to provincial machine-building industries by the central authorities. A primary goal of the authorities must have been to aid localities in obtaining technical skills. Certainly more sets of production equipment could have been produced had tools been ordered from preexisting machine building centers such as Shanghai. As a result of this regional development strategy, the proliferation of small plants in the FSIs has given rise to a sizable machine-building industry spread across many localities.

## Conclusion

Decentralized production using intermediate technologies has succeeded in achieving a number of objectives of China's development program. First, it has led to a more equitable regional distribution of industrial growth. Second, it has built up local machine-building industries as well as fostered the development of rural research networks in many areas. In addition, it has reduced China's dependence on foreign technology. Because of the more dispersed pattern of industrial growth, a network of small and medium cities has expanded gradually. Although labor intensity was not an immediate objective of the FSIs, the plants have provided more employment than their modern large-scale counterparts.

As different inputs are utilized it is extremely difficult to compare costs of production between small-scale rural and large-scale urban enterprises. In cement and fertilizer production, for example, locally mined, low-quality coal cannot be compared to coal mined from large-scale state mines. Local hydraulic sources tapped by small hydroelectric stations cannot be used in large-scale power plants. Interestingly, where small plants *do* use the same inputs as large, state-run plants, costs seem to play an important role in the choice of technology. This is especially true in the post-Mao period where more narrowly defined, short-run, economic efficiency criteria are receiving greater emphasis. The guideline seems to be that as long as small plants can produce a usable product without infringing upon state supplies of key materials, they are to be promoted. Where small plants compete with large plants for the same resources and their costs are higher—as in iron and steel, diesel engine, and tractor production—they are to be rectified, consolidated or closed down.

After over a decade of rapid growth, the time has come for the FSIs to be reviewed and altered as necessary. After a prolonged period of political turmoil, management of local plants in many areas needs to be revamped and improved. Industrial growth has outstripped infrastructural support, causing bottlenecks to emerge in the supplies of coal, electricity, and transport facilities. Ironically, many of the management problems in the FSIs, such as low product quality and high production costs, are the direct result of the regional development strategy. In the zeal to equalize regional distribution, many plants were built in areas without the necessary resources. In addition, operating costs tend to be higher in areas with little experience in running industry. Unfortunately, rural industrialization programs in less-developed regions are likely to be scrapped in the future. Instead, resources will be concentrated in expanding plants in areas with better conditions, and in raising their technical level. Although this will not lead to a general abandonment of intermediate technologies, the reordering of priorities in China's development strategy may lead to a new choice of technique in such industries as iron and steel, diesel engines, walking tractors, and perhaps phosphorus fertilizers.

## Notes

1. "Western" is used here to refer to all advanced industrial countries including Japan and the Soviet Union.

2. Alexander Gerschenkron, *Economic Backwardness in Historical Perspective* (Cambridge: Harvard University Press, 1962).

3. The 958 million figure was given in Hua Guofeng, "Report on the Work of the Government," in Renmin Ribao (People's Daily) (hereafter RMRB), July 19, 1979. Labor force estimate is based on the C.I.A. estimate of the demographic composition of the population, which shows 55.4 percent of the population to be between the ages of 15 and 59. U.S. Central Intelligence Agency, "China: Economic Indicators," December 1978, ER 78-10750.

4. Alice Amsden, "The Division of Labor is Limited by the Type of Market: The

Case of Taiwanese Machine Tool Industry," *World Development* (March 1977); Frances Stewart, *Technology and Underdevelopment* (London: Macmillan, 1975).

5. Information given by French experts constructing the Xixiashan Chemical Fertilizer Plant on outskirts of Nanjing, 1977, in an interview with Hugh Thomas, a Canadian exchange student at the University of Nanjing.

6. Richard Eckaus, *Appropriate Technologies for Developing Countries* (Washington, D.C.: National Academy of Sciences, 1977), p. 49.

7. For a summary of Great Leap Forward activities in rural industries, see Carl Riskin, "Small Industry and the Chinese Model of Development," *China Quarterly* (June 1971).

8. Dwight Perkins et al., *Rural Small-Scale Industry in the People's Republic of China* (Berkeley: University of California Press, 1977), p. 176.

9. *Jingji Daobao* (Economic Newspaper) (Hong Kong), March 15, 1965, pp. 15–16.

10. This section is summarized from detailed investigations of the FSIs in Christine Pui Wah Wong, *Rural Industrialization in China: Development of the "Five Small Industries,"* Ph.D. dissertation, University of California, Berkeley, 1979.

## Readings

Clark, N. Gardner. *Development of China's Steel Industry and Soviet Technical Aid.* Ithaca, N.Y.: Cornell University Press, 1973. A detailed study of China's steel industry in the 1950s and 1960s.

Eckous, Richard. *Appropriate Technologies for Developing Countries.* Washington, D.C.: National Academy of Sciences, 1977. A good reference on appropriate technologies.

Gerschenkron, Alexander. *Economic Backwardness in Historical Perspective.* Cambridge, Mass.: Harvard University Press, 1962.

Perkins, Dwight, et al. *Rural Small-Scale Industry in the People's Republic of China.* Berkeley, Calif.: University of California Press, 1977. This is the report of the 1975 American Rural Small-Scale Industry Delegation, with some good technical and economic data on selected enterprises.

Riskin, Carl. "Small Industry and the Chinese Model of Development," *China Quarterly.* June 1971. This is an excellent article on the development of small-scale industry, particularly for the Great Leap period and the 1960s.

Sigurdson, J. "Rural Industrialization in China," in U.S. Congress Joint Economic Committee, *China: A Reassessment of the Economy.* Washington, D.C.: U.S. Government Printing Office, 1975. This is a good introductory article on the "five small industries."

Stewart, Frances. *Technology and Underdevelopment.* London: Macmillan, 1975. An excellent basic book on the importance of technology choice in economic development.

Wong, Christine Pui Wah. *Rural Industrialization in China: Development of the "Five Small Industries."* Ph.D. dissertation, University of California, Berkeley, 1979. A detailed, industry-by-industry study of the "five small industries," during the Cultural Revolution decade (1966–1977).

# 10
# Food Consumption in the People's Republic of China

*Nicholas R. Lardy*

Since the Communist Party rose to power, China's economy has undergone significant economic growth and structural change, yet that growth has been highly imbalanced, emphasizing industry and particularly the producer goods sector rather than agriculture. Consequently, for most of the past three decades average food consumption has been somewhat below the level achieved prior to the Sino-Japanese War. After 1949, agriculture recovered rapidly from wartime devastation and by 1957–1958 per capita food consumption reattained the prewar level. However, in the subsequent two decades the quantitative and qualitative standard of the average Chinese diet was significantly below that of 1957–1958. Average food consumption surpassed the mid-1950s level only at the end of the 1970 decade.

The absence of growth in average per capita food consumption indicates that significant improvement in the diet of most Chinese could have occurred only through a more egalitarian distribution of food. Collectivization of agriculture and introduction of rationing of basic foods in the urban sector in the 1950s, in fact, did improve the distribution of food. But recent evidence suggests that in the last twenty years the production and consumption of food grains may have become increasingly uneven, particularly in rural regions.

This unevenness in the regional distribution of food might explain the difference between the rather optimistic appraisal of the Chinese food situation by Western visitors and the pessimistic assessment by the Chinese toward the end of the 1970s. Visitors to China throughout the 1970s noted the absence of beggars or other evidence of widespread malnutrition, and frequently suggested absolute deprivation had been eliminated. But such generalizations were almost always based on observations of urban areas or of atypical rural areas. In retrospect, these assessments appear to have been overly optimistic.

Increased inequality in the distribution of food grains could have stemmed from two sources. On the one hand, given the regional diversities in natural resources and factor endowments, differential rates of growth in agricultural output are not surprising. Certain aspects of agricultural development policy since the mid-1960s appear to have accentuated the pattern of differential regional agricultural growth, compared to the 1950s. On the other hand, compared to the 1950s, the state, as part of its policy of promoting regional self-sufficiency in food grains, appears to have played a reduced role in redistributing food grains within and among provinces to maintain a minimum food standard in grain deficit rural areas. A central hypothesis of this chapter is that the state's development and marketing policies both contributed to increased inequality in the distribution of food grains and led to a critical food supply situation in many regions in China, especially in 1976–1978. A decline in the per capita production of some important nongrain crops, such as edible soybeans, and other food products must have further reduced both average caloric consumption and the quality of the diet.

## Average Consumption

Many estimates of Chinese food consumption have been made. Although these studies have advanced our knowledge, until the Chinese release more production and population data it will be impossible to provide a detailed analysis of changes over time in the quality and quantity of food consumption. The following paragraphs summarize the most comprehensive estimates that have been made, pointing out in passing major deficiencies in each of the studies.

The two most important sources of information relating to consumption in the 1930s are the surveys of 2,728 households in 136 rural communities conducted by John Lossing Buck and the Food Balance Sheets for China for 1931–1937. The latter were based on crop reports compiled by the National Agricultural Research Bureau of the Nationalist Government. Both of these sources have been considered by some scholars to err on the side of overestimation. Revised estimates produced by Liu and Yeh and by Wiens are presented in Table 10.1 together with the original estimates. These three authors estimate that average per capita intake of food in China in the early 1930s was between 2000 and 2100 calories per day.

Unlike the 1930s, no detailed countrywide food consumption surveys for the post-1949 period have been published. As a result, Western estimates of

Table 10.1  Food Consumption in Prewar China

| Sources | Calories from food grains[a] | Percent of total calories from food grains | Total caloric consumption |
|---|---|---|---|
| John Lossing Buck[b] | 2072 | 90 | 2313 |
| Food and Agricultural Organization/National Agricultural Research Bureau[b] | 1771 | 80 | 2226 |
| Liu and Yeh[c] | 1936 | 91 | 2127 |
| Wiens[d] | 1789 | 90 | 1998 |

a/  Includes grains, tubers (at grain equivalent weight), soybeans and other legumes. Buck's data are for the rural population only and refer to 1929-1933. The FAO/NARB data are for the total populations and refer to the period 1931-1937. Both the Liu and Yeh and Wiens data are for the total population and refer to 1933.

b/  Peter Schran, The Development of Chinese Agriculture, 1950-59 (Urbana: University of Illinois Press, 1969), p. 98.

c/  Ta-chung Liu and Kung-chia Yeh, The Economy of the Chinese Mainland, National Income and Economic Development, 1933-1959 (Princeton, N.J.: Princeton, University Press, 1965), p. 29.

d/  Thomas Wiens, "Agricultural Output," in Alexander Eckstein (ed.), Quantitative Measures of China's Economic Output, Ann Arbor: University of Michigan Press, 1980), p. 76.

caloric intake since 1949 have been based almost entirely on production data. Two alternative approaches have been used. The most common is to estimate the per capita caloric intake from food grains and then to assume that comprises the same share of total caloric intake as in Buck's data for the 1930s. Wiens's estimate for 1957, using this procedure and the official population of 646 million, is 2053 calories per capita. The alternative approach has been used by Vaclav Smil.[1] He estimates total caloric supply by constructing food balance tables incorporating data on production, trade, nonfood uses (for example, grains used for seed and feed), and extraction rates for grains, vegetables, tubers, fish, and animal products. His estimate of per capita caloric intake in 1957 (again based on official population data) is 2057 calories per day, almost exactly equal to Wiens's estimate.

The central conclusion emerging from both these studies is that average per capita consumption in 1957 was much the same as in the early 1930s. There was almost certainly a decline in agricultural output and consumption levels during the Sino-Japanese and Civil wars, but by 1957 both production and consumption seem to have recovered. Furthermore, the majority of the population probably consumed a more adequate diet than in the 1930s since the redistribution of land and the introduction of rationing of grains and edible oils in urban areas significantly reduced the skewness in food consumption.

In marked contrast to the positive trend of 1949–1957, per capita food consumption deteriorated after 1958. Reductions were most drastic in the crisis caused by the Great Leap Forward. The magnitude of the consumption decline and the consequent loss of life have been the subject of considerable, although inconclusive, debate in the West. In the late 1970s, the Chinese released important new evidence suggesting the scope of the disaster had been underestimated. On the production side the Chinese have disclosed that grain output dropped by 26.4 percent, or more than 50 million tonnes, in 1960 compared to 1957, the last year of the First Five Year Plan. The 1960 production level of 143.5 million tonnes is roughly equal to the 1951 output and is 12–16 million tonnes less than the most widely accepted earlier Western estimates. Newly released figures for 1958 and 1962, as well as 1960, are incorporated in Table 10.2. Consumption, of course, did not fall quite so dramatically because food grain stocks were drawn down, grain was diverted to human use as the number of draft animals was reduced, and after 1960 China became a net importer of food grains from the West. Despite these palliatives, average food grain consumption fell precipitously. In 1960, for example, per capita consumption was 163.5 kilograms, 20 percent below the level of 1957.[2]

The decline in cereal consumption both reduced fertility and increased the death rate. The magnitude of population loss has now been estimated using Chinese demographic data. In 1979, a survey of the 1975 age distribution, reflecting a sharp decline in the number of births in the crisis years, was released. In addition, in the spring of 1980 the Chinese published a graph indicating the number of births annually from 1949 through 1977. Using these new data and the previously available mid-year 1964 census data, John Aird has constructed a new model of demographic developments in the critical years.[3] A model that follows the Chinese data most closely shows a net loss of 28 million persons in 1960–1961 and a total population cost (the sum of reduced births as well as increased mortality) of 64 million. An alternative model assumes that the 1975 age distribution data were constructed considering children one year of age at birth. This makes the peak birth rate year 1964 rather than 1963, and the level of mortality required to link the official year-end 1957 and mid-year 1964 totals (given the numbers of births per year) is substantially smaller. The net loss of population based on this assumption is cut almost in half, to 16 million. Regardless of which set of assumptions leads to a closer approximation of the true underlying population trend, the preliminary conclusion is

10.2. The Balance Between Food Grain and Population in China, 1952-1979

| | Food Grain Output[a/] (million tonnes) | Population[b/] (millions, at year-end) | Food Grain Output/Capita (kilograms) |
|------|------|------|------|
| 1952 | 164 | 575 | 285 |
| 1957 | 196 | 647 | 302 |
| 1958 | 200 | (661-662) | (303-302) |
| 1960 | 144 | (659-673) | (218-213) |
| 1962 | 160 | (659-664) | (243-241) |
| 1965 | 195 | (702-703) | (277-278) |
| 1976 | 284 | 933 | 305 |
| 1977 | 283 | 945 | 299 |
| 1978 | 305 | 958 | 318 |
| 1979 | 332 | 971 | 342 |

Sources: 1952, 1957: State Statistical Bureau, Ten Great Years (Beijing: Foreign Languages Press, 1960), pp. 119, 124. 1958: Xue Muqiao, "An Arduous Thirty Years of Pioneering Work," Hongqi (Red Flag) no. 10, 1979, p.44. 1960: Zhang Qingwu, "Controlling Urban Population Growth," People's Daily, August 21, 1979, p. 3. 1962, 1965, 1976: Ge Zhida, "Raise the Effectiveness of Financial Funds Used to Support Agriculture," Jingji Yangiu (Economic Research) no. 2, 1980, p. 12. 1977, 1978: State Statistical Bureau, "Communique on the Fulfillment of the 1978 Economic Plan," People's Daily, June 28, 1979, p. 2. 1979: State Statistical Bureau, "Communique on the Fulfillment of the 1979 Economic Plan," People's Daily, April 30, 1979.

a/ Food grain output, by Chinese statistical definition, includes grains, tubers (at grain equivalent weight), soybeans, and legumes. Output and output per capita data in this table are measured in unprocessed form.

b/ Source: John S. Aird, "Reconstruction of an Official Data Model of the Population," Table 1, unpublished paper, May 1980. Aird's tables give official data for all years but 1958, 1960, 1962, and 1965. Aird's estimates for the population in these four years are based on population data for year-end 1957 and for midyear 1964 and a new series indicating the number of births in the intervening years.

that outside observers grossly underestimated the magnitude of the famine of 1960-1962.

From the low point of 1960, grain output grew at an annual average rate of over 4 percent for the next two decades. But, as reflected in Table 10.2, even at this pace it was not until 1976 that per capita production regained the 1957 level. Despite continuing imports, consumption recovered even more slowly — as late as 1978, when per capita output was well above the 1957 level, actual consumption of processed grain was still below that of 1956 and 1957.[4] Furthermore, throughout this period consumption standards remained vulnerable to a sequence of no growth harvests such as occurred in 1970-1972. By 1972 per capita consumption had fallen to 173 kilograms, only marginally above the depths of consumption levels in the 1960 famine.[5]

Because data on the availability of nongrain foods begin to appear for the years after 1976, it is possible to make a preliminary estimate of whether

Table 10.3  Output of Nongrain Food, 1957, 1977, 1978, and 1979[a]

| Nongrain food | 1957[b] | 1977[c] | 1978[c] | 1979[d] |
|---|---|---|---|---|
| | (thousand tonnes) | | | |
| Fish | 3,120 | 4,700 | 4,660 | 4,305 |
| Sugarcane | 10,393 | 17,753 | 21,117 | 21,508 |
| Sugar beets | 1,501 | 2,456 | 2,702 | 3,106 |
| Oil seed crops[e] | 3,806 | --- | 4,568 | 5,641 |
| Tea | 115 | 252 | 268 | 277 |
| Fruit | 3,250 | --- | 6,600 | 7,250 |
| Soybeans | 10,045 | 7,300 | 8,300 | 8,300 |
| Meat[f] | 3,985 | 7,800 | 8,160 | 10,624 |

a/  All data, except 1977, 1978 and 1979 soybean output, are from official sources.
    Soybean production listed for these years is estimated by the United States
    Department of Agriculture.  -- indicates data not available.
b/  State Statistical Bureau, Ten Great Years (Beijing: Foreign Languages Press,
    1960), pp. 100, 124, 125, and 127.
c/  State Statistical Bureau, "Communique on the Fulfillment of the 1978 Economic
    Plan." People's Daily, June 28, 1979, p.2. Xinhua, December 1, 1979, Foreign
    Broadcast Information Service, December 3, 1979, p. 116. United States Depart-
    ment of Agriculture, People's Republic of China Agriculture Situation Review of
    1979 and Outlook for 1980, June 1980, p. 40.
d/  State Statistical Bureau, "Communique on the Fulfillment of the 1979 Economic
    Plan," People's Daily, April 30, 1980.
e/  Includes only peanuts, sesame seed, and rapeseed.
f/  State Statistical Bureau, Main Indicators, Development of the National Economy
    of the People's Republic of China (1949-1979), Beijing, 1980. Meat includes
    pork, beef, and mutton.

the slight decline in grain consumption between the mid-1950s and
1976–1978 was offset by increased consumption of nongrain foods. Consumption of some important nongrain foods clearly declined. Per capita
consumption of vegetable oils pressed from peanuts and oil-bearing seeds
such as rape and sesame was down by a third between 1957 and 1978.[6]
Judgments on other nongrain foods must be based on trends in production,
as shown in Table 10.3. Per capita consumption of soybeans, an important
source of protein, must have fallen substantially, because shifting from being a net exporter in the 1950s to being a net importer by the mid-1970s
compensated for only, part of the 50 percent decline in per capita production
between 1957 and 1977–1978. Judging from official production figures,
average per capita fish consumption in 1977–1978 was about the same as in
1957. Consumption of sugar, fruit, and meat, however, did increase
significantly because production rose considerably.

Increased per capita consumption of meat, fruit, and sugar must be placed in perspective. The share of total calories supplied by these foods is dwarfed by the huge share derived from grains — 80 to 90 percent according to recent Chinese statements. The lack of diversity implied by the high share of calories derived from grain is confirmed by the small quantities of nongrain foods consumed. China's per capita meat consumption averaged 8.4 kilograms annually in 1976–1977, placing it ninety-eighth in world consumption. Per capita sugar consumption, 2.8 kilograms in 1976–1977, is only a tenth that of the world average and is well below the levels of many developing countries. In 1978 fruit production was less than 7 kilograms per capita. Consumption of other food products was also quite small. Per capita consumption of eggs and dairy products in 1976–1977 averaged 2.2 kilograms and 1.1 kilograms per year, respectively.[7] Because adult Han Chinese do not consume dairy products, the average consumption figure is somewhat misleading, but the Chinese say that current levels of milk production are inadequate to supplement the diets of infants and to supply the needs of the several tens of millions of minority races living in China who do consume milk.

On balance, in comparing 1976–1978 with the mid-1950s, it seems quite unlikely that increased supplies of meat, sugar, and fruit were sufficient to offset the sharp decline of edible vegetable oils and beancurd and the slight reduction in cereal consumption. Consequently, average caloric intake in 1976–1978 was probably somewhat below the 1957 range of 2000 to 2100 calories per day.

The quality of diet, or at least the people's perception of it, might have gone down because of the rising share of grain accounted for by potatoes and coarse grains, particularly corn. Corn, barley, and other coarse grains are generally considered to be inferior foods. However, this factor alone should not affect caloric intake more than marginally because caloric values among grains do not differ much.

## Distribution of Food

The draft of a Chinese Communist Party Central Committee report, presented in a meeting in December 1978, stated that 1977 per capita grain production was slightly less than in 1957 and, more significantly, that more than 100 million peasants had "insufficient amounts of food grains."[8] A communist-controlled periodical published in Hong Kong painted an even bleaker picture, stating that "the annual food grain ration of 200 million peasants in China is less than 300 jin [150 kilograms], that is to say they are living in a state of semistarvation."[9] The final Central Committee Report adopted in late September 1979, however, deleted the estimate of the number of peasants that were inadequately fed and merely pointed out that

1978 per capita grain output was equivalent only to that of 1957. Subsequent Chinese press reports, however, have placed the number of peasants with inadequate food supplies at between 100 and 130 million.[10]

Yet, when net imports are included, annual per capita grain supplies in 1976, 1977, and 1978 were somewhat greater than in 1957 or, for that matter than in 1956 or 1958. Although there were official reports of localized food shortages in some years in the mid-1950s, there is no evidence that a comparably large segment of China's rural population was similarly underfed in that earlier period. Under the circumstances, the official and semiofficial statements imply that supplies of food may have been much less equitably distributed in the mid- to late 1970s than in the mid-1950s. That worsening distribution, in turn, appears to have been the consequence of a skewed regional pattern of agricultural growth over the previous decade and government policies that severely curtailed both private and state marketing of food grains and perhaps other food products as well.

Trends in provincial grain output are not fully known, but the constancy of national per capita output between 1957–1958 and 1976–1977, shown in Table 10.2, probably masks increased variation in production trends among provinces. The slowest-growing provinces are widely dispersed geographically and have significantly differing cropping patterns. They include the northwestern provinces Xinjiang and Gansu; Neimonggol (Inner Mongolia) in north China; the entire southwest — Sichuan (at least through 1976), Guizhou, and Yunnan; and Guangdong in the south. Per capita food grain production in Neimonggol in the late 1970s was only half the level of 1956. The decline in per capita production in Gansu and Xinjiang between 1957 and 1978 was 25 and 20 percent, respectively. Sichuan was another extreme case. Between 1957 and 1976 the population grew almost a third from 72 million to approximately 95 million, while grain output rose less than 10 percent from 23 to 25 million tonnes. By 1976 the food shortages were so severe that diets had to be supplemented with sorghum and other animal feeds.

In sharp contrast to declining per capita food production in the provinces mentioned above, in widely separated provinces such as Jiangsu in east China, Hunan in central China, and Guangxi in south China, growth in grain output since 1957 has been far above the national average.

In a different policy milieu, private marketing, centrally directed redistribution of grains from surplus to deficit regions, or interprovincial migration might have alleviated the effects of increasingly disparate trends in regional grain production. But after the onset of the Cultural Revolution in 1966 private rural marketing was attacked as a remnant of capitalism in the countryside and private grain trading was suppressed. Furthermore in a March 1966 speech to an enlarged Politbureau meeting Mao Zedong opined that it was "dangerous" for individual provinces to rely on grain transfers from other provinces to meet basic consumption requirements. Thus a strategy of food grain self-sufficiency emerged after 1966 that required each locality to supply its basic grain needs before allocating land and other resources to animal husbandry or the production of nongrain crops. The impetus for local self-sufficiency appears to have been reinforced after 1967 or 1968 with the onset of an intense campaign for preparedness against potential Soviet military invasion. Lacking any significant military deterrent, the leadership sought to create regions that could survive independently if cut off by military action.

To enforce local self-sufficiency the government actually reduced its commitment to supply food grains to chronically grain deficit rural areas, many of which tended to specialize in production of cotton or other nongrain crops, or in animal husbandry. In spite of a huge increase in total output, the state actually procured less grain from the countryside in 1977–1978 than in the mid-1950s (Table 10.4). More significantly, as explained below, in per capita terms the resupply of food grains to rural areas was reduced significantly between 1957 and 1978.

Information on resupply to food deficit rural areas since the 1950s has not been reported, but this decline in the resupply of food grains can be supported only by a loose order-of-magnitude estimate. The 1977 urban population was reported to be 120 million and it is also said that 40 percent of all urban food grain requirements were supplied by imports. In the 1950s an urban population of 83 million was fed with average procurements (net of resupply to grain deficit rural areas, net exports, and net additions to stocks) of 24.7 million tonnes. As a broad approximation, in 1977 the urban population not fed imported grain would have required about 23.6 million tonnes of grain from domestic sources. Thus, in 1977 the maximum quantity of grain available for resupply to grain-deficit rural areas would have been 19.9 million tonnes. Although this is well above the average resupply in the 1950s, the rural population increased by more than 50 percent over the period. In short, the average per capita quantity of grain available for resupply to rural areas probably declined by at least one-quarter compared to the First Five Year Plan. This should be considered as the minimum estimate of the decline in the quantities of food grains available for resupply to rural areas because it is based on an urban population figure (from a Chinese source) that seems unreasonably low. If the urban population is actually larger, the estimated supply to urban areas would be higher and the resale to rural areas lower.

Finally, migration might have alleviated the effects of increasingly divergent trends in grain production. Yet in recent decades strict controls on intrarural migration have foreclosed this prospect. Most of the inter-

Table 10.4.  State Food Grain Procurement, 1953–1980[a/]

| | Total Procurement[b/] | Resale to Rural Areas | Supply to Urban Areas[c/] |
|---|---|---|---|
| | (million tonnes) | | |
| 1953–54 | 42 | 13 | 29 |
| 1954–55 | 45 | 19 | 26 |
| 1955–56 | 43 | 13 | 30 |
| 1956–57 | 42 | 19 | 23 |
| 1957–58 | 48 | 15 | 33 |
| Average | 44 | 16 | 28 |
| 1977–78 | 44 | 20 | 24 |
| 1978–79 | 47 | 23 | 25 |
| 1979–80 | 52 | 27 | 26 |

Sources:  1953-1954 through 1957-1958:  David L. Denny, "Soviet Economic Policies in Rural China," unpublished paper, 1975, and Alexander Eckstein, China's Economic Revolution (Cambridge, England:  Cambridge University Press, 1977), p. 117.  1977-1978:  Shigeru Ishikawa, "China's Economic Issues in 1980 and 1981:  A Prospect," unpublished paper, December 1979. 1978-1979 and 1979-1980:  "The Development of Our Country's Rural Situation is Surpassing People's Expectations," Guangming Daily, February 8, 1980; "Our National Economy is Advancing Amidst Adjustment," Guangming Daily, May 2, 1980, p. 1.

a/  Food grains procured include grains, tubers (at grain equivalent weight of 5-1, soybeans, and other legumes.  Measurement is in terms of trade grain, which in 1950s included rice and millet in processed form but other grains in unprocessed form.  Data are all expressed in terms of the procurement year, which in the 1950s ran from July 1 to June 30 and which in the late 1970s ran from April 1 to March 31.  Supply to urban areas is calculated as a residual and also includes net grain exports and additions to state stockpiles.  Total procurement for 1979-1980 is preliminary and does not include a reported 5 million tons of grain sold in rural markets.

b/  Includes agricultural tax collected in kind.  Excludes transactions on so-called free markets or rural collective markets.

c/  Includes supply from domestic sources only.  Imports, which are used almost exclusively to feed urban areas, would have to be added to derive total urban grain supplies.

regional migration that has occurred since the mid-1950s has been the forced relocation of urbanites in rural areas. Many have been resettled on the periphery of China, where agriculture generally has been growing relatively slowly. The long-run rates of population growth in these areas have been substantially above average, partially because of this internal migration.

The procurement system in the late 1970s not only appears to have done

Table 10.5.  Food Grain Distribution in Rural Communes by Province, 1977–1979[a/]

| | 1977 | 1978 | 1979 |
|---|---|---|---|
| | (kilograms per capita) | | |
| Zhejiang | 240 | 280 | 350 |
| Henan | | 189 | 199 |
| Hunan | 252 | 278 | |
| Jiangsu | 220 | 250 | |
| Jiangxi | | | 300 |
| Jilin | 209 | 250 | 261 |
| Liaoning | 205 | 220 | |
| Ningxia | 152 | 187 | |
| Xinjiang | 169 | 185 | 193 |
| Sichuan | 218 | 246 | 260 |

a/  Based on official provincial data published in or broadcast from China.
    Although it is not clear from Chinese sources, these data are probably
    measured in unprocessed weight.

little to alleviate interprovincial variations in average rural per capita consumption (Table 10.5), but clearly exacerbated urban-rural inequality compared to the mid-1950s. The reported average consumption of 196 kilograms of grain in 1978 (Table 10.6) should have supplied 1770 calories daily. Assuming that grains supply 80 to 90 percent of the total (as Chinese sources have recently stated), overall food intake should have been between 1965 and 2210 calories daily. Even the lower end of this range, if distributed equitably, probably would be adequate to meet the minimum nutritional needs of China's population. Therefore, one is initially puzzled by assertions that more than 100 million peasants had inadequate supplies of food grains.

Part of the disparity may arise because stagnation in grain production in 1975–1977 reduced 1977 per capita grain output to the lowest level since 1972. Skewness in the distribution of foods, however, may be a primary source of malnutrition in the mid- to late 1970s. While 1978 national per capita grain consumption showed a 3.2 percent reduction from 1957 (Table 10.6) rural consumption declined by almost 6 percent and urban consumption rose by 10 percent or more. A parallel development occurred in edible vegetable oils — per capita rural consumption fell more than 40 percent between 1957 and 1978 while urban consumption increased slightly.[11] In short, urban food standards were protected by large imports of grain and vegetable oils and declining consumption in the countryside. This period marked the culmination of a decade in which private and state marketing of grains were curtailed and in which agricultural development policy

Table 10.6.  Estimated Urban and Rural Consumption of Food Grains, 1956–1957
             and 1978 [a/]

|  | 1956–57 | 1978 | Percent Change |
|---|---|---|---|
|  | (kilograms, fine grains) | | |
| National | 203 | 196.5 | – 3.2 |
| Urban | 218 | 253.0 | +15.8 |
| Rural | 200 | 188.0 | – 5.9 |
| Urban as a Percent of Rural | 109 | 135 | |

Source:  Data Office, Statistical Work, "The Basic Situation of Unified Purchase
         and Sale of Foodgrains in China," Tongji Gongzuo (Statistical Work),
         no. 19, 1957.  Liu Fangyu and Wang Gengjin, see note 7.  1978 Urban
         Population: Bao Guangqian, "The State Cannot Take Full Responsibility
         for Urban Housing," People's Daily, June 1, 1980, p. 2.

[a/]  Consumption is expressed in processed or fine grains for both periods.  All
      data are taken directly from Chinese sources except urban consumption in
      1978.  Urban consumption in 1978 can be derived once urban population is
      known.  I have used a figure of 125 million urban out of a total 1978 popu-
      lation of 958 million.  The reported decline in national consumption of 3.2
      percent to 196.5 kilograms and the reported 5.9 percent decline in rural
      consumption are consistent only if the consumption of 125 million urbanites
      rose to 253 kilograms.  If the actual urban population was larger than 125
      million, the implied rise in consumption in urban areas would be smaller
      than that shown in the table.  For example, if the urban population was
      actually 200 million, the increase in urban consumption required to make the
      the other data consistent would be only 5.7 percent.  However, regardless of
      the actual urban population the data released to date by the Chinese imply
      that in per capita terms urban consumption has risen while rural consumption
      has fallen.

contributed significantly to disparate trends in per capita food production.

## Policy Changes Since 1977

   After autumn 1976 the shortcomings of agricultural development policy
were discussed widely in the Chinese press. That process led to a fundamental shift in strategy in 1978 and 1979. The new strategy attempts to
provide greater incentives for production and marketing to increase the efficiency of resources used within the agricultural sector and to raise living
standards. State expenditures on agricultural modernization have been increased and, more importantly, the prices the state pays for grains and
other food crops were raised in 1979 by record amounts. The state has also
sought to restore the decision-making authority of production teams by
relaxing the sown area and output targets they previously were required to
meet. Production units are being encouraged to make their own cropping

decisions based on local conditions and the relative prices set by the state. Changes in agricultural development policy, better weather, and increased supplies of modern inputs, especially chemical fertilizers, have led to a substantial increase in the output of food grain and other agricultural products as well as a sharp rise in state procurements.

Grain output in 1979 was 332 million tonnes, or 17 percent more than in 1977; oil-bearing crops rose by 2.4 million tonnes, or 60 percent; sugarcane and sugar beet by 4.4 million tonnes, or 22 percent; and meat production by more than 35 percent. Among important foods, only fish production declined — by about 10 percent as a result of planned reduction to restore badly depleted stock. Average per capita food consumption by 1979 seems to have risen substantially, exceeding both the prewar and mid-1950s levels for the first time.

Several policies have created a potential for reducing the proportion of the rural population without adequate food supplies. First, the state curtailed grain extractions in China's poorest agricultural regions in order to alleviate rural malnutrition. Where average per capita distribution of food grains was less than provincially established minimum levels ranging from 150 to 180 kilograms, production teams were exempted from all grain taxes. In 1979 reduced procurement targets and tax exemptions totaled more than five million tonnes. Second, beginning in 1979 the state eased previous restrictions on private sales of grain and an estimated five million tonnes were sold in rural farm markets.

Finally state procurement rose significantly in 1978 and 1979, substantially increasing the quantity of grains available to resupply grain-deficit rural regions (Table 10.4). Much of this grain is being sent to regions that are either allocating more of their sown area to cotton, oil-bearing seeds, and other nongrain crops or are restoring their cultivated land to pastures. An increase in specialized production is crucial for increasing the efficiency in the use of resources in agriculture. The shift away from regional self-sufficiency in food grain production toward cropping along lines of comparative advantage will, through increased efficiency, clearly expand output even with the present level of labor and other inputs. This shift will be undertaken by peasants only when they are assured of adequate supplies of basic food grains and reasonable prices for their own commercial production. As mentioned above, these conditions are gradually being met through higher prices for nongrain crops, increased state resale of procured grain to grain-deficit rural areas, and the sale of grain on rural free markets.

## Conclusion

Except for a few years in the mid-1950s and late 1970s, average per capita food consumption since 1949 does not appear to have reached the prewar level. In several short periods grain consumption fell to such low levels that mortality almost certainly increased. The per capita availability of other foods probably declined, particularly between 1966 and 1977 when official policy emphasized grain at the expense of cash crops, livestock products, and other nongrain foods.

Over the long run China's food population balance is potentially more favorable. If the policy changes initiated in 1978 and 1979 are sustained and implemented satisfactorily, agriculture will likely grow somewhat more rapidly than the 2 to 2.5 percent rate achieved during the Cultural Revolution period (1966–1976). Clearly it will not be possible to sustain the rates of increase of 1978–1979 and China will remain vulnerable to years of adverse weather, such as occurred in 1980, when the output of some crops fell. But on average it might be reasonable to expect a rate of growth of from 2.5 to 3 percent for the agricultural sector as a whole.

Many questions remain to be answered concerning China's population growth, but there is no doubt that the birth rate has fallen in the past decade. Official data suggest the rate of natural increase has declined from well over 2 percent at the beginning of the last decade to just over 1 percent more recently. If this low rate is confirmed by China's 1982 census and can be sustained, there is a genuine prospect that average food consumption in the 1980s will surpass the prewar levels on a sustained rather than episodic basis. Average consumption might rise by 20 percent in the current decade. This would put China roughly on par with the consumption level achieved in South Korea and Japan in the mid-1970s. More importantly, this pattern of agricultural and population growth would allow a significant improvement in the quality of the average diet, particularly some diversification away from cereals and an increase in protein and other nutrients.

## Notes

1. Vaclav Smil, "Food Energy in the PRC," *Current Scene,* vol. 15, nos. 6 and 7 (June-July 1977).

2. Yang Jianbai and Li Xuezeng, "On the Historical Relationship Between Agriculture, Light Industry and Heavy Industry in China," *Zhongguo Shehui Kexue* (Chinese Social Science), no. 3 (1980), p. 8.

3. John S. Aird, "Reconstruction of an Official Data Model of the Population of China," unpublished paper, May 1980.

4. Liu Fangyu, "A Discussion of the Position and Role of Consumption in a Socialist Economy," *Jingji Kexue* (Economic Science), no. 1 (1980), p. 20; Wang Gengjin, "The Rule in Socialist Construction Is to Respect Agriculture as the Foundation," *Jingji Yanjiu* (Economic Research), no. 12 (1979); Pei Yuanxiu, Liu Bingying, and Li Bingzhang, "An Inquiry into the Optimum Rate of Accumulation," *Guangming Daily,* June 23, 1980, p. 4.

5. Yang and Li, "On the Historical Relationship," p. 8.

6. Wang Gengjin, "The Rule in Socialist Construction," p. 37.

7. Yu Guoyao, "Animal Husbandry Production Must Strive to Increase Meat Output," *Guangming Daily,* June 7, 1980, p. 4.

8. Chinese Communist Party Central Committee, "Decisions on Some Problems in Accelerating Agricultural Development," draft. The Chinese text was published in Hong Kong, *Zhangwang,* no. 417, June 16, 1979, pp. 21–24 and no. 418, July 1, 1979, pp. 23–25 and in Taiwan *Zhonggong Yanjiu,* vol. 13, no. 5, pp. 149–162. The quotation is from page 151. A garbled translation of the document appeared in Foreign Broadcast Information Service, *Daily Report China,* August 31, 1979, pp. 122–137.

9. Lin Shen, "The Inside Information on China's Economic Readjustment," *Zhengming* (May 1979), pp. 9–13. Quote on page 11. According to the standard caloric conversion factor used by FAO, 150 kilograms of processed food grains supplies about 1350 calories per day. For the least well fed portion of China's rural population that is probably the source of at least 90 percent of total caloric intake, implying a total supply ceiling of 1500 calories. It is estimated that in the 1970s a quarter of India's population fell below that critical level of 1500 calories. See Fred H. Sanderson and Shyamal Roy, *Food Trends and Prospects in India* (Washington, D.C.; The Brookings Institution, 1980), p. 83.

10. Niu Ruofang, "Does 'Taking Grain as the Key Link' Suit Measures to Local Conditions?" *Guangming Daily* December 8, 1979. Wang Zhenzhi and Wei Yunlang, "On the Scissors Differential Between Industrial and Agricultural Production," *Baike Zhishi* (Encyclopedic Knowledge), no. 2 (1980), p. 7. Jiang Junchen, Zhou Chaoyang, and Shen Jun, "Problems in the Relation Between Production and Livelihood," *Jiangji Yanjiu* (Economic Research), no. 9 (1980), p. 53.

11. Wang, "The Rule in Socialist Construction," p. 37.

## Readings

Buck, John Lossing. *Land Utilization in China.* Nanking: University of Nanking, 1937. Chapter 14 of this classic study analyzes the nutritional status of peasants in the years prior to the Sino-Japanese War.

Ishikawa, Shigeru. "China's Food and Agriculture: A Turning Point." *Food Policy,* May 1977, pp. 90–102. A clear analysis of relative supply and demand for food grains and the prospects for raising grain output through improved agricultural development policies at both the macro and micro levels.

Smil, Vaclav. "Food Energy in the People's Republic of China." *Current Scene,* vol. 15, nos. 6 and 7 (June-July 1977), pp. 1–11. Constructs food balances for 1957 and 1974 based on estimated output data, seed and feed needs, waste, and extraction rates. Estimates for 1974, however, are dependent on many unwarranted assumptions.

Walker, Kenneth R. "Grain Self-Sufficiency in North China, 1953–1975." *The China Quarterly,* September 1977, pp. 555–590. A perceptive examination of how a national policy of local self-sufficiency led to declining food consumption in Henan, Hebei, and Shandong between the 1950s and the first half of the 1970s.

Wiens, Thomas B. "Agricultural Statistics in the People's Republic of China," in Alexander Eckstein, ed., *Quantitative Measures of China's Economic Output*. Ann Arbor: University of Michigan Press, 1980. Estimates per capita consumption of food grains and total caloric intake for the 1930s, 1952, and 1957 as part of a broader analysis of total grain output in the 1930s and 1950s.

# 11
# Prospects for Growth in Grain Production

*Randolph Barker*
*Daniel G. Sisler*
*Beth Rose*

China's capacity to increase production and economic efficiency in agriculture in the decade ahead will depend on its ability to adopt appropriate policies and to overcome technical and environmental constraints. With respect to policy, it has been argued that agricultural growth has been retarded by a lack of incentives and by poor state planning. Insistence on local and regional self-reliance led to an overemphasis on grain production at the expense of cash crops — such as oilseeds, cotton, and soybeans — and fodder. Many observers believe that recent policy changes will lead to a more rational allocation of resources, but that further improvement could be achieved if China were to adopt price and production planning based on Western concepts of comparative advantage.

The effectiveness of policy changes will depend on the ease with which technical and environmental constraints can be overcome. Is there a backlog of technology that can be readily disseminated, or are further improvements likely to require significant investments in technology development and infrastructure with a long gestation period?

The outlook for grain production is a matter of central concern in this discussion because of the dominant role of grain in the agricultural economy. Approximately 50 percent of gross agricultural product is derived from grain, and grain provides close to 90 percent of all calories consumed. It seems that for political and economic reasons China cannot increase food grain imports much beyond the current level of about 15 million tonnes or 5 percent of total yearly requirements.[1]

Until recently, data on which to base judgments regarding the past performance or future potential of Chinese agriculture have been sparse. Even

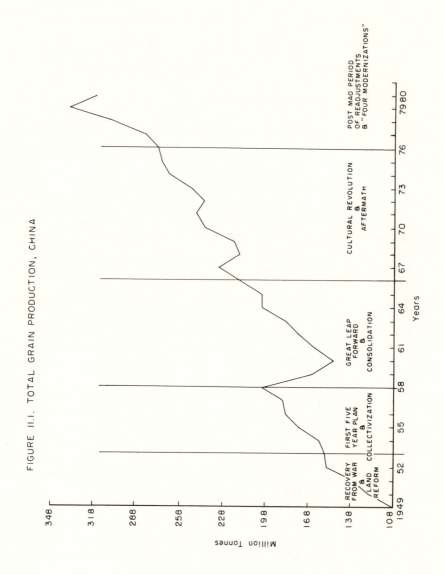

FIGURE II.I. TOTAL GRAIN PRODUCTION, CHINA

now available data are spotty and frequently of variable quality, rendering any attempts at quantitative analysis suspect. For a large and climatically diverse country such as China, national aggregates provide no clear understanding of technical constraints and growth potentials. The limitations of data notwithstanding, this chapter will focus on regional trends in grain production. First, we examine the national growth in grain production since 1949 and the policies affecting grain production.

## Growth in Grain Production Since 1949

Between the late 1950s and the late 1970s grain output grew at about 2.4 percent annually, or slightly faster than population growth. Per capita production of food grains in China changed very little if at all during this period (see Chapter 10). Technical change, policy measures, and social reforms helped cause uneven growth rates across regions and over time. Important socioeconomic and political movements included land reform (1950-1953), collectivization (1954-1958), Great Leap Forward (1958-1961), Cultural Revolution period (1966-1976), and the "four modernizations" (1977 to present). Figure 11.1 illustrates the growth of national grain production against the background of political change. It is virtually impossible to disentangle the effects of political and social reform from other factors, such as weather, on the rate of growth of agricultural production.

Rice is the dominant grain crop, accounting for 45 percent of total unmilled grain production (Table 11.1), followed by wheat and corn.[2] Corn production rose rapidly in the 1970s, slightly surpassing wheat production in some years. Although we know the bulk of corn is utilized as a food rather than a feedgrain, we do not know how this use is changing over time. However, because of increased emphasis placed on improving diets, we can assume that feedgrain utilization is likely to grow.

Long-term growth in grain production varies, depending on the base year chosen. Differences in estimated annual growth rates for selected time periods are substantial.

| | |
|---|---|
| 1949-1951/1955-1957 | 6.7% |
| 1955-1957/1977-1979 | 2.4% |
| 1952-1953/1977-1979 | 2.8% |
| 1949-1951/1978-1980 | 3.3% |

Between 1949 and 1957, as agriculture recovered from the devastating effects of war, resistance, and revolution, production increased very rapidly

Table 11.1  Specified Crops as Percentage of Total Food Grain Production

| | 1957 | | 1977 | |
|---|---|---|---|---|
| | million tonnes | percent | million tonnes | percent |
| All grains | 195 | 100 | 285 | 100 |
| Rice (unmilled) | 87 | 45 | 129 | 45 |
| Wheat | 24 | 12 | 41 | 14 |
| Coarse grains and pulses[a] | 52 | 27 | 86[b] | 30 |
| Corn | 21 | 11 | 48 | 17 |
| Tubers | 22[c] | 11 | 19[c] | 7 |
| Soybeans | 10 | 5 | 10 | 4 |

Source:   Anthony Tang and Bruce Stone, "Food Production in the People's
          Republic of China."  Research Report No. 15, International Food
          Policy Research Institute, May 1980, pp. 157-158.

[a]  Includes millet, corn, sorghum, barley, buckwheat, oats, proso-millet,
     small beans, small green beans, broad beans, peas, and others.
[b]  The 1977 estimates for coarse grain and tubers were calculated as a
     residual.  The coarse grain figure appears too low and the tuber
     figure too high.  For example, USDA estimates 1977 coarse grain pro-
     duction at 74.5 million tonnes and 1976 tuber production at 24
     million tonnes.
[c]  Tubers are valued on a 1-to-4 grain equivalent basis in 1957 and a
     1-to-5 basis in 1977.


(6.7%). The 1949–1957 recovery period skews long-term growth rates
markedly. For this reason we regard the period 1955–1957 to 1977–1979 as
most appropriate for measuring long-term growth.


## Policies Affecting Grain Production

Over the past three decades China maintained low food grain prices and
rationed basic necessities so as to insure a more equitable distribution of
supply. Although the government subsidized grain prices to consumers,
producer prices remained well below international levels and low relative to
prices of nongrain crops. An adequate supply of grain was insured through
production planning based on area targets. As a further incentive to grain
production, prices for grain sold above the quota were about 30 percent
above the quota price. "Squeezing agriculture" with low prices for
primary products has been practiced in developing agricultural economies

worldwide. Utilization of collective labor for land and water development and compost as fertilizer, coupled with significant technological advances for the major grain crops, allowed the government to maintain low prices.

Whether shifts in policy following the death of Mao were a consequence solely of political factors or were caused by a combination of both basic economic forces and politics is a matter of debate. One hypothesis suggests that there were already signs of stagnation in the agricultural sector that would have necessitated a change in agricultural policy even without the political upheaval.

Be that as it may, since 1976 there have been significant changes in policy with future directions still unclear. In 1978 China announced a ten-year plan (1975–1985) that was intended to lay the groundwork for achieving success in the "four modernizations" (agriculture, industry, national defense, and science and technology). The 1985 target for grain production was set at 400 million tonnes, which implied a growth in output of 4 percent per year over the ten-year period, considerably above the 2.4 percent annual growth rate achieved since 1957.

In December 1978 the Third Plenum of the Chinese Communist Party adopted new policies that gave high priority to agriculture. Changes in agricultural policy have taken three forms: (1) price incentives (the quota prices for grain were raised by 20 percent, and the above-quota prices were set at 50 percent above that), (2) higher allocation of industrial goods and resources to agriculture (e.g., electrical power and chemical fertilizer), and (3) a restructuring of agriculture within the commune to allow for greater resource mobility and flexibility in production decision making.

The likely impact of these incentives on agricultural production as a whole and upon production among various crops and regions is difficult to ascertain. Prices rose not only for grain crops, but for nongrain crops as well. Inputs such as fertilizer are distributed by the government. Hence, a more favorable fertilizer-to-crop price ratio does not indicate that fertilizer will be allocated toward those crops and regions where it will give the highest return. Likewise, the degree to which farmers can now choose what they would like to produce is a matter of debate and probably varies considerably from area to area.

In terms of the overall performance of agriculture, the immediate response to the new agricultural strategy was positive. The production of both grain and nongrain crops rose sharply in 1979, partly because of very favorable weather conditions. Record increases occurred despite a decline in total grain hectarage, as producers cut back on triple cropping and shifted some land to more profitable nongrain crops such as cotton and oilseeds.

Unfavorable weather in north and central China in 1980 has resulted in a decline in grain production from the record levels of 1979, and grain imports have reached record levels. Despite this, nongrain crop production continued to rise.

Following the reduced grain harvest of 1980, agricultural policy has swung toward a reemphasis on grain production targets. Policymakers are likely to favor production targets rather than further increases in producer prices as a means to insure adequate consumer supplies and to avoid overdependency on world markets. However, the ease with which grain production targets can be met without serious sacrifice of economic efficiency is certainly related to the technical capacity for gains in production.

## Regional Growth in Grain Production

Following the work of Buck (1937) it is common to distinguish between north and south China, wheat being the dominant crop in the north and rice in the south. The dividing line is set between the Yangtze and Huai rivers and extends westward at approximately 33° north latitude. Historically, the balance of progress in agricultural development has tended to shift back and forth between the drier north and the more humid south.

Agricultural innovation has often been accompanied by shifts in population and political power.[3] For example, a technological revolution in milling in the eighth and ninth centuries made possible the widespread cultivation of wheat in place of millet. This was followed by the development of the technology of wetland rice culture (in the eighth to twelfth centuries), involving the flooding, puddling, and transplanting of paddy fields, which is such a familiar part of the Asian landscape today. This development contributed significantly to population growth in south and central China. It is estimated that in the seventeenth century rice accounted for 70 percent of all food grains grown. The introduction of food plants (corn, peanuts, sweet potato, and irish potato) from the Americas in the sixteenth and seventeenth centuries, coupled with the growing demand for industrial cash crops such as cotton and sugar cane, allowed agriculture to expand into hillier and less well-watered areas that were unsuitable for rice. The contribution of rice to total food production declined relative to crops such as wheat and corn. However, the success of intensive cultivation methods in irrigated central and south China helped rice maintain its role as the dominant food grain of China, although by 1930 rice comprised less than half of the total.

Since 1949 growth in agricultural production has varied over time and among regions. An understanding of this variation is important in making an assessment as to the future potentials for growth. In a country of the size and diversity of China, no regional delineation will accurately combine areas of similar agricultural potential perfectly; however, it is felt that the regional designation adopted here does foster valuable insights when considering the past performance and potential of grain production within China.

We have divided China into eight agricultural regions: I. northeast, II. north, III. east, IV. central, V. south, VI. southwest, VII. Sichuan, and VIII. northwest. Figure 11.2 delineates the provincial boundaries of the eight agricultural regions. In general, these are the designations used by Western agriculturalists since Buck in 1937, with the exception of the province of Sichuan, shown as a separate region (VII). We feel that agriculture within Sichuan is unique and cannot logically be combined with any adjacent regions.

Important agro-climatic characteristics of each region, with the exception of the northwest, are summarized in Table 11.2. The northwest is excluded from this table because the agro-climate of this vast area is too varied.

In calculating regional and national growth rates, we have relied principally on official production estimates compiled by Tuan (USDA, 1981)[4] for the 1970s and on provincial information gathered by the Committee on the Economy of China, Social Science Research Council[5] for the 1950s. From 1957 until the middle 1970s almost no official provincial figures were released so that we have chosen to estimate growth rates between the years of 1955–1957 and 1977–1979 (Table 11.3). In addition these years were not marked by any major political or social upheaval. Regional estimates were obtained by summing provincal estimates within the respective regions.

Table 11.3 presents annual growth rates in grain production for China in total and for the eight regions.[6] The growth rate in grain production has varied widely from 3.1 percent per annum in northeast China to 1.3 percent per annum in southwest China. Regions I to IV have grown much more rapidly than regions V to VIII. There is, of course, considerable variation in growth rate among provinces within regions, as is illustrated in Table 11.4 where provinces have been ranked by annual growth rate. Guangxi in south China has shown remarkable growth compared to its neighboring provinces. Conversely, Anhui's growth is extremely low compared to its neighbors in east China.

Figure 11.3 shows the growth of grain production for selected regions for the periods 1949–1957 and 1974–1979. The southwest and the northwest have been excluded from this figure due to data problems (see Table 11.3, Footnote b). Regions II, III, and IV evidenced similar growth patterns and have been combined. The region of most rapid growth, the northeast, is

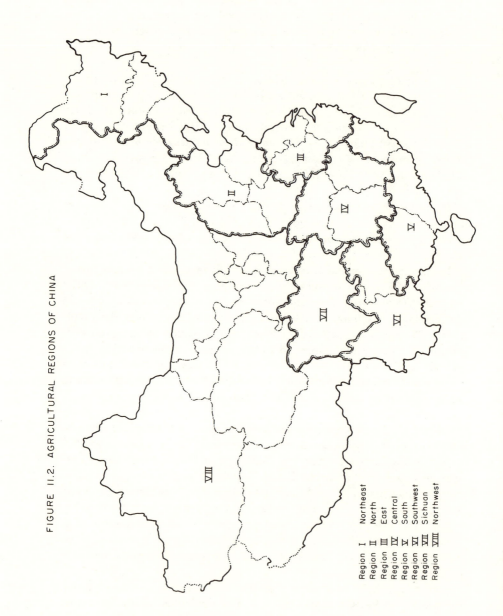

FIGURE II.2. AGRICULTURAL REGIONS OF CHINA

Region I    Northeast
Region II   North
Region III  East
Region IV   Central
Region V    South
Region VI   Southwest
Region VII  Sichuan
Region VIII Northwest

Table 11.2  Selected Agro-climatic Characteristics of Seven Agricultural Regions of China

| Region | Cropping index | Frost free period (days) | Average July temperature (C degrees) | Average January temperature (C degrees) | Precipitation (mm/yr) | Cultivated land irrigated (percent)* | Major crops |
|---|---|---|---|---|---|---|---|
| I. Northeast | 100 | 140 to 180 | 22 to 23 | -13 to -23 | 500 to 700 | 14 | Corn, millets, soybeans, sorghum |
| II. North | 110 | 210 to 250 | 26 to 28 | -4 to -7 | 600 to 800 | 53 | Wheat, corn, soybeans |
| III. East | 170 | 230 to 250 | 25 to 27 | 3 to 5 | 700 to 1000 | 68 | Rice, cotton, wheat |
| IV. Central | 180 | 240 to 320 | 27 to 29 | 7 to 10 | 700 to 1500 | 73 | Rice, wheat, soybeans, cotton |
| V. South | 180 | 340 to 365 | 27 to 28 | 14 to 15 | 1500 to 2000 | 73 | Rice, tubers, corn |
| VI. Southwest | 145 | 260 to 300 | 21 to 25 | 5 to 9 | 1000 to 1200 | 42 | Rice, tubers, corn, cotton |
| VII. Sichuan | 170 | 290 to 340 | 27 to 29 | 6 to 8 | 800 to 1000 | 50 | Rice, corn, tubers |

Sources:  C. Chen and M. Y. Nuttonson, The Agricultural Regions of China (Washington, D.C.:  American Institute of Crop Ecology, 1969).

T. R. Tregear, An Economic Geography of China (London:  Butterworths, 1970).
A.Y.M. Yao, "Characteristics and Probabilities of Precipitation in China" USDA Environmental Services Administration, Technical Report No. EDS8.

*Percent irrigated calculated from data in Zhongguo Nongye Dili Zonglun (General Treatise on Agricultural Geography) translation appearing in JPRS No. 78034, May 8, 1981.

Table 11.3  Annual Growth in Total Grain Output by Region, PRC [a]

| Region [b] | | 1955–1957 (million tonnes) | 1977–1979 (million tonnes) | 1957–1979 (percent) |
|---|---|---|---|---|
| I. | Northeast | 17.1 | 33.3 | 3.1 |
| II. | North | 37.7 | 68.5[c] | 2.8 |
| III. | East | 31.4 | 52.7 | 2.4 |
| IV. | Central | 27.7 | 49.6 | 2.7 |
| V. | South | 21.6 | 34.3 | 2.1 |
| VI. | Southwest | 10.7 | 14.2 | 1.3 |
| VII. | Sichuan | 21.9 | 30.2 | 1.5 |
| VIII. | Northwest | 15.6[d] | 22.4[e] | 1.7 |
| | TOTAL–all regions | 183.7 | 305.2 | 2.3 |
| | USDA–TOTAL GRAIN | 180.8 | 306.5 | 2.4 |

Sources:  "Provincial Agricultural Statistics for Communist China,"
Committee on the Economy of China, Social Science Research
Council, Ithaca, New York, 1969, and Francis Tuan, "Provin-
cial Total Grain Production 1969–1979," Research Notes on
Chinese Agriculture No. 2, USDA, Economics and Statistics
Service, International Economics Division, Asia Branch Peo-
ple's Republic of China section, 1981.

[a]  Growth percent calculated with an average of 1955–1957 as a beginning period and an average of 1977–1979 as an end period.
[b]  There are several problems in the raw data that may affect our
regional growth percents to varying degrees.  Administrative bound-
ary changes between provinces may have altered results slightly.
Tuan's report assumes that provinces have made adjustments themselves.
There is also a possibility that 1979 production includes private
plot production.  This could account for as much as five million metric
tons.  For 16 cases data were not available and an estimate was made
based on the best information available.  The problem of missing data
was most serious in the southwest and northwest rendering those growth
rates suspect.
[c]  Tianjin municipality was created in 1967 and further enlarged in 1973
for Hebei province.  This should not alter regional growth as no area
was moved outside the region.
[d]  Xizang and Ningxia were not included.
[e]  Ningxia not included.

Table 11.4  Annual Growth in Total Grain Output for Selected Provinces,
PRC, 1955-1957 and 1977-1979

| Province | Region | Average 1955-1957 (million tonnes) | 1977-1979 | Annual growth (percent) |
|----------|--------|------------|-----------|-------------|
| Heilongjiang | Northeast | 6.4 | 13.9 | 3.6 |
| Shanxi | North | 3.6 | 7.3 | 3.3 |
| Hebei | North | 8.7 | 16.7 | 3.0 |
| Hunan | Central | 10.9 | 20.8 | 3.0 |
| Guangxi | South | 5.7 | 10.8 | 2.9 |
| Jilin | North | 4.7 | 8.8 | 2.9 |
| Xinjiang | Northwest | 1.9 | 3.6 | 2.9 |
| Zhejiang | East | 7.7 | 13.9 | 2.7 |
| Jiangxi | Central | 6.5 | 11.7 | 2.7 |
| Jiangsu | East | 12.2 | 21.6 | 2.6 |
| Shandong | North | 12.6 | 22.1 | 2.6 |
| Liaoning | Northeast | 6.1 | 10.6 | 2.5 |
| Fujian | South | 4.2 | 7.0 | 2.3 |
| Hubei | Central | 10.3 | 17.1 | 2.3 |
| Henan | North | 12.0 | 19.5 | 2.2 |
| Shaanxi | Northwest | 4.8 | 7.6 | 2.1 |
| Neimonggol | Northwest | 3.4 | 5.1 | 1.9 |
| Qinghai | Northwest | 0.6 | 0.9 | 1.9 |
| Yunnan | Southwest | 5.9 | 8.4 | 1.6 |
| Anhui | East | 10.5 | 14.7 | 1.5 |
| Guangdong | South | 11.7 | 16.4 | 1.5 |
| Sichuan | Sichuan | 21.9 | 30.2 | 1.5 |
| Gansu | Northwest | 4.8 | 4.8 | 0 |

Source:  See Table 11.3, Sources.

also the region of greatest variability in year-to-year production. There was apparently no growth in grain production in Sichuan and southwest China between 1957 and the mid-1970s. However, growth has been rapid in the last five years. Between 1957 and 1975 the annual growth rate for south China was equal to that for north, east, and central China, but production seems to have stagnated since.

Fluctuations in annual grain production are extremely important. Uncertainty induces stresses on available food supply and places additional burdens on transportation, storage, and imports. Many observers of Chinese agriculture have concluded that total grain production is relatively stable with less year-to-year swings than in many other important grain producing nations. This observation is reinforced by the fact that in China

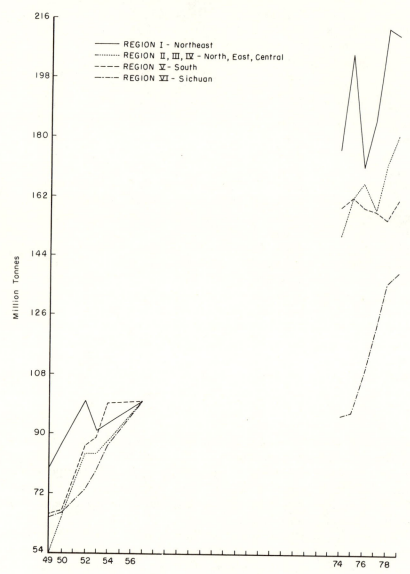

FIGURE II.3. INDEX PRC TOTAL GRAIN PRODUCTION BY REGION, 1957=100
(Southwest and Northwest not included)

REGION I - Northeast
REGION II, III, IV - North, East, Central
REGION V - South
REGION VI - Sichuan

Million Tonnes

Table 11.5  Per Capita Production of Rough Grain, kg/capita/yr, 1955-1957 and 1977-1979

| Region | | 1955-1957 | 1977-1979 | Percent change |
|---|---|---|---|---|
| I. | Northeast | 332 | 347 | 4.5 |
| II. | North | 225 | 294 | 30.7 |
| III. | East | 283 | 342 | 20.8 |
| IV. | Central | 324 | 384 | 18.5 |
| V. | South | 300 | 300 | 0.0 |
| VI. | Southwest | 297 | 246 | -20.7 |
| VII. | Sichuan | 303 | 311 | 2.6 |
| VIII. | Northwest | 326[a] | 306[b] | -6.5 |
| | TOTAL | 285 | 320 | 12.3 |

Source:  Production:  See Sources, Table 11.3.
Population:  John Aird, "Recent Population Figures," China Quarterly, no. 7, 1978, and John Jowett, "China: The Provincial Distribution of Population," China Quarterly, March 1980.

a/  Ningxia and Xizang omitted
b/  Ningxia omitted.

over 45 percent of the land used for grain (representing about two-thirds of production) is irrigated, thereby lessening uncertainty of yield associated with erratic rainfall patterns. We have computed yearly deviations from trend for China as a whole and for seven regions (omitting the northwest) from 1957 to 1979. The regional estimates were based on only 13 years of data in this period. The average yearly deviation from the value predicted by a fitted trend line over the same period was 13.1 million tonnes. This means that for the nation as a whole, the standard error of the estimate from the fitted line amounted to about 5 percent of average grain production. The northeast showed the highest year-to-year fluctuations during the 1970s. Grain production dropped sharply in Sichuan and the southwest in 1974, which was otherwise a good weather year, and in the northeast in 1972 and 1976, which were poor weather years countrywide.

The government procures very little grain for shipment to deficit rural areas. Thus trends in grain production can be presumed to have an influence on regional consumption. Estimates of per capita unmilled grain production for 1955-1957 and 1977-1979 are shown in Table 11.5. The recovery rate for milled rice is typically about 72 percent, which is lower than wheat (85 percent), or corn (92 percent). Hence, in relative terms the predominantly rice-eating regions of southern China have a lower per capita availability than is suggested by the data in Table 11.5. Those regions with the lowest per capita production in 1955–1957, the north and the east, showed the largest gains over the last two decades. Regions I to IV all showed significant increases, while regions V to VIII showed little increase (or in the case of the southwest, a decline) over the period.

## Crop Yields

The recent decline in some regions in the intensity of cropping — e.g., shifts from triple to double cropping — make it appear that the limit of land intensification has been reached. As a consequence, future production gains will be determined almost entirely by increases in single crop yields. There is very little reliable data on crop yields even at the national level. For example, in the most widely used series from the U.S. Department of Agriculture it is impossible to compare or link yield estimates up to 1976 with those after 1976. National yield growth for major cereal grains from 1955–1957 to 1974–1976 are as follows:

|       | *China* | *India* | *U.S.* |
|-------|---------|---------|--------|
| rice  | 1.6     | 1.3     | 2.0    |
| wheat | 2.8     | 3.1     | 1.9    |
| corn  | 2.3     | 1.6     | 3.3    |

The most notable technological achievements have been made in the area of rice and wheat. This includes the introduction of modern fertilizer-responsive varieties in the 1960s and the development of the world's first $F_1$ hybrid rices in the 1970s, both of which are discussed in more detail in Chapter 7. The slow growth in rice yields, despite these achievements, may be explained in part by overzealous efforts to intensify production through the expansion of triple cropping.

On a regional level, crop yield and hectarage data are sparse and sometimes unreliable. We can make some assessment of regional yields by looking at climatic analogues. Climatically the lower Yangtze River valley is similar to southern Japan, and Guangdong Province to Taiwan. As best we can determine from the information available, rice yield levels in these two regions are similar to those achieved in Japan and Taiwan 15 to 20 years ago. As we look back on the development experience of Japan and Taiwan, we are reminded of the substantial incentives, including the raising of rice prices well above the world market, that brought rice yields in these two regions to their current high plateau.

Both the level of wheat yield and the rate of increase in yield are almost identical with those of India and Pakistan. Significant yield gains have been achieved through the extensive use of modern varieties and fertilizers and the expansion of irrigated area. China's largest wheat area is the North China Plain and this area accounts for almost three-quarters of total production. The growth of irrigation in this area, as in the Indo-Gangetic Plain, has occurred largely through the use of tubewells. Currently more than 80 percent of the wheat in this area is said to be irrigated, while the 1950 level was probably less than 20 percent. Despite this progress, the national wheat yield is currently only 2 tonnes per hectare. In Mexico and Egypt, where most of the wheat production is also under irrigation, yields are approaching 3.5 tonnes per hectare.

As noted previously, corn production has risen significantly in China over the past three decades. Between 1957 and 1977 it rose from 11 to 17 percent of total production. Unlike rice and wheat, a substantial portion of the increase in production was due to area expansion, as higher-yielding corn was substituted for lower-yielding sorghum (gaoliang) and millet, principally in north and northeast China. Corn yields have improved significantly over this period, from 1.5 to 2.5 tonnes per hectare, but even today are considerably less than half those of the United States (6 tonnes per hectare).

## Inputs

The principal sources of future yield growth in grain production can be identified as: (1) varietal improvement, (2) use of fertilizers, and (3) irrigation. Varietal improvement depends on research or on the transfer of technology. Research is needed to develop new varieties of grain with greater yield potential and resistance to insects and diseases and to develop new cultural and management practices. The potential does exist for borrowing from the experience of others. However, new agricultural technology must be adapted not only to local climatic conditions but also to the particular factor endowments and socioeconomic conditions of China. For example, historically it has been difficult to introduce new foreign plant varieties to China because the intensive crop rotations demanded an early maturity not found in most exotic plant materials.

It would appear that in the recent past research priority has been given to rice, followed by wheat, with corn and other grain crops getting much less attention. It is difficult to assess the degree to which the Cultural Revolution and its aftermath may have set back agricultural research, and how long it will take to overcome this deficiency. It is equally difficult to judge China's capacity to transfer appropriate technology from other parts of the world. China did import significant amounts of Mexican wheat seed in the 1970s. Mexican wheat and Chinese-Mexican crosses are being grown on approximately a quarter of the total wheat area, principally in the northeast and south of the Yangtze River. At present the most active program of scientific exchange and manpower training involves extensive interaction with the International Rice Research Institute in the Philippines.

In the initial steps to modernize agriculture after 1949 principal emphasis was placed on organic compost as the primary source of plant nutrients. With development of small-scale rural industries following the Great Leap Forward, ammonium bicarbonate became an important source of nitrogen fertilizer. The importation of thirteen modern urea plants in the 1970s led to a near doubling in the production of chemical fertilizer (5.5 million tonnes nutrient weight in 1975 to 10.7 million tonnes in 1979). The national fertilizer application rate now exceeds 100 kilograms per cultivated hectare. However, over half of fertilizer by nutrient weight is still supplied by organic materials, an extremely large share compared with that of other developing countries.

Although the Chinese have emphasized the production of nitrogen fertilizer, many soils, particularly those in the south, are deficient in phosphorus and potassium. Increased application of these elements could help boost stagnant rice yields.

The rate of fertilizer application per hectare will continue to increase. China must expand domestic capacity of modern fertilizer plants, not only to meet this growing demand, but also to replace ammonium bicarbonate plants and organic fertilizers, which could become increasingly obsolete because of the high opportunity cost of land and labor used in their production. The ten year plan has set a target of one large chemical fertilizer plant for each province and autonomous region plus an additional ten plants (for a total of 39). However, it is unlikely this target will be met by 1985. In any event, China will certainly encounter many difficulties in changing the structure and scale of fertilizer production so as to meet ever-growing demands.

The third major technical constraint in the expansion of grain production is water availability. Here again, as in the case of fertilizer, there has been a shift away from local self-reliance. The national government has taken increasing responsibility for decision making in the construction and improvement of irrigation facilities. Emphasis has moved from small-scale projects under county, commune, and brigade control to more capital-intensive and large-scale endeavors. This is a reflection of the fact that opportunities for development of small-scale systems have been almost fully exploited. Further expansion may require the development of major projects with relatively long gestation periods. There is a growing reluctance to exploit local labor for the construction of projects of this type. Although the PRC is still considering some large-scale water management projects, many prominent scientists suggest that more research, particularly environmental investigation, is necessary before actual building commences, and current capital constraints make it difficult for China to proceed.

A major objective of the proposed irrigation projects is to provide northern China with more water. Rhoads Murphey (Chapter 4) notes that water is the major constraint to increased agricultural production in this area. Expansion of irrigation in the North China Plain led to rapid growth in wheat production and yields in the last two decades. However, there have been major salinity problems associated with poor drainage in the development of these water resources, necessitating the withdrawal of as much as 2 million hectares of land from agricultural production.

The kinds of problems that have been outlined above are by no means insurmountable. However, it does suggest the need not just for appropriate policies, but also for skillful management at all levels of planning and production. Shortage of management skills would seem to be a major constraint to agricultural production in the short run.

## Conclusions

Grain occupies a dominant position in the Chinese agricultural economy. What happens in the grain sector will have a critical effect on the rate of agricultural and economic development in the future. If production slows and imports increase markedly, then resources will have to be diverted away from potentially more profitable activities to boost production.

The growth in grain production over the past two decades has been slightly above the rate of growth of population and close to the average of the performance of other developing countries. However, there is a general consensus that overemphasis on local grain self-sufficiency has led to a sacrifice in efficiency.

Recent policy changes have resulted in significantly higher price incentives to grain producers and in more flexibility in decision making at the local level regarding the choice of crops and crop rotations. Despite the higher grain prices, there has been a shift of some land and resources to more profitable alternatives. As a consequence of the reduced grain harvest of 1980, the Chinese are finding it necessary to reevaluate their policies.

It is our contention that, in spite of these policy shifts due largely to short-run weather effects, the Chinese will face serious technical and environmental constraints to increased grain production in the immediate future. These constraints are best viewed in the context of specific crops and regions.

Over the longer period, the prospects for growth in wheat and corn production appear to be more favorable than for rice. The consequence of this must be evaluated in the context of shifts in demand for grain, which are as difficult to forecast as shifts in supply. The population growth rate will probably continue to decline. At the same time, if incomes rise there will probably be an increasing demand for livestock products and consequently feedgrains, particularly corn. Feedgrains can be supplied by either domestic production or the export market. Furthermore, there is ample opportunity for substitution of wheat for rice in food grain consumption.

In summary, the question is not whether grain production can grow in the future, but whether needed supplies can be obtained without slowing the rate of growth of the rest of the economy. The efficient growth of domestic grain production in a severely overpopulated country depends on the development of new technology and infrastructure. The underinvestment in scientific manpower and agricultural infrastructure over the past two decades will make it more difficult to overcome the technical constraints to growth in grain production in the near future.

## Notes

1. According to recent USDA estimates, 1980/1981 wheat and coarse grain imports reached 14.7 million tonnes.

2. The current Chinese definition of food grain covers a wide range of plant products including grains (such as corn, wheat, rice, oats, barley, buckwheat, sorghum, millet), soybeans, tubers (irish and sweet potatoes), and pulses (for example, field beans and field peas). Tubers are currently valued on a 1-to-5 grain equivalent basis.

3. For a more detailed discussion of these issues see Ping-ti Ho, "The Introduction of American Food Plants into China," *American Anthropologist,* vol. 57 (1955), pp. 191–199, and Ping-ti Ho, "Early Ripening Rice in Chinese History," *Economic History Review,* vol. 9 (1956), p. 200–218.

4. Francis C. Tuan, "PRC Provincial Total Grain Production, 1969–1979," *Research Notes on Chinese Agriculture No. 2,* USDA Economics and Statistics Service (January 1981).

5. Committee on the Economy of China, Social Service Research Council, "Provincial Agricultural Statistics for Communist China" (Ithaca, N.Y.: 1969).

6. Although we have relied on official provincial information in the calculation of the 1955–1957 through 1977–1979 growth rates, the tenuousness of these data cannot be overemphasized. Provincial production estimates are based on a combination of scattered official estimates and on government statements regarding the level of production relative to a previous year. Information is almost totally missing after 1957 until the 1970s. Much more data have become available in the latter part of the 1970s. However, even at the national level there is a great deal of uncertainty about estimates. For example, the USDA points out that there is an inconsistency in their national estimates between the years up to 1976 and those following 1976.

## Readings

A detailed discussion of various sources of statistics on national production, area, and yield by crop since 1949 can be found in Appendix A and B. We have used the most recent U.S. Department of Agriculture grain series.

The most comprehensive data for provincial grain production are found in Francis C. Tuan, "PRC Provincial Total Grain Production, 1969–79." *Research Notes on Chinese Agriculture No. 2,* USDA, Economics and Statistics Service, January 1981. The most detailed regional description of Chinese agriculture, although increasingly out of date, is John Lossing Buck, *Land Utilization in China.* Chicago: University of Chicago Press, 1937.

For an historical perspective on the early development of grain production in China see Mark Elvin, *The Pattern of China's Past,* "The Revolution in Farming," Chapter 9, Palo Alto: Stanford University Press, 1973 and Ping-ti Ho, "Early Ripening Rice in Chinese History," *The Economic History Review,* vol. 9 (1956), p. 200–218.

General literature for grain production is more extensive for rice and wheat than for corn and other grain crops. A very detailed study of rice cultivation was completed in China in the early 1960s and recently has been translated into English. Ting Ying, *Cultivation of Chinese Paddy Rice,* U.S. Joint Publication Research Service, June 1, 1979 (JPRS #73599). Other useful reports include National Academy of Sciences, Committee on Scholarly Communication with the People's Republic of China, *Wheat in the People's Republic of China,* CSCPRC #6, Washington, D.C., 1977 and Chinese Academy of Sciences and International Rice Research Institute, "Proceedings of International Rice Research Workshop," Guangzhou, People's Republic of China, October 1979, Los Banos, Philippines: International Rice Research Institute, 1980.

# 12

# Foreign Trade and China's Agriculture

*Frederic M. Surls*

China's foreign trade has grown rapidly since the death of Mao Zedong and the emergence of new leadership oriented toward economic growth. Between 1976 and 1979 imports rose at an average annual rate of 37 percent, reaching $15.6 billion by 1979, and exports jumped by 24 percent per year to $13.8 billion. The growth of total trade is only one aspect of major changes in the character and role of foreign trade in China's economy.

Trade has been assigned a crucial role in China's new development strategy. The drive for modernization now underway has prompted China's leaders to acknowledge technological backwardness and the importance of foreign technology. As a consequence, use of foreign expertise has grown and Western capital goods and technology have been purchased for critical sectors of the economy.

New development policies have also had an important impact on agricultural trade. Between 1977 and 1979 agricultural imports rose at an average rate of 33 percent per year and China became a leading importer of both wheat and cotton. The rise in agricultural imports is driven by policies to raise living standards and the emergence of demand growth as an important factor influencing trade levels.

Significant changes in traditionally conservative financial policies have accompanied the growth of imports. Trade deficits are now built into foreign trade plans and substantial lines of credit have been arranged to finance the deficits. In addition, the Chinese have also eased their traditional aversion to government-to-government credits and have obtained low interest government-guaranteed credits from Western countries as well as some direct development assistance loans. China has also sought direct foreign investment in joint venture operations, a remarkable departure from past practices.

On the export side, a new and vigorous export drive includes expanded marketing efforts coupled with greater sensitivity to foreign market demand. Experiments in decentralization of export contracting, relaxed foreign trade and exchange controls, and establishment of export processing zones are also underway. The export emphasis has also led to shifts in domestic investment. State support for industries, particularly light industry and textiles, that promise rapid increases in export capacity has increased. Efforts to attract foreign joint-venture investment have focused on export-oriented industries. In part because of the export drive, exports of agricultural products rose and China remained a net exporter of agricultural products through 1979 despite sharply higher agricultural imports. These changes in trade patterns and policies are important departures from those of the past.

Recently the momentum of trade growth has slowed and questions about future growth have arisen. This chapter will first examine developments in overall trade, which are important both in their own right and because they have an impact on agricultural trade. Second, past patterns of agricultural trade will be outlined and the nature and causes of growth in the past several years explored. Finally, prospects for China's future agricultural trade will be examined. It will be argued that, for both agricultural and nonagricultural trade, China's leaders are taking a cautious approach to future trade expansion and that some elements of continuity with conservative trade policies of the past still remain.

For agricultural products in particular, the leadership is not likely to promote continued rapid growth of imports as this would certainly result in the erosion of agriculture's contribution to the finance of high priority nonagricultural imports. A policy of agricultural import substitution designed to hold down import growth appears to be emerging. However, pressures to import are substantial and there are serious questions about the extent to which agricultural import growth can be curtailed.

## Patterns in Total Trade

Historically, China's foreign trade has been small in relation to total domestic economic activity. Exports, for example, have amounted to only several percent of gross national product, a very low level by world standards. This in part reflects the large continental nature of China's economy, but is also an outgrowth of conservative foreign trade policies. Foreign trade is a state monopoly with imports largely limited to filling shortfalls in domestic economic plans. Although China has consciously avoided participation in international specialization, trade has aided the introduction of new technologies, supplied capital goods to key sectors of the economy, and provided critical industrial materials and some consumer goods, including basic agricultural products.[1]

The importance and role of foreign trade has varied over the past 30 years. These variations resulted from the interplay of conflicting forces that shaped trade policies and patterns. When China's leadership stressed economic development and modernization, trade tended to grow in importance. Efforts to generate high rates of economic growth require heavy imports of capital goods for critical bottleneck sectors of the economy, new technology to raise productivity, and expanded imports of industrial raw materials. However, trade has been restrained by an unwillingness to become heavily dependent on foreign sources for supplies of critical materials and a desire to remain self-reliant. Although the precise emphasis placed on self-reliance has varied, even during periods of trade expansion, it has been an important factor contributing to policies of import substitution, aversion to participation in international specialization, and a generally conservative view of foreign debt. During other periods, self-reliance has been a potent political issue and an important factor restricting trade. This was evident during the virulent campaign against Deng Xiaoping between 1974 and 1976, when strong criticism of the impact of trade on national independence contributed to a sharp slowdown in imports.

Trade grew rapidly during the fifties and the seventies, but the decade of the sixties was one of stagnation (Figure 12.1). Capital goods imports during the fifties provided the core for China's heavy industrial sector. Trade played a critical role during the rapid expansion of the economy during this period as foreign trade grew faster than the economy as a whole. During these years industrial equipment and supplies financed by Soviet loans formed the largest share of imports.

The importance of trade decreased during the sixties, and growth rates declined. With the sharp downturn in the economy following the Great Leap Forward, excess capacity in industry reduced the demand for capital goods imports. Export capacity also fell off, particularly as a result of the fall in agricultural production. During the Cultural Revolution the importance of economic development and trade was again downgraded. For the decade as a whole, trade showed little overall growth, the importance of machinery and equipment imports dropped sharply, and China accumulated no significant international debt.

Economic growth reemerged in mid-1972 as an important goal of the leadership and a new trade expansion began. This expansion was marked by the first large-scale purchases of complete plants for key sectors of the economy since the fifties. About $2.5 billion in foreign credits were used for financing plant purchases between 1972 and 1975, the first major use of foreign funds since the fifties. Although trade growth and contracts for new plants were temporarily interrupted between 1974 and 1976 by a combina-

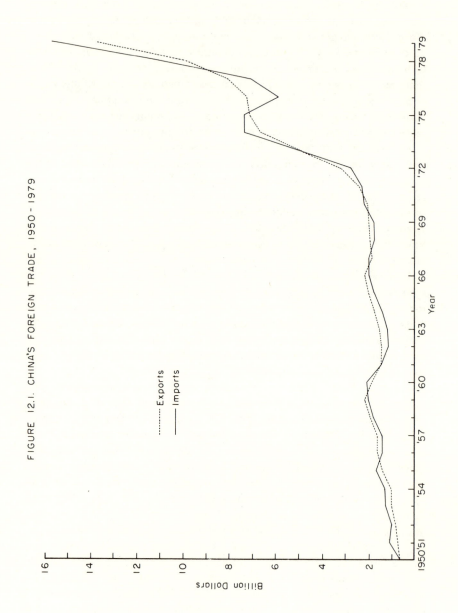

FIGURE 12.1. CHINA'S FOREIGN TRADE, 1950 - 1979

tion of domestic political turmoil and unanticipated shocks from the world recession, the decade as a whole saw substantial growth in trade.[2]

Since 1979 the nature and pace of trade expansion has changed. The growth of trade, although still substantial, has slowed. Contracts for turnkey plants have declined markedly and a further slowdown is planned for the next several years. The trade deficit has fallen below planned levels and, although credit lines of nearly $30 billion have been arranged, only limited amounts of credit actually have been drawn. This slowdown in the growth of trade mainly reflects economic developments, but also to some extent is a result of the resurgence of the same conservative forces that exerted a strong impact on foreign trade policies over the past 30 years.[3]

An important element in the slowdown is an ongoing reassessment of domestic investment levels and priorities as part of what is labeled a "period of readjustment," scheduled to extend for the next several years. The rate of capital formation has been reduced, giving way to greater emphasis on higher living standards. The reassessment has also meant a shift away from investment in large-scale, capital-intensive projects to smaller scale projects promising more rapid returns. These changes have depressed demand for capital goods imports. The shift stems from growing concern with both the appropriateness of widespread applications of capital-intensive Western technology to China's labor abundant economy, and with China's ability to absorb and effectively utilize large amounts of foreign capital goods and technology.

A second element in the reduced momentum of foreign trade is a hard look at feasible future export growth rates coupled with increased caution about assuming foreign debt. This reassessment has constrained the willingness to import.

Finally, along with these economic factors, questions of appropriate trade policy and the extent to which it is feasible to open the Chinese economy continue to be raised in policymaking circles. There seems to be no major dispute over the general upward direction of foreign trade, but questions of how far and how fast the expansion should be pushed have not been fully resolved.

## Agricultural Exports

Chinese discussions of trade place greatest emphasis on trade of industrial products and technology, but agriculture is consistently an important component of overall foreign trade (Table 12.1). Exports of Chinese agricultural commodities have exceeded agricultural imports for most years since 1949. This net export surplus is an important source of financing for

Table 12.1. Agricultural Exports and Trade Balance, 1970-1979 a/

| | 1970 | 1971 | 1972 | 1973 | 1974 | 1975 | 1976 | 1977 | 1978 | 1979 |
|---|---|---|---|---|---|---|---|---|---|---|
| | | | | (Million dollars) | | | | | | |
| Foodstuffs | 645 | 740 | 955 | 1,530 | 1,995 | 2,125 | 1,945 | 1,960 | 2,275 | 2,630 |
| Live animals | 65 | 90 | 110 | 135 | 195 | 215 | 230 | 245 | 255 | 250 |
| Meat and fish | 150 | 185 | 225 | 335 | 335 | 415 | 430 | 375 | 525 | 635 |
| Grains | 110 | 95 | 155 | 445 | 715 | 720 | 450 | 395 | 350 | 335 |
| Fruits and vegetables | 170 | 155 | 180 | 245 | 315 | 360 | 385 | 500 | 580 | 720 |
| Tea and spices | NA | NA | NA | NA | 100 | 100 | 140 | 180 | 230 | 315 |
| Other agricultural products | 335 | 420 | 515 | 645 | 590 | 730 | 725 | 775 | 980 | 1,290 |
| Oilseeds | 65 | 65 | 70 | 110 | 135 | 140 | 85 | 85 | 95 | 200 |
| Textile fibers | 100 | 120 | 205 | 330 | 190 | 250 | 285 | 290 | 400 | 510 |
| Crude animal materials | 115 | 105 | 115 | 170 | 200 | 230 | 260 | 335 | 375 | 445 |
| Vegetable oils | NA | NA | NA | NA | 40 | 40 | 40 | 30 | 55 | 65 |
| Total, agricultural | 980 | 1,160 | 1,470 | 2,175 | 2,585 | 2,855 | 2,670 | 2,735 | 3,255 | 3,920 |
| Total, all exports | 2,155 | 2,535 | 3,220 | 5,100 | 6,730 | 7,130 | 7,260 | 8,110 | 10,120 | 13,750 |
| Agricultural trade balance b/ | 380 | 625 | 645 | 425 | 240 | 1,500 | 1,720 | 625 | 605 | 175 |
| Overall trade balance b/ | (55) | 220 | 420 | 75 | (645) | (265) | 1,240 | 985 | (1,065) | (1,810) |

Sources: Central Intelligence Agency, China: International Trade Quarterly Review, Second Quarter, 1980. ER CIT 81-001, Feb. 1981, and earlier CIA trade review. R. E. Batsavage and J. L. Davie, "China's International Trade and Finance," in Chinese Economy Post-Mao, Congress of the United States, Joint Economic Committee, 1976. Vol. I: pp. 707-741. Some minor adjustments have been made to the data presented in these sources.

( ) = negative value.
NA = not available.

a/ Export values f.o.b. basis. All figures rounded to the nearest $5 million.
b/ Exports minus imports.

high priority nonagricultural imports. For the first half of the seventies, the agricultural trade surplus financed, on an average, about 20 percent of nonagricultural imports. Even between 1977 and 1979, when agricultural imports grew rapidly, the agricultural trade surplus continued, although at a reduced level.

China's agricultural exports cover a wide range of commodities. Live animals, meat and animal products, fruits and vegetables, textile fibers (mainly silk), and grain are consistently the leading agricultural export categories. China's grain exports consist almost entirely of rice, which is the largest bulk export item. China has consistently ranked among the world's top rice exporters. The remainder of agricultural exports are spread across a wide range of commodities.

Agricultural exports have risen over time, but they have not kept pace with the overall growth of trade, particularly during periods of rapid expansion. Consequently agricultural exports have slipped from more than 60 percent of total exports during the mid-fifties, to an average of about 44 percent between 1970 and 1974, and only about one-third of total exports during the last half of the seventies.[4] Despite this lower share in total trade, exports of agricultural commodities continue to be an important part of Chinese foreign trade plans.

Indirect exports of agricultural commodities also make up a crucial share of total exports. Agriculture provides large amounts of raw materials for the light industrial sector. For example, when textile yarns, fabrics, and clothing are added to exports of agricultural commodities, the resulting total of "agriculture-related" exports accounted for about 65 percent of total exports during the first half of the seventies and 58 percent for 1975–1978.[5]

Despite the importance of agriculture, Chinese policies toward agricultural exports have not been clearly stated and the precise determinants of total agricultural export levels and of exports of individual commodities are difficult to identify. The proportion of total production of most agricultural commodities that is exported is very small and there is probably only a loose relationship between year-to-year changes in production levels and exports. Rice is an extreme case. Although rice exports are an important part of international trade in rice, they amount to only about 1 percent of China's total rice production.

A variety of other factors—particularly producer incentives and domestic procurement policies—play a dominant role in year-to-year fluctuations in agricultural export levels. Foreign exchange pressures also serve as a stimulus to increase exports of agricultural as well as other commodities. Thus a relationship between import growth rates and agricultural exports seems likely. Over longer periods of time, however, the growth of agricultural production will be a major factor limiting exports. This has clearly been the case for soybeans. Per capita production of soybeans has dropped by half over the past two decades and exports have declined markedly. This decline has reached the point where China, an exporter of over one million tonnes annually in the late 1950s, is now a net importer of soybeans (Figure 12.2). The slow growth of agriculture in relation to the rest of the economy is probably the major reason for agriculture's declining share of China's exports.

The recent export drive and significantly improved agricultural production have contributed to a substantial rise in agricultural exports (Table 12.1). Institutional and incentive changes have also played an important role. These changes have included higher state procurement prices for at least some commodities, decentralization of controls over foreign trade, and more intensive efforts by Chinese marketing agencies to open foreign markets. Decentralization of foreign trade decision making, which has given increased autonomy and flexibility as well as a share of foreign exchange earnings to lower-level government, is a particularly important development for agricultural exports. Specific export-oriented projects may also have an impact. Joint venture operations now underway for poultry and dairy production in southern China and for grain and soybean production in the northeast are examples of projects using foreign capital and technology and aimed, at least in part, at export markets.[6]

Even with these changes it will be difficult for China to maintain the average 1976–1979 annual growth rate of 14 percent for agricultural exports. For the next several years the trend rate of growth of agricultural production will be well below that of 1978 and 1979. This will tend to have a depressing effect on export supplies. Additionally, rising domestic demand will increase competition for available supplies of many commodities. On balance, it seems unlikely that the growth rate of agricultural exports will increase significantly in the next several years. Fairly rapid growth in production and export of some minor commodities is likely as production is geared specifically to export markets. But a sustained increase in exports of major commodities does not seem likely. For these commodities — for example, rice — world market conditions will be as much a limiting factor as domestic availabilities in China.

Given the relatively slow growth of agricultural exports, a continued rapid rise in agricultural imports would eliminate the surplus that has characterized China's agricultural trade for most of the period since 1949. Unless import growth slows, the agricultural sector will emerge as a net claimant on scarce foreign exchange resources during a period when China is attempting to increase nonagricultural imports and hold down debt levels.

FIGURE 12.2. TRADE BY COMMODITY, 1960-1980

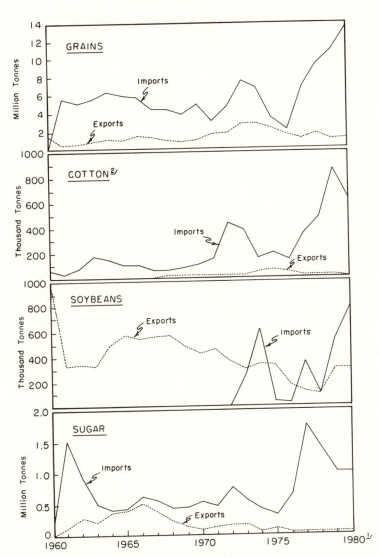

1 1980 FIGURES ARE PRELIMINARY ESTIMATES
2 MARKETING YEAR BEGINNING AUGUST 1

### Agricultural Imports

Agricultural imports have passed through at least three distinct phases, each reflecting policy changes. Agricultural imports during the fifties were modest, consisting primarily of cotton, rubber, and small amounts of sugar. With the exception of sugar, very few foodstuffs were imported and total agricultural imports amounted on an average to no more than 10 percent of total imports.[7]

The first major change in agricultural import policy occurred in 1961. China began a major program of grain imports, following the sharp decline in agricultural production stemming from the failure of the Great Leap Forward. Through this program foreign wheat, and to a lesser extent corn and other coarse grains, came to provide an important share of grain supplies for coastal cities of northern China. As agricultural production levels recovered during the mid-sixties, these imports were institutionalized as a supplement to state grain procurements from the rural areas. During the sixties, the share of agricultural imports increased to perhaps one-third to one-half of total imports.[8] This increase was primarily due to higher grain imports. Somewhat higher sugar and cotton purchases were the only other noticeable changes.

Beginning in late 1972 agricultural imports jumped again (Table 12.2). Grain and cotton imports reached record levels in 1973. The first significant imports of soybeans and edible oils also occurred and China temporarily became a net importer of soybeans. The expansion of agricultural imports was likely part of initial steps to raise domestic consumption and allow a somewhat greater role for imports in meeting domestic requirements. Although the 1972 harvest was poor, the sudden growth of agricultural imports cannot fully be explained by lower domestic supplies of agricultural products. Rather it seems to reflect a more liberalized approach to foreign trade and economic policy. This surge in imports was interrupted in 1975 and 1976 as foreign trade was curtailed because of balance-of-payments problems and the disruptions caused by political attacks on relaxed domestic and foreign economic policies. The most recent expansion of agricultural trade, which began in 1977, seems to have its roots in the 1973–1974 period.

Since 1977 agricultural imports have risen to record levels and growth continued through 1980. Grains and cotton again led the expansion of trade. Grain imports have increased steadily and in 1980 exceeded 13 million tonnes, a level more than 30 percent above the average for the previous two years and 80 percent above the average for 1973 and 1974. Long-term agreements now in effect with major suppliers, including a recent agreement for 6–9 million tonnes of U.S. grain annually between 1981

Table 12.2.  Agricultural Imports, 1970-1979 a/

| | 1970 | 1971 | 1972 | 1973 | 1974 | 1975 | 1976 | 1977 | 1978 | 1979 |
|---|---|---|---|---|---|---|---|---|---|---|
| | | | | (Million dollars) | | | | | | |
| Foodstuffs | 395 | 320 | 500 | 1,015 | 1,440 | 885 | 560 | 1,105 | 1,460 | 1,945 |
| Grain | 280 | 215 | 345 | 840 | 1,180 | 675 | 325 | 720 | 1,060 | 1,575 |
| Sugar | 80 | 70 | 135 | 135 | 175 | 180 | 200 | 330 | 290 | 220 |
| Other agricultural products | 205 | 215 | 325 | 735 | 905 | 470 | 390 | 1,005 | 1,190 | 1,805 |
| Oilseeds | --- | --- | 10 | 65 | 160 | 15 | 5 | 125 | 40 | 125 |
| Rubber | 80 | 60 | 70 | 170 | 155 | 145 | 150 | 215 | 95 | 325 |
| Textile fibers | 95 | 125 | 215 | 450 | 520 | 260 | 190 | 460 | 760 | 1,095 |
| Crude animal and vegetable materials | NA | NA | NA | NA | 25 | 20 | 20 | 40 | 40 | 50 |
| Animal and vegetable fats and oils | NA | NA | NA | NA | 45 | 30 | 25 | 165 | 155 | 210 |
| Total, agricultural imports | 600 | 535 | 825 | 1,750 | 2,345 | 1,355 | 950 | 2,110 | 2,650 | 3,750 |
| Total, all imports | 2,210 | 2,315 | 2,800 | 5,025 | 7,375 | 7,395 | 6,025 | 7,120 | 11,185 | 15,560 |

Sources:  See Table 12.1.  Import data for 1977 and 1978 have been adjusted to the seame C.I.F. basis as that for earlier years.

--- = none or negligible.
NA  = not available.

a/  Import values C.I.F. basis.  All figures are rounded to the nearest $5 million.

and 1984, suggest planned imports for the next several years of a minimum of 12 million tonnes and possibly as much as 17 million tonnes. The bulk of these imports will be wheat; plans do not appear to envision increases in corn imports above the current level of about 2 million tonnes annually. These levels of imports rank China and the USSR as the world's leading wheat importers.

Soybean imports are also up and China's traditional position as a net soybean exporter has clearly shifted to a net import position. Soybean imports are now consistently supplemented by imports of soybean oil. Finally, for the past four years China's sugar imports have been at a considerably higher level than previously.

Along with higher food imports, cotton imports have also reached record levels. China became the world's largest importer of cotton during the 1979/1980 cotton marketing year.[9] These imports were supplemented by large imports of synthetic fibers. Although import levels dropped somewhat in 1980/1981, China remained a major factor in the world cotton market.[10]

This recent growth in agricultural imports clearly indicates a substantial modification of constraints on agricultural imports. These changes stem from new demand pressures in China, which are being generated by domestic economic policies. The shifts underway in domestic policy would not be possible without the relaxation of trade constraints.

The primary demand pressure affecting agricultural imports is a commitment to raise Chinese standards of living following two decades of minimal growth. Wage increases for urban workers and higher state purchase prices for agricultural products raised incomes significantly in both 1978 and 1979. Increased purchasing power has led to more demand for basic farm commodities and consumer goods such as textiles.

A second part of the explanation for higher imports is state procurement of farm products. The central government has not pressed rural areas to increase sales of farm products to the state, choosing instead to permit higher retention of food products and thus higher rural consumption. In the case of grain, for example, although total grain production increased by 49 million tonnes between 1977 and 1979, state grain procurements increased by only 8 million tonnes, and the proportion of the total crop procured by the state remained unchanged or declined slightly. The proportion of the crop procured is now below that of the fifties, the last period for which comparative data are available.

The government is also actively promoting regional specialization and encouraging key areas of the country to concentrate on production of specific economic crops and livestock. To insure success for these policies the central government will have to provide increased supplies of grain to these areas. Past attempts to promote specialization have failed, at least in part, because localities were not assured of grain supplies to replace crop area shifted to other uses. These developments all add up to significant increases in demand for state supplies of basic food items at the same time that domestically procured supplies are growing only slowly. This gap appears to be a major reason behind the surge in imports of grain, soybeans, edible oils, and sugar.

Rising textile production caused by higher domestic and export demands resulted in an average 9 percent per year growth in cotton yarn production between 1977 and 1979. Domestic cotton production grew at less than half this rate during the same period. The growing gap between domestic supply and demand, together with the high priority awarded to the textile industry, clearly explain the surge in imports of both cotton and synthetic fibers.

## The Future of Agricultural Trade

Pressures will continue for higher imports as long as domestic policies emphasize economic development, modernization, and higher standards of living. While domestic investment is currently being cut, and imports of high technology capital goods, particularly of complete plants, are being temporarily curtailed, rising imports will be crucial to future economic growth. These imports will increase sharply as domestic economic readjustments are completed in the next several years.

The extent to which demands for agricultural products translate into higher imports will depend on developments in the foreign trade sector and on agricultural performance. Import capacity will be shaped by both the overall growth of exports and by China's willingness and ability to borrow. Export growth rates are not likely to increase substantially. In fact, sources of growth that will permit the average 24 percent per year growth rate of total exports of 1976–1979 are unlikely to be sustained. This assumption is borne out by what little is known of foreign trade plans. Plans indicate a declining rate of growth for trade in 1980 and 1981.

Additional use of foreign credit could also finance Chinese imports. China's access to substantial amounts of credit is clear; less certain is its willingness to assume increases in foreign debt. Use of credit lines and accumulation of debt will probably increase over the next several years as the period of readjustment ends. However, events of 1979 suggest that the Chinese will be reluctant to see debt levels rise too rapidly. This reluctance is due to a more sober look at export prospects, but also indicates some reassertion of concern about self-reliance. Given this scenario, competition for limited foreign exchange will grow as the eighties progress. With a high priority for industrial imports, there is potential for conflict between agricultural and nonagricultural imports.

Other than what can be inferred from past increases in agricultural imports and existing contracts, there is no information about China's plans for future agricultural trade. However, Wang Renzhong, a Secretary of the Chinese Communist Party recently stated, "At this time we are striving to end our imports of cotton and sugar and to gradually free ourselves from grain imports in the foreseeable future."[11] This suggests that self-reliance remains important in Chinese thinking about agricultural trade, and that they view rising agricultural imports as temporary.

To aid programs of regional specialization, larger state supplies of grain are necessary. Supplemental state allocations of grain to several provinces involved in these programs were reported during 1980. The effort to increase state grain supplies seems to be one important reason behind the planned growth in grain imports for the next several years. If this is the case, then the rise in grain imports can be viewed as the first phase of a program of agricultural import substitution. Grain imports are used temporarily to permit greater expansion of production of nongrain crops, such as cotton, oil-seeds, and sugar, resulting in lower imports of nongrain farm products.

Further reductions in the growth of imports will ultimately require a higher rate of growth of grain production and larger state procurements. For import demand, state procurements are as important as the overall growth of grain production. Two agricultural policies are targeted specifically at increasing procurements. Large increases in procurement prices instituted in 1979 have thus far had little effect. Development of grain bases with substantially above average marketing rates may also aid in boosting procurement rates. Large increases in grain procurements would be the second phase in a program of agricultural import substitution, permitting lower grain imports.[12]

The real costs of import substitution are certain to be substantial and the programs may be reevaluated as this becomes evident. Also, progress in increasing domestic supplies is likely to be slower than anticipated, especially for grains. Production increases may be sufficient to hold down import levels of some crops, particularly cotton. Efforts to restrain imports will be aided by a planned slowdown in the rate of growth of the textile industry and by growing production of synthetic fibers. However, pressures seem likely to remain for continued substantial levels of agricultural imports, especially grains. The Chinese may slow import growth enough to maintain a small agricultural export surplus, but agriculture is not likely to make a significant contribution to financing other imports.

This analysis has ignored the possibility of increased imports of feedstuffs for livestock. To date, China has mainly imported grain for food use and soybeans for processing of oil, industrial purposes, or human consumption. Livestock feed has not been an important source of import demand. In view of the small share of corn in the grain agreements with the United States and other countries, China does not seem to intend to increase feedgrain imports. This fits with recent modifications in livestock programs that emphasize diversified livestock development and pasture improvement.

Nevertheless, China's livestock program does include expansion of production in near-urban areas and some concentrated feeding operations. The faster these programs are pushed, the greater the likelihood that feed demand will spill over into greater imports, particularly during years of low production and reduced state procurements. The livestock program still has the potential to be an additional factor upsetting trade plans.

Finally, although China may slow the growth of agricultural imports, particularly of items other than grains, the new importance of domestic demand has implications for the stability of agricultural imports. Stabilization of consumption levels in the event of a shortfall in domestic production appears to have a higher priority than in the past. Because state-held stocks of most commodities are likely quite low, China's imports of agricultural products may well show greater responsiveness to annual fluctuations in agricultural production than in the past. This variability will be even greater if livestock programs outrun the domestic supply of feedstuffs.

## Notes

1. China's foreign trade since 1949 is surveyed in Alexander Eckstein, *China's Economic Revolution* (New York: Cambridge University Press, 1977), pp. 233–276.

2. Some of the growth of trade during the seventies resulted from inflation and depreciation of the U.S. dollar, but real growth was substantial. A deflated trade series is available for 1970–1976. This series shows exports rising by 12 percent annually between 1970 and 1976 and imports increasing at 16.5 percent annually through 1974, then dropping in both 1975 and 1976. The series is presented in Richard E. Batsavage and John L. Davie, "China's International Trade and Finance," *Chinese Economy Post-Mao* (Congress of the United States, Joint Economic Committee, 1978), vol. 1, pp. 736–737.

3. China's traditional debt policies are explored in David L. Denny and Frederic M. Surls, "China's Foreign Financial Liabilities," *The China Business Review,* vol. 4, no. 2 (March-April 1977), pp. 13–21.

4. No consistent historical trade series broken down by commodity for the entire 1949–1979 period is available. The figure for the fifties is based on data presented in Robert F. Dernberger, "Prospects for Trade Between China and the United States,"

in Alexander Eckstein, ed., *China Trade Prospects and U.S. Policy* (New York: Praeger, 1971), pp. 276–277, 308–309.

5. Data on this and other components of trade during the seventies are available in the sources cited for Table 12.1.

6. Joint venture operations are projects between Chinese governmental units and foreign investors. The foreign investors typically provide hard currency financing, equipment, and technology. Repayment is often in the form of exports from the project.

7. Dernberger, "Prospects for Trade," pp. 276–277, 310–311.

8. Incomplete data presented in Nai-ruenn Chen, "China's Foreign Trade, 1950–74," *China: A Reassessment of the Economy* (Congress of the United States, Joint Economic Committee, 1975), p. 646, give an average of 35 percent for 1965–1969. The figure was undoubtedly higher in the early sixties.

9. Calendar year quantity data for cotton trade are unavailable. The cotton marketing year begins August 1.

10. Data on agricultural production and trade for recent years are available in U.S. Department of Agriculture, Economics, Statistics, and Cooperative Service, *People's Republic of China Agricultural Situation, Review of 1979 and Outlook for 1980,* Supplement 6 to World Agricultural Situation No. 21, June 1980. This report is published annually.

11. Interview translated in U.S. Department of Commerce, National Technical Information Service, Foreign Broadcast Information Service, *Daily Report: People's Republic of China,* vol. 1, no. 200 (October 14, 1980), pp. L1–L4.

12. Factors determining agricultural import levels are more fully discussed in Frederic M. Surls, "New Directions in China's Agricultural Imports," *American Journal of Agricultural Economics,* vol. 62, no. 2 (May 1980), pp. 350–355.

## Readings

Batsavage, Richard E., and John L. Davie. "China's International Trade and Finance," *China's Economy Post-Mao.* Congress of the United States, Joint Economic Committee, 1978, vol. 1, pp. 704–741. A useful survey of foreign trade in the 1970–1976 period. Includes a deflated trade series for the period. The Joint Economic Committee volumes on China, published every third year, are indispensable references on all aspects of China's economy.

Central Intelligence Agency (CIA). *China: International Trade Quarterly Review.* The most comprehensive source of up-to-date information on quantity, value, composition, and direction of China's foreign trade.

Eckstein, Alexander. *China's Economic Revolution.* New York: Cambridge University Press, 1977. An important analysis of China's economic development through the mid-seventies with considerable attention to the role of foreign trade.

U.S. Department of Agriculture, Economics, Statistics, and Cooperatives Services. *People's Republic of China Agricultural Situation, Review of 1979 and Outlook for 1980.* Supplement 6 to World Agricultural Situation No. 21, June 1980. An annual publication containing both analysis of current developments and up-to-date data on agriculture and agricultural trade.

# Epilogue

*Randolph Barker*
*Radha Sinha*

As this book goes to press, China continues in a period of adjustment and change following the death of Mao Zedong and the downfall of the "Gang of Four." In our judgment the changes that are occurring in the agricultural economy are not simply the reflection of political forces, but have an underlying economic rationale. To emphasize this point and at the same time to summarize the preceding chapters, we pose three key questions that both Chinese policymakers and Western analysts are exploring:

1. Will the direction of new policies lead to greater efficiency in agricultural production?
2. Will there be radical changes in basic social organization and rural institutions?
3. What will be the nature of change in rural employment, income, and consumption?

Our purpose is not to provide answers, for indeed at this time there can be no definitive answers, but rather to examine the questions in the context of the diverse views expressed by the authors of this book.

## Agricultural Production

Given China's land resource constraints and the disparate topography and climate, as well as the already high levels of agricultural technology in the premodern sense (Chapters 2 and 4), the attainment of an overall growth rate of agricultural output of close to 3 percent between 1957 and 1979 has been a remarkable achievement (Chapters 7 and 11). This rate of growth of output is comparable to that of India and Southeast Asia. However, at a regional level, growth in agricultural production has varied widely over time and among areas, with serious implications for disparities in income and consumption levels (Chapters 10 and 11).

Agricultural production dropped sharply after the formation of the communes and implementation of Great Leap policies (1958–1961), but then rapidly recovered with important weather improvements and the relaxation of strict policies. Throughout the 1960s "Green Revolution" technology fueled significant production improvements, as in other parts of Asia. However, the Chinese independently developed their own fertilizer-responsive varieties of rice and wheat, supplying the necessary fertilizer inputs through labor-intensive composting and small-scale ammonium bicarbonate plants. During the Cultural Revolution period (1966–1976) agricultural growth does not appear to have fallen, although the decline of statistical and research organizations has led some to refer to the period as "the ten wasted years."

Despite the favorable growth record, the efficiency of agricultural production, measured by growth in output relative to growth in inputs, has been declining (Chapters 7 and 8). Whether this has been due to the process of collectivization itself or to limits imposed by diminishing returns on an already highly developed land base is a matter of open debate among scholars. Some have argued that low labor and land productivity in the precommunist period were rooted in the stagnancy of agricultural technology rather than in the land tenure system (Chapter 3). However, the alternative to collectivization, i.e., division into small private holdings, would almost certainly have led to a growth in landless labor, as has occurred in other densely populated regions of developing Asia. Although collectivization facilitated the development of crucial small-scale rural industries (Chapter 9), it also aided the "squeezing" of agriculture for industrial development (Chapter 5). Thus, it is unclear whether the net effect of collectivization on agricultural efficiency has been positive or negative.

With the passage of time, the returns to labor in private and sideline activities relative to collective activities has apparently increased, bringing economic pressure in many areas for a change in the organization of agriculture. The development of transportation and industry to serve the needs of agriculture has brought further economic pressure to replace the policy of local self-reliance in food production and resource use with one seemingly more in line with Western concepts of comparative advantage. At the same time, development of transportation and industry has rendered some small-scale industries obsolete (Chapter 9).

Will the new policy directions lead to greater efficiency in agricultural production? Several authors see great scope for improvement in agricultural productivity through policy changes and modifications in the organization and management of agricultural resources (Chapters 5, 7, and 10). However, the related question of the relative importance of technical improvements remains to be answered. Concern has been expressed that severe resource constraints, coupled with setbacks in agricultural research and technology development associated with the Cultural Revolution, could seriously limit future growth in agricultural productivity (Chapter 11). At this writing, it is still virtually impossible to assess the magnitude and impact of those policy changes that have been implemented, although the Chinese press reports a favorable response in the rural areas.

## Social Organization

Rural institutions were created under the communists to increase equality and social justice in the countryside, to provide incentives for rural development, and to provide capital, commodities, and labor for the development of the industrial sector (Chapter 6). Equity was valued as an important end in itself as well as a means to increase production and capital accumulation. To enforce equality the government first abolished private property and then reorganized rural life around the commune system, which, by and large, insured basic minimum employment, income, and consumption standards for all.

China's rural institutions have been particularly successful at mobilizing vast amounts of surplus labor in the creation of rural infrastructure (Chapter 8). The tripartite collective institution has been reasonably successful at providing leadership, labor, and funds for development activities of many kinds. These range from farm production activities controlled largely by individual teams to small-scale industrial plants organized at the commune and county level for the production of agricultural inputs and the processing of agricultural products.

Since 1949 there has been an ongoing conflict between stress on equity and stress on productivity (Chapters 5 and 6). This debate has carried over into policy decisions affecting the structure of rural institutions. Rapid collectivization in 1958 shifted responsibility for decision-making to higher echelons and undermined local initiative. However, as a more equitable balance was achieved in the early 1960s, much decision making power was again delegated to the team level. Although some efforts were made to raise the level of accounting to the brigade during the Cultural Revolution, this was resisted by teams who preferred to retain control over income distribution among members. This generally has meant that efforts at greater equalization of income between teams and brigades have not made appreciable progress. Income levels continue to differ considerably from team to team because of varying land resources, geographical placement, access to inputs, and management skills. In recent years pressure toward delegating decision-making responsibility and income sharing to lower levels has continued.

Will there be radical changes in social organization and rural institutions? Since the Cultural Revolution the tides of political and economic pressure appear to have been flowing in the same direction. As mentioned previously, the rising profitability of private and side-line activities, the development of transportation and industry to serve the needs of agriculture, and the desire to move away from a policy of local self-reliance in food production have all affected existing rural institutions. Older institutions, such as People's Communes, may begin to obstruct, rather than encourage, progress (Chapter 8). For example, policies that emphasize local decision making and a greater degree of personal freedom may also require some relaxation of laws that restrict rural-urban migration. However, adequate urban employment opportunities could not be easily created to match an unrestricted population flow. Obviously Chinese decision makers must move slowly when considering policy changes.

It seems almost certain that rural institutions will undergo some changes (Chapter 6). How radical or pervasive these changes will be is difficult to predict, as China at present still seems to be in an experimental mood. The lack of unity and decisiveness in recent policy decisions may be a healthy sign that old solutions, no matter how successful in the past, may not be entirely appropriate for the future (Chapter 8). For a country as large and diverse as China, different regional patterns of rural organization may be completely consistent with political, economic, and social realities.

At present, several forms of the "responsibility system" are being experimented with throughout China. Under the "responsibility system," teams, families, or individuals contract with the state to produce a certain quantity of goods on a piece of communal land. This system delegates increased decision-making power to the lower levels. However, collective ownership of farmland is certain to continue as China seeks to develop a more efficient organization of local production and management systems.

## Employment, Income, and Consumption

It is commonly agreed that collectivization and the rural industrialization facilitated by it have enabled China to use both its land and labor with growing intensity (Chapters 8 and 9). Intensification of cropping practices, sometimes pushed beyond desirable limits (Chapter 7), adoption of labor-using plant and animal products, and extensive farmland construction campaigns led to massive absorption of labor. Admittedly, underemployment is prevalent in the rural areas, although outright unemployment is largely absent. Consequently, labor productivity has declined steadily since 1952 and is likely to continue to decline in the decade ahead as even more people join the work force (Chapter 8). However, sharing of limited employment opportunities, which is an essential feature of the commune organization, also amounts to a more equitable sharing of underemployment.

The system of work-related income distribution, widespread employment, insured access to minimum food requirements regardless of ability to pay, and relatively low prices of basic consumer necessities has meant that even at low levels of income and consumption, health standards and expectation of life are high, compared to other developing countries.

However, the Western assessment of China's success in solving her food problem has changed considerably in recent years as more information has become available and as the Chinese themselves have admitted to serious problems of malnutrition, especially during the Great Leap period (Chapter 10). The data suggest that there has been no significant improvement in the per capita level of food consumption during the two decades from the late 1950s to the late 1970s and that current consumption is not much different than the prewar level, although dietary variety seems to have improved. Furthermore, despite greater equity within communes, regional and rural-urban disparities in production, income, and consumption are similar to those found in other developing Asian countries. The policy of local self-reliance in food production plus the unevenness of regional distribution of food would explain these sharp regional differences.

What will be the nature of change in employment, income, and consumption? There are two essential aspects of this question: Will the overall level improve? Will the distribution be more or less equitable than in the past?

The most encouraging sign for overall improvement relates to population control policy. Government policy to restrict the size of families to one or two children, backed by strong sanctions and rewards, is apparently having an effect even in the rural areas where there is still a strong desire for a male heir. Even with these population control measures, however, employment problems will continue for more than a decade as children born prior to the 1980s enter the labor force.

Ultimately, a reduction in population growth, coupled with rising incomes, will lead to demands for a more diverse diet. Increased diversification and specialization of agriculture should help meet some of these rising consumer demands. However, the government may also have to resort to an even greater use of the world market to both fulfill consumer expectations and make more efficient use of agricultural resources. Under current policies, China seems to be willing to continue importing large quantities of grain in order to meet the urban demand and to make up deficits resulting from crop failures caused by unfavorable weather (Chapter 12). As a result, balance of payment will continue to be a serious constraint. At least in the foreseeable future, imports of grain for animal feed will not rise significantly.

Policies designed to increase the efficiency of agricultural resource use by allowing an economically more rational pattern of resource allocation and commodity production should reduce income disparities among regions, although those areas with low quality land and overcrowding will still have to rely on government assistance to raise their living standards. Policies that are designed to give more decision-making authority to teams or private households, such as the "responsibility systems" currently in use, are likely to increase income differentials locally as well as between regions. Just how far such policies will be pushed is difficult to say. Occasional weather-related shortfalls could create a more conservative mood in policy planning, leading to reinforcement of production targets to insure adequate grain supplies and avoid excessive dependence on imports. As stated at the outset, however, underlying economic forces are likely to continue to bring pressures for policy change over the longer run.

# The Use of Agricultural Statistics:
# Some National Aggregate Examples and
# Current State of the Art

*Bruce Stone*

There are four broad problems economists must consider when using statistical material. These are:

1.  Which organizations or researchers are in the best positions to gather and aggregate the most accurate statistical material?
2.  What are the exact definitions of the statistical categories employed, and are they consistent over time and geographic area?
3.  What is the quality of these materials and what methodologies are used in collecting or producing them? What are the probable margins of error?
4.  How can the available data be put to productive use in economic analysis?

Most applied economists spend the majority of their energies solving the fourth problem. Here theoretical skills can be employed to produce results leading to practical conclusions. It is evident, however, that addressing the fourth question in a responsible fashion requires careful scrutiny of the first three questions. In contrast, until recently, foreign analysts of the Chinese economy (perhaps of Chinese agriculture in particular) have spent a majority of their time searching for accurate statistical material or in making circuitous estimates when the data were unavailable.

The quality of Chinese statistical series has varied widely through time for historical reasons. Unlike many developing countries where statistical collection has made steady, if slow, progress, Chinese statistical collection has both advanced and regressed. The rudiments of a national system were established in 1952 with the formation of the State Statistical Bureau (SSB), and subsequently destroyed during the Great Leap Forward, (1958–1961) when statistics were declared "a weapon of class struggle." Although the Chinese statistical system recovered to a certain extent during the early 1960s, it was dealt a staggering blow during the Cultural Revolution, especially the first stage (1966–1969), when responsibility for record keeping was withdrawn from professionals and charged to cadres, whose promotions depended on the records in their own ledgers. In a 1979 Chinese publication it was stated that during the 1960s "many statistical agencies were abolished, many statistical workers persecuted, and plenty of statistical data destroyed, with the whole country's statistical work nearly brought to a halt for a time." There are reportedly half as many trained statisticians now as before the Cultural Revolution.

The ups and downs of the statistical system are reflected in the availability of official numbers. Between 1960 and 1979, especially 1960–1962, 1968–1969, and 1976, unified statistical material was largely unavailable. Since the publication of a modest set of official statistics for 1977 and 1978, the quantity and purported accuracy (more decimal places) of statistics have rapidly increased. Brief summaries of unified provincial statistics for several provinces have appeared, and the Chinese news media have increased publication of quantitative information. In addition, considerable official data for 1975–1980 and for a few benchmark years (1952, 1957, 1965, and one or two years in the early 1970s) have been released. Recently the *Agricultural Yearbook of China 1980* has provided complete data series in a limited number of categories for the entire People's Republic.

Progress in defining statistical categories, analyzing methodologies, and assessing relative quality of data has been slow because Chinese collecting, aggregating, and synthesizing methodology is still poorly understood. Information about changes in operating procedures over time is particularly sketchy. We do know of specific cases in which statistical definitions have varied across time periods or among constituent reporting groups. In some cases statistics published as consistent series may use different parameters over the span of benchmark years. Systematic biases, especially at local levels, introduce additional distortions. For example, since grain production is a local success indicator, cadres may report inflated statistics. On the other hand, teams and brigades may underreport grain production to escape higher grain quotas. In spite of these problems Chinese statistical data are still very useful and are undoubtedly superior to those of the majority of developing countries.

In general, the most reliable agricultural statistics are generated by state farms, followed by the collective sector, with only sketchy estimates for private production. Because grains occupy the bulk of cultivated area and are produced primarily on state farms and collective lands, basic output data are better than for some other kinds of farm production, such as hogs or vegetables. On the other hand, data for economic crops grown predominately on state farms, or for exclusive purchase by state organs, are of better quality.

Presently China's national statistical system consists of three major and not necessarily related systems: (1) a central system operating at the national, provincial, and county levels; (2) a statistical system associated with specialized ministries at the national, provincial, and county levels; and (3) statistical collection in communes and factories.

The State Statistical Bureau (SSB), the national level central statistical agency, is responsible for organizing and directing statistical work countrywide. Prior to the formation of the SSB in 1952, statistics gathering was uncoordinated, presumably relying upon the crop report network left by the Nationalist government and information provided by tax data, the land reform, and commercial organizations.

The SSB utilizes data from two primary sources. It carries out periodic stratified surveys on output, peasant household income and expenditure, and agricultural cost of production. Representative communes, brigades, and teams from about 10 percent of the counties within each province are selected to complete surveys conducted directly by the SSB. The SSB also issues standard reporting forms for various aspects of agricultural production and rural development. Theoretically these forms are completed at the local level using primary data obtained from each team for every commune in China. However, in reality, complete and easily accessible records are rarely kept at brigade or team levels. When forms are aggregated at the commune level, empty cells are often estimated by accountants. The SSB has no direct control over these procedures and has been clearly suspicious of the accuracy of lower level statistics, particularly during periods of disorder, such as the Great Leap Forward. Thus the SSB has relied primarily on the stratified surveys over which it has greater control.

The Ministry of Agriculture, as well as the other specialized ministries, also collect, aggregate, and occasionally release estimates. The ministries establish their own standards and collection procedures independently of the SSB, although in principle the SSB is responsible for overseeing ministerial statistical work. In many cases the SSB endorses or adjusts ministry figures.

Although SSB and ministry statistical collection has improved substantially, stumbling blocks still exist. County-level units find they still exert little control over grass-roots statistical collection. Statistical forms generated at higher levels place a strain on local units, which find themselves struggling to accommodate even modest demands. Most Chinese statistical collection and aggregation, particularly at the local levels, are still carried out without the aid of trained personnel or machines. Considerable room remains for improvement of basic methods and coordination between independent systems.

The remainder of this appendix provides national aggregated series for basic statistical data categories relevant to agricultural production and consumption.[1] The primary purpose is to provide the reader with a quick impression of a wide range of estimates and a brief introduction to the difficulties incurred in their use. Official statistics are reported when available.[2] In years for which official statistics are unavailable, some idea of general trends may be obtained from estimates derived by foreign researchers. These figures are typically the researcher's attempted reconstruction of official data series, although they are occasionally supplemented, especially in the case of USDA or FAO series, with interpolations, trended material, or guesses based on incomplete provincial figures or non-quantitative information. The included foreign series have been selected either because they are well known, or because they contribute additional information unavailable in collections of Chinese source material.

Space limitations prevent the inclusion of a complete collection of national aggregated data categories, disaggregated material, and a thorough descriptive and analytic treatment of data and data sources. The reader is directed to Appendix B, where references for more complete information are listed. Also included are the names and addresses of organizations publishing statistics or quantitative studies on Chinese agriculture. Finally, Appendix B lists English language periodicals in which recently published statistical information may appear.

## Population

Until recently, population estimates for China were quite divergent. However, with the appearance of SSB estimates for 1975–1980, the communication of unpublished national estimates for 1969–1979 to international delegations, and the appearance of increasingly believable official provincial figures, analysts' estimates have converged. After the 1950s, few official estimates for population were made. Foreign analysts were dependent on rough figures published in nonofficial source material, or on an occasional casual reference to population in government reports or public speeches.

There have been two official midyear censuses with provincial breakdowns, one in 1953 and one in 1964. A census using computer tabulation is planned for midyear 1982. In addition, there have been other sets of official provincial estimates: one appearing outside of China in 1967–1968 totaling 710 million, one appearing after Mao's death in 1976 totaling 855 million, one for 1979 given to visiting international delegations, and an incomplete set for 1980 based on provincial SSB communiques. These provincial reports should be used with care as there are some important inconsistencies. For example, SSB estimates for vital rates in the 1977–1980 period do not match population totals on a national or provincial level.

Most official total population estimates are not derived from census data, but are based on example surveys, which are rather unlikely to be accurate, or on local registration materials subject to local reporting and aggregating difficulties. Estimates based on local materials may be expected, in general, to understate the true population owing to the likelihood of incomplete reports, but there are reasons for suspecting other systematic biases. As the rationing mechanism utilizes registration materials, there may be a tendency to underreport deaths. On the other hand, since the renewed emphasis on population policy, there may be incentive for cadres to exaggerate the success of local birth control programs.

The population series of the Foreign Demographic Analysis Division (FDAD) of the Department of Commerce are revised annually by John Aird, the foremost expert on Sino-demography outside China. The present approximated official estimates by Aird incorporate the recent official figures, adjusted as necessary to a year-end basis, for 1953, 1964, and 1969–1979. These data may still underestimate China's true population, although to a much lesser extent than series of several years ago. The three FDAD model estimates are all based on varying assumptions of higher birth and death rates, with the low estimate similar to the approximated official figures (Table A.1). Current FDAD figures are slightly lower than those previously estimated, owing in part to the recent disclosure by the Chinese of a large net population loss through premature death and fertility declines during the agricultural failures of the early 1960s.

United Nations estimates have suffered from the political necessity of conforming with the unrealistically low figures that the Chinese have reported in the past. Since population figures emanating from official sources have purportedly included Taiwan province in the past, so have U.N. figures. The U.N. series appearing in Table A.1 is substantially higher than previous versions, but well below other estimates despite the fact that it includes the population of Taiwan (17 million in 1979). The series thus assumes substantially lower rates of natural increase over the 1970s than do even the official or FDAD series. U.N. estimates are not discussed or documented in readily available publications, so justification for retention of such low figures is left open to question.

## Food Grain Production

The *Agricultural Yearbook of China 1980* food grain production series is the first complete production series published by the Chinese since 1959. Ex-

Table A.1. Population and Labor Force Estimates, 1949-1980

| Year | Total Population | | | | | | Total Labor Force | |
|---|---|---|---|---|---|---|---|---|
| | "Reconstructed Official"[a] (year-end total) | FDAD (year-end totals) (1980) | | | | U.N.[b] (midyear total) | Commune Labor Force "Reconstructed Official"[a] (year-end) (1980) | Agricultural Labor Force Agricultural Yearbook of China 1980 (1981) (year-end) |
| | | Approximated Official | Low Model | Intermediate Model | High Model | | | |
| | (million persons) | | | | | | (million persons) | |
| 1949 | 542 | | | | | | | |
| 1950 | 552 | | | | | | | |
| 1951 | 563 | | | | | | | |
| 1952 | 575 | 576 | 576 | 576 | 576 | | | |
| 1953 | 583[c] | 589 | 589 | 589 | 589 | | 207[c] | 173 |
| 1954 | 602 | 603 | 605 | 604 | 604 | | | |
| 1955 | 615 | 616 | 618 | 619 | 620 | | | |
| 1956 | 628 | 630 | 631 | 634 | 636 | | | |
| 1957 | 647[d] | 647 | 647 | 650 | 653 | | 238[c] | 193 |
| 1958 | 670[d] | 660 | 661 | 665 | 669 | | | |
| 1959 | | 666 | 674 | 679 | 684 | | | |
| 1960 | | 658 | 674 | 684 | 694 | | | |
| 1961 | | 641 | 663 | 679 | 695 | | 259[c] | 213 |
| 1962 | 673[e] | 659 | 665 | 684 | 703 | | | |
| 1963 | | 681 | 680 | 700 | 721 | | | |

|  | | | | | | | | |
|------|------|-----|-----|-----|-----|-----|--------|-----|
| 1964 | 691 c/ | 702 | 703 | 725 | 746 | | | |
| 1965 | **725** | 722 | 725 | 747 | 770 | | 287 c/ | 234 |
| 1966 | | 741 | 746 | 770 | 793 | | | |
| 1967 | | 761 | 765 | 791 | 816 | | | |
| 1968 | | 782 | 786 | 813 | 840 | | | |
| 1969 | 803 e/ | 803 | 808 | 837 | 866 | 812 | | |
| 1970 | 825 e/ | 826 | 829 | 860 | 890 | 826 | 345 c/ | 278 |
| 1971 | 844 e/ | 847 | 849 | 882 | 914 | 840 | | |
| 1972 | 868 | 868 | 902 | 936 | 854 | | | |
| 1973 | | 887 | 886 | 921 | 957 | 868 | | |
| 1974 | 905 e/ | 904 | 903 | 941 | 978 | 882 | 382 c/ | 295 |
| 1975 | 920 | 920 | 919 | 959 | 999 | 895 | | |
| 1976 | 933 | 933 | 932 | 975 | 1,017 | 908 | | |
| 1977 | 945 | 945 | 945 | 990 | 1,034 | 921 | | |
| 1978 | 958 | 958 | 958 | 1,005 | 1,051 | 933 | 406 c/ | 294 |
| 1979 | 971 | 971 | 971 | 1,020 | 1,069 | 945 | | |
| 1980 | 983 | 982 | 983 | 1,034 | 1,086 | | | |

Note: All estimates have been rounded to the nearest million persons and exclude Taiwan Province population unless otherwise noted.

a/  See Note 2 for definition.
b/  Includes Taiwan Province population.
c/  Not year-end figures; results of 1953 and 1964 midyear census.
d/  Coverage for estimate was unspecified. It probably was intended to include Taiwan Province population.
e/  These estimates were calculated from indirect data appearing in Chinese publications.

Table A.2.  Estimates of Total Food Grain Production in China, 1949-1980

| Year | Food Grain Production (including soybeans) (million tonnes) | | | | | Soybean Production (million tonnes) | | |
|---|---|---|---|---|---|---|---|---|
| | Agricultural Yearbook of China 1980 (1981) a/ | "Reconstructed Official" b/ | Wiens c/ (1980) | USDA (1980,1981) | FAO d/ (1975,1978) | "Reconstructed Official" e/ | Wiens (1980) | USDA (1980,1981) |
| 1949 | 113 | 111 | 133 | 113 | | 5.1 | 6.0 | 5.1 |
| 1950 | 132 | 130 | | 133 | | | | 8.1 |
| 1951 | 144 | 141 | | 144 | | | | 8.6 |
| 1952 | 164 | 164 | 167 | 164 | | 9.5 | 9.7 | 9.5 |
| 1953 | 167 | 163 | 170 | 167 | | 9.9 | 10.1 | 9.9 |
| 1954 | 170 | 166 | 171 | 170 | | 9.1 | 9.2 | 9.1 |
| 1955 | 184 | 180 | 185 | 184 | | 9.1 | 9.2 | 9.1 |
| 1956 | 193 | 188 | 187 | 193 | | 10.2 | 10.2 | 10.2 |
| 1957 | 195 | 191 | 195 | 195 | | 10.0 | 10.0 | 10.0 |
| 1958 | 200 | 196 | | 211 | | 10.5 | | 10.5 |
| 1959 | 170 | 166 | | 177 | | 11.5 | | 11.5 |
| 1960 | 144 | 139 | | 158 | | | | 8.2 |
| 1961 | 148 | 144 | 162/155 | 170 | 183 | | | 7.9 |
| 1962 | 160 | 155 | 174/160 | 182 | 196 | | | 7.7 |
| 1963 | 170 | 170 | 183 | 190 | 200 | | | 7.0 |
| 1964 | 188 | 188 | 200 | 207 | 212 | | | 6.9 |
| 1965 | 195 | 195 | 200/191 | 207 | 222 | 6.2 | | 6.8 |
| 1966 | 214 | 214 | 220 | 222 | 236 | | | 6.8 |
| 1967 | 218 | 218 | 230 | 237 | 242 | | | 7.0 |
| 1968 | 209 | 209 | | 222 | 237 | | | 6.5 |
| 1969 | 211 | 211 | | 226 | 245 | | | 6.2 |
| 1970 | 240 | 240 | 240 | 247 | 255 | 9.2 | | 6.9 |
| 1971 | 250 | 250 | 246 | 254 | 258 | | | 7.9 |
| 1972 | 240 | 240 | 240 | 249 | 252 | | | 8.7 |
| 1973 | 265 | 265 | 257 | 260 | 275 | 8.4 | | 10.0 |
| 1974 | 275 | 275 | 265 | 275 | 287 | | | 9.5 |
| 1975 | 285 | 285 | | 280 f/ | 298 | 10.0 | | 10.0 |
| 1976 | 286 | 286 | | 281 h/ | 306 | 6.6 | | 6.6 g/ |
| 1977 | 283 | 283 | | 283 h/ | 298 | 7.3 | | 7.3 g/ |
| 1978 | 305 | 305 | | 305 h/ | 310 | 7.6 | | 7.6 g/ |
| 1979 | 332 | 332 | | 332 h/ | | 7.5 | | 7.5 g/ |
| 1980 | 318 | 318 | | 318 h/ | | 7.9 | | 7.9 g/ |

*213*

Note: Although most countries exclude soybeans from total food grains, the Chinese do not. Thus, soybean production estimates (including green, yellow, and black soybeans) have been provided to allow calculation of Chinese total grain series excluding soybeans. All total food grain production series value tubers at one-fourth natural weight except the Agricultural Yearbook of China 1980 series (1963-1980) and the "reconstructed official" series (1949-1980) which use 1:5.

a/ This is the first up-to-date, complete and continuous food grain series published by the Chinese since 1959.

b/ These figures are the author's attempted reconstruction of an official series adjusted to consistently value tubers at 1:5. This series includes several debatable estimates and does not attempt to correct for hypothesized biases in the official estimation procedures.

c/ These figures have been adjusted by Wiens to correct the hypothesized biases in estimation of cultivated area, cropping intensity and yields. These data have not been adjusted for constant tuber valuation. The series includes competing estimates for 1961, 1962, and 1965.

d/ These figures are sums of all categories of FAO data included in the Chinese definition of food grains. Taiwan Province production has been deducted as necessary.

e/ See Note 2 for definition of "reconstructed official."

f/ The USDA has accepted official figures for rice, wheat, corn, and soybeans from 1976-1980. However, a revised total food grain production figure for 1976 has not yet appeared.

g/ USDA accepts official figures for 1976-1980. However, 1976-1980 soybean production numbers form a discontinuous series with pre-1976 estimates.

h/ USDA accepts official figures for 1977-1980. However, 1977-1980 total food grain production numbers form a discontinuous series with pre-1977 USDA estimates.

cept for minor adjustments, these figures will undoubtedly be accepted by the foreign research community unless further versions are published in China.

Currently Chinese food grains include rice, wheat, corn, millet, sorghum, barley, buckwheat, oats, proso-millet, small beans, green beans, broad beans, field peas, sweet and white potatoes, minor tubers (notably cassava), and green, yellow, and black soybeans. Tubers have been valued at both one-fourth and one-fifth of their natural weight. At present a one-to-five ratio is used. Soybean production has been included or excluded depending on the years under consideration. Confusion over when soybeans became part of food grain production accounts for some of the divergence in individual estimates. Recently Chinese officials have indicated that soybeans were included in total food grain production from 1958 and that tubers were valued at one-fifth their weight from 1963. The "reconstructed official" series is based on these assumptions. The Chinese have adjusted the *Agricultural Yearbook of China 1980* series to include soybeans since 1949, but continue to value tubers at differing rates. There has also been some confusion over which soybean production the Chinese count. According to official statements made to a 1979 Japanese delegation, only soybeans used for direct human consumption are included in total grain numbers. Occasionally it has been alleged that only marketed soybean output has been counted, and most recently Chinese officials reported that all soybean production is included in food grain output statistics.

It should be noted that definitions for food grain in general have varied among reporting localities, and the SSB may not have been able to make all of the appropriate adjustments. The "reconstructed official" series attempts to correct for definitional changes, but it still may not be the most accurate, especially for the 1950s. A considerable Western literature and a number of Chinese articles discuss systematic biases in estimation, especially for the 1949–1955 period. Wiens's figures for these years are an attempt, based on Chinese materials, to correct these problems, which include an underestimation of cultivated area (1949–1955), an overestimation of area sown to fine grains (1956), and an underestimation of yields (1949–1951). His efforts suggest that official figures do indeed underestimate significantly for the 1949–1951 period, but that by 1952 biases were corrected. Wiens's work, therefore, represents a general vindication of the official production estimates for the 1952–1957 period. Unfortunately, as the work was completed several years ago, most of the 1960–1974 entries are now obsolete.

The U.S. Department of Agriculture (USDA) and the U.S. Central Intelligence Agency (CIA) have regularly produced independent estimates less directly linked to Chinese media statements. Over time, however, and with the clear exception of the original 1958 and 1959 Great Leap inflated figures, these agencies have come to accept numbers increasingly close to the official ones. For the time being, however, there are serious discontinuities with the recently released SSB information, now generally accepted by USDA, and the department's previous series, sections of which are often included in current publications for years prior to 1977. The discontinuities are especially telling when grain statistics disaggregated by crop are examined (Table A.3).

The Food and Agriculture Organization (FAO) of the United Nations has included Taiwanese production in its figures for China since 1972. It should be noted that FAO figures with Taiwan subtracted and with tubers valued at one-fifth of their natural weights are still higher than the official series.

As with the USDA data on individual crops, the FAO disaggregated series exhibits discontinuities. This is especially true when, as opposed to their data supply tape, a series is constructed on the basis of individual *FAO Production Yearbook* entries. FAO delegations are beginning to receive new information from the Chinese that has not been available in the past, and the organization will no doubt accept the recent SSB figures, but previous entries must be regarded with great care.

### Livestock

In Table A.4 the "reconstructed official" and Groen and Kilpatrick livestock numbers are based on Ministry of Agriculture and State Statistical Bureau publications or indirect Chinese media information. Tang's series is a combination of official statements and a least-squares regression analysis of the relationship between livestock numbers and livestock exports and grain production. This is a useful approach if estimates must be made to supplement official data, but some of the reconstructions Tang used as bases are now outdated in some cases.

Although the quality of official estimates clearly declined for several years after midyear 1957 with the onset of the Great Leap Forward and resulting disruption in the agricultural sector, in most cases there appears to be no strong reason to reject official figures in favor of other estimates. The "reconstructed official" series, which makes use of the *Agricultural Yearbook of China 1980* estimates, appear to be the best available, with the possible exception of year-end 1957 hog stock figures, which may be exaggerated. The Groen and Kilpatrick year-end 1957 figure, also based on Chinese sources, is probably an improvement.

Another difficulty involving all reconstructions for 1960 through 1975 is the ambiguity over the date of stock estimates. Although official estimates

Table A.3.  Production of Major Food Grains, 1949-1980

| Year | Wheat | | | Rice (rough) | | | Maize | | Tubers a/ | | |
|---|---|---|---|---|---|---|---|---|---|---|---|
| | Agricultural Yearbook of China 1980 (1981) | USDA (1980) (1981) | Wiens (1980) | Agricultural Yearbook of China 1980 (1981) | USDA (1980) (1981) | Wiens (1980) | "Reconstructed Official" b/ | USDA (1980) (1981) | "Reconstructed Official" b/ (1981) | USDA (1980) (1981) | Wiens (1980) |
| | | | | (million tonnes) | | | | | | | |
| 1949 | 13.8 | 13.8 | 14.1 | 48.6 | 48.6 | 56.9 | (11.8) | 9.0 | 9.9 | 9.8 | 11.0 |
| 1950 | 15.0 c/ | 14.5 | | 55.1 | 55.1 | | | 11.8 | 12.4 | 12.4 | |
| 1951 | 17.2 | 17.2 | | 60.6 | 60.6 | | | 14.6 | 14.0 | 14.0 | |
| 1952 | 18.1 | 18.1 | 18.4 | 68.4 | 68.4 | 69.7 | 16.8 | 17.3 | 16.4 | 16.4 | 16.7 |
| 1953 | 18.3 | 18.3 | 18.6 | 71.3 | 71.2 | 72.6 | 16.7 | 17.4 | 16.7 | 16.6 | 17.0 |
| 1954 | 23.3 | 23.4 | 23.6 | 70.9 | 70.8 | 71.5 | 17.1 | 17.6 | 17.0 | 17.0 | 17.2 |
| 1955 | 23.0 | 23.0 | 23.2 | 78.0 | 78.0 | 78.7 | 20.3 | 21.4 | 18.9 | 18.9 | 20.3 |
| 1956 | 24.8 | 24.8 | 24.2 | 82.5 | 82.4 | 78.0 | 23.1 | 24.3 | 21.9 | 21.8 | 21.8 |
| 1957 | 23.6 | 23.6 | 23.7 | 86.8 | 86.8 | 86.8 | 21.4 d/ | 21.8 | 21.9 d/ | 21.9 | 21.9 |
| 1958 | 22.6 | 25.0 | | 80.9 | 93.0 | | 21.4 d/ | 23.7 | 45.4 d/ | 30.0 | |
| 1959 | 22.2 | 24.0 | | 69.4 | 79.0 | | | 15.1 | | 21.0 | |
| 1960 | 22.2 | 21.0 | | 59.7 | 73.0 | | | 13.0 | | 20.0 | |
| 1961 | 14.3 | 16.0 | | 53.6 | 78.0 | | | 16.0 | | 24.0 | |
| 1962 | 16.7 | 20.0 | | 63.0 | 78.0 | | | 19.1 | | 23.0 | |
| 1963 | 18.5 | 22.0 | | 73.8 | 80.0 | | | 20.2 | | 25.0 | |
| 1964 | 20.8 | 25.0 | | 83.0 | 90.0 | | | 21.3 | | 26.0 | |
| 1965 | 25.2 | 25.0 | 25.1 | 87.7 | 90.0 | | 23.7 | 23.0 | 24.8 | 25.0 | |
| 1966 | 25.3 | 28.0 | | 95.4 | 96.0 | | | 24.1 | | 25.0 | |
| 1967 | 28.5 | 28.0 | | 93.7 | 100.0 | | | 26.9 | | 26.0 | |
| 1968 | 27.5 | 24.0 | 27.5 | 94.5 | 95.0 | | | 24.7 | | 25.0 | |
| 1969 | 27.3 | 27.0 | | 95.1 | 99.0 | | | 25.0 | | 25.0 | |
| 1970 | 29.2 | 31.0 | | 110.0 | 110.0 | | 30.7 | 28.2 | 31.9 | 24.0 | |
| 1971 | 32.6 | 31.0 | | 115.2 | 117.0 | | | 27.8 | | 23.0 | |
| 1972 | 36.0 | 36.0 | 35.8 | 113.4 | 112.0 | | | 25.5 | | 23.0 | |
| 1973 | 35.2 | 35.0 | | 121.7 | 118.0 | | (38.6) | 29.9 | | 24.0 | |
| 1974 | 40.9 | 38.0 | | 123.9 | 127.5 | | | 33.2 | | 25.0 | |
| 1975 | 45.3 | 41.0 | | 125.6 | 126.5 | | 50.6 | 35.6 | | 25.0 | |

| 1976 | 50.4 | 50.5[e/] | 125.8 | 126.0[e/] | 48.2 | 48.0[e/] | 33.3 | 24.0[f/] |
| 1977 | 41.1 | 41.0[e/] | 128.6 | 128.6[e/] | 49.4 | 49.0[e/] | 37.1 | |
| 1978 | 53.8 | 54.0[e/] | 136.9 | 137.0[e/] | 55.9 | 55.9[e/] | 39.7 | |
| 1979 | 62.7 | 60.7[e/] | 143.8 | 143.7[e/] | 60.0 | 60.0[e/] | 35.6 | |
| 1980 | 54.2 | 54.2[e/] | 139.3 | 139.3[e/] | | 59.7[e/] | 34.8 | |

Note: Figures in parentheses were not given directly as absolute figures by Chinese officials or in official publications. All figures are reported in unprocessed form.

a/ All tuber figures are given on a one-to-four grain equivalent basis. All tubers include sweet potatoes, white potatoes, and small amounts of cassava, taro, and other minor roots and tubers.

b/ See Note 2 for definition of "reconstructed official."

c/ The only substantial revision made by the Chinese in the 1950s is for wheat production in 1950. Wheat production was revised upward from 14.5 million tonnes to 15.0 million tonnes.

d/ Due to extreme difficulties in reporting control during the Great Leap Forward period, these figures may be particularly unreliable.

e/ USDA figures for 1976-1980 adopted from official sources, predating the publication of the Agricultural Yearbook of China 1980, form a discontinous series with pre-1976 estimates.

f/ USDA has not yet revised its tuber series.

Table A.4.  Livestock, 1949-1980

(million head)

| Year | Hogs "Recon-structed Official" b/ | Hogs Groen and Kilpatrick (1978) | Hogs Tang c/ (1980) | Sheep & Goats "Recon-structed Official" b/ | Sheep & Goats Groen and Kilpatrick (1978) | Sheep & Goats Tang c/ (1980) | Large Animals a/ "Recon-structed Official" a/b/ | Large Animals a/ Groen and Kilpatrick (1978) | Large Animals a/ Tang c/ (1980) |
|---|---|---|---|---|---|---|---|---|---|
| 1949* | 57.8 | 57.8 | | 42.3 | 42.3 | | 60.0 | 59.8 | |
| 1950* | 64.0 | 64.0 | | 46.7 | 46.7 | | 65.4 | 65.3 | |
| 1951* | 74.4 | 74.4 | | 52.9 | 52.9 | | 70.4 | 70.4 | |
| 1952* | 89.8 | 89.8 | 93.0 | 61.8 | 61.8 | 66.9 | 76.5 | 76.2 | 78.3 |
| 1953* | 96.1 | 96.1 | 98.9 | 72.0 | 72.0 | 76.7 | 80.8 | 80.5 | 82.7 |
| 1954* | 101.7 | 101.7 | 94.8 | 81.3 | 81.3 | 82.8 | 85.3 | 85.0 | 86.2 |
| 1955* | 87.9 | 87.9 | 86.0 | 84.2 | 84.2 | 87.9 | 87.7 | 87.4 | 87.4 |
| 1956* | 84.0 | 84.0 | | 91.7 | 91.7 | | 87.7 | 87.4 | |
| 1956** | 98.0 | 97.8 | 98.0 | | | 93.9 | | | 86.1 |
| 1957* | 115.3 d/ | 115.3 | | (96.5) | | | (83.0) | | |
| 1957** | 145.9 | 127.8 | 115.0 | 98.6 | 98.6 | 98.6 | 83.8 | 83.5 | 83.5 |
| 1958** | 138.3 | | 160.0 | 95.7 | 108.0 | 108.9 | 77.7 | 85.1 | 85.1 |
| 1959** | 120.4 | | 136.1 | 111.7 | | 82.9 | 79.1 | | 81.8 |
| 1960** | 82.3 | | 105.5 | 112.8 | | 78.3 | 73.4 | | 79.6 |
| 1961** | 75.5 | | 101.7 | 123.9 | | 78.3 | 69.5 | | 73.4 |
| 1962** | 100.0 | | 115.5 | 134.7 | | 100.1 | 70.2 | | 70.9 |
| 1963** | 131.8 | | 136.6 | 137.5 | | 97.0 | 75.1 | | 76.8 |
| 1964** | 152.5 | | 148.3 | 136.7 | | 104.4 | 79.4 | | 82.9 |
| 1965** | 166.9 | 160.2 | 167.7 | 139.0 | | 115.7 | 84.2 | | 91.2 |
| 1966** | 193.4 | | 183.1 | 138.1 | | 119.4 | 87.4 | | 92.4 |
| 1967** | 190.1 | | 198.7 | 144.3 | | 130.6 | 89.8 | 85.0 | 86.4 |
| 1968** | 178.6 | | 198.3 | 144.2 | | 119.4 | 91.8 | | 83.8 |
| 1969** | 172.5 | | 190.8 | 140.2 | | 123.2 | 92.3 | | 87.0 |
| 1970** | 206.1 | | 210.4 | 147.0 | | 138.1 | 94.4 | | 87.8 |
| 1971** | 250.4 | 196.2 | 230.9 | 150.1 | | 130.1 | 95.4 | | 92.1 |
| 1972** | 263.7 | 217.8 | 259.9 | 149.3 | 147.0 | 148.2 | 95.8 | 95.0 | 95.0 |
| 1973** | 257.9 | 248.3 | 233.5 | 157.3 | | 145.6 | 97.2 | | 97.9 |
| 1974** | 260.8 | 241.9 | 252.8 | 160.9 | | 157.8 | 97.5 | | 100.8 |
| 1975** | 281.2 | 260.0 | 268.2 | 163.4 | | 160.6 | 96.9 | | 103.8 |

|         |       |     |       |       |     |       |      |       |
|---------|-------|-----|-------|-------|-----|-------|------|-------|
| 1976**  | 287.2 |     | 272.1 | 158.2 |     | 162.1 | 95.0 | 106.9 |
| 1977**  | 291.8 |     | 273.5 | 161.4 |     | 160.6 | 93.8 | 110.1 |
| 1978*   | 297.0 | 280 |       | 176.9 | 160 |       | 93.8 |       |
| 1978**  | 301.3 |     |       | 169.2 |     |       | 93.9 |       |
| 1979*   | 309.5 |     |       | 190.2 |     |       | 94.3 |       |
| 1979**  | 319.7 |     |       | 183.1 |     |       | 94.6 |       |
| 1980*   | 314.0 |     |       | 206.1 |     |       | 95.3 |       |
| 1980**  | 305.4 |     |       | 187.3 |     |       | 95.2 |       |

* Midyear
** Year-end
*/** Apply to "reconstructed official" and Groen and Kilpatrick series only.

a/ These include cattle, oxen, yaks, buffalo, horses, mules, asses, and camels except for the Groen and Kilpatrick series and Tang series for 1949 and 1952-1957, which exclude camels.

b/ See Note 2 for definition. Parenthesized figures have been calculated and rounded from indirect quantitative data.

c/ Year-end figures throughout.

d/ The 1957 hogstock figure is subject to greater skepticism than most of the current official 1950s livestock data. All the included "reconstructed official" 1958 figures and the 1959 figures for hogs and large animals are recent official downward revisions.

were shifted from midyear to a year-end basis in 1957, both midyear and year-end estimates are available from 1977 and were probably synthesized in China for at least a portion of the intervening years. Chinese material upon which previous foreign estimates for 1960-1975 have been based has seldom specified the month of the stock estimate. There may be important differences between midyear and year-end stocks of hogs, sheep, and goats. Hog numbers, in particular, sometimes drop by large percentages in a single year, depending upon slaughter rates. Recent Chinese publications, such as the *Agricultural Yearbook of China 1980* and the *Annual Economic Report of China 1981,* have linked midyear estimates for 1949-1956 with year-end estimates for 1957 and 1977-1979 in their purportedly year-end series. This implies, but does not guarantee, that the 1958-1976 year-end figures from these publications are indeed year-end estimates.

Little work has been done to approximate the margin of error of the official estimates once their numerical value is ascertained. Because most draft animals are collectively owned, and because sheep and goat herds are higly concentrated geographically, estimates for these stocks are likely to be more accurate than for hogs that have been raised primarily on private plots for most of PRC history. Poultry stock figures for China are particularly unreliable and hence not included. Total poultry stocks, predominantly chickens, but including several hundred million ducks and geese, are probably well over one billion birds.

### Cultivated and Sown Area and Multiple Cropping

Chinese cultivated area figures, especially for the 1950s, have been the subject of debate and criticism. Several scholars, represented here by Chao (Table A.5), have maintained that increases in official cultivated area statistics were not the result of land reclamation, as the Chinese claimed, but simply the discovery and addition of unregistered lands. In contrast, Wiens's analysis of the data has led him to believe that most increases between 1949 and 1956 were real, with the exception of two million hectares clearly identified in Chinese publications as previously unregistered land. This debate has not been fully resolved.

Although most scholars, including the Chinese, agree that cultivated area remained the same or decreased slightly since 1956, questions remain as to the level at which cultivated hectarage stabilized. Official Chinese statistics currently place total cultivated area from the late 1960s to the present at about 100 million hectares, although 107 million hectares was retained as the official figure throughout the '60s and most of the '70s. More recently Chinese government sources are said to be considering an upward revision of cultivated area to about 2 billion mou (133 million hectares) on the basis of their analysis of U.S. satellite photographs. Although figures based on satellite information are highly questionable, the idea that cultivated land is probably underestimated under present statistical collection methods is not unfounded. Several important coincident reporting biases probably exist. Farmers are motivated to conceal producing land to escape taxation, and cadres may also underreport so as to improve per area yields on paper. Nevertheless, the best available current cultivated area statistics are official figures as reported.

Throughout much of China, sown area exceeds cultivated area because more than one crop per year is planted on a given plot of land. This practice is particularly common in rice-growing areas, where two and sometimes three crops can be harvested each year. The multiple-cropping index is a measure of total sown hectarage as a percentage of cultivated area (Table A.5).

Multiple-cropping statistics, especially for the post-1960 period, are so scarce that there is no reasonable basis for questioning the recent Chinese figures for 1965–1979. In particular, Tang's assumption of increase in the late 1970s seems suspect. Although there was official pressure to raise cropping intensity, many localities had difficulty in making the shift. In some cases total production even fell, and in others production rose, but the additional costs were so great that net incomes declined, and cropping reverted to previous patterns.

Most of China's sown area is planted to food grains (Tables A.5, A.6). All estimates roughly agree that food grains, including soybeans and tubers, have occupied 80 to 90 percent of total sown area throughout PRC history, declining somewhat in recent years. The clearest shift among grains since the 1950s has been an increase in hectarage sown to corn at the expense of other coarse grains, such as millet and sorghum, and a fall in soybean sown area, which is only gradually being redressed.

### Irrigated Area

Although historically China had very developed irrigation systems, most were located in the south and central provinces where paddy rice is traditionally grown. Thus, since 1949, expansion in irrigated area has been concentrated in north China where returns are greater. However, significant improvements in the quality of irrigation throughout China as a whole have made steady yield increases possible (Table A.7).

Even though irrigated area has grown markedly since 1949, year-to-year expansion has varied with the political climate. When the Communist party came to power they found China's irrigation systems in disarray. Subsequently considerable rural labor was mobilized, both to improve existing systems and to build new small-scale facilities at the local level. However,

Table A.5. Cultivated Area, Multiple Cropping Index and Food Grain Sown Area, 1949-1980.

| Year | Cultivated Area | | | Multiple Cropping Index | | | Food grain Sown Area (including soybeans) | | |
|---|---|---|---|---|---|---|---|---|---|
| | "Reconstructed Official" a/ b/ | Chao (1970) | Wiens (1980) | "Reconstructed Official" a/ | Wiens(1980) and Jones(1967) | Tang (1980) | Agricultural Yearbook of China 1980 (1981) | Wiens (1980) | USDA (1980, 1981) |
| | (millions hectare) | | | (percent) | | | (million hectares) | | |
| 1949 | 97.9/97.8 b/ | 111.1 | 99.9 | | 121.1 c/ | | 110.0 | 112.4 | 109.9 |
| 1950 | 100.4 | 111.1 | 102.4 | | | | 114.4 | | 114.4 |
| 1951 | 103.7 b/ | 111.0 | 105.7 | | | | 117.8 | | 117.8 |
| 1952 | 107.9/108 b/ | 110.9 | 109.9 | 130.9 | 133.5 c/ | 130.9 | 124.0 | 126.3 | 124.0 |
| 1953 | 108.5 | 110.8 | 110.5 | 132.7 | 134.8 c/ | 132.7 | 126.6 | 129.0 | 126.7 |
| 1954 | 109.4 | 110.8 | 110.4 | 135.3 | 136.8 c/ | 135.3 | 129.0 | 130.2 | 129.0 |
| 1955 | 110.2 | 111.5 | 111.2 | 137.2 | 137.6 c/ | 137.2 | 129.8 | 131.0 | 129.8 |
| 1956 | 111.8 | 112.4 | 111.8 | 142.3 | 139.7 c/ | 142.3 | 136.3 | 133.4 | 136.3 |
| 1957 | 111.8/112 b/ | 111.8 | 111.8 | 140.6 | 140.6 c/ | 140.6 | 133.6 | 132.2 | 133.6 |
| 1958 | 107.8 | 107.8 | | 145.0 | | 145.0 | 127.6 | | 131.2 |
| 1959 | 107.3 | 106.7 | | | | 141.2 | 116.0 | | 118.7 |
| 1960 | | 105.7 | | | 133.0 d/ | 137.0 | 122.4 | | 128.3 |
| 1961 | | 104.0 | | | | 132.8 | 121.4 | | 127.2 |
| 1962 | 106.7 | 103.3 | | | | 136.1 | 121.6 | | 126.8 |
| 1963 | | 102.2 | | | | 139.4 | 120.7 | | 126.7 |
| 1964 | | 102.2 | | | | 142.6 | 122.1 e/ | 119.2 | 130.1 |
| 1965 | 102.2/103.6 b/ | 102.2 | | 138 | 143.1 d/ | 145.8 | 119.6 e/ | 120.2 | 130.7 |
| 1966 | | | | | | 145.4 | 121.0 | | 131.9 |
| 1967 | | | | | | 145.6 | 119.2 | | 135.3 |
| 1968 | | | | | | 145.9 | 116.2 | | 135.9 |
| 1969 | | | | | | 146.4 | 117.6 | | 137.1 |
| 1970 | 101.1 b/ | | | 142 | | 147.2 | 119.3 | | 137.8 |
| 1971 | 106 | | | | | 148.9 | 120.8 | | 139.6 |
| 1972 | | | | | | 149.9 | 121.2 e/ | | 140.6 |
| 1973 | 107/100 b/ | | | 149 | | 151.6 | 121.2 e/ | | 141.7 |
| 1974 | 107 | | | | | 153.2 | 121.0 | | 143.5 |
| 1975 | 99.7 b/ | | | 151 | | 154.9 | 121.1 | | 145.6 |

| | | | | | |
|------|--------|-----|-------|-------|----------|
| 1976 | | | 156.4 | 120.7 | 146.5 f/ |
| 1977 | 99.3 b/ | 150 | 157.9 | 120.4 | f/ |
| 1978 | 99.4 b/ | 151 | | 120.6 | 120.6 f/ |
| 1979 | | 149 | | 119.3 g/ | 119.0 f/ |
| 1980 | 99.5 b/ | | | 115.3 g/ | |

a/ See Note 2 for definition of "reconstructed official."
b/ Figures have been quoted recently. All others in the cultivated area series appeared at the time for which they are listed. This explains the large differences in some years between the two essentially separate series.
c/ These figures are revisions of official estimates by Thomas Wiens (1980).
d/ These figures are estimates by Edwin Jones (1967).
e/ Crop distribution percentages in a recent Institute of Geography publication would put the 1965 figure at around 128 million hectares and the 1973 figure at 120.4 million hectares.
f/ Although the USDA has revised its series for rice, wheat, corn and soybeans for 1976-1980, revised total food grain sown area figures for 1976, 1977 and 1980 have not yet appeared. The 1978-1979 figures adopted here are inconsistent with the prior data.
g/ This figure did not appear in Agricultural Yearbook of China 1980. It is based on media sources that claim a 5.3 million hectare decline since 1978.

Table A.6. Estimates of Area Sown to Major Food Grains, 1949–1980

(million hectares)

| Year | Wheat — Agricultural Yearbook of China 1980 (1981) | Wheat — USDA (1980)(1981) | Wheat — Wiens (1980) | Rice — Agricultural Yearbook of China 1980 (1981) | Rice — USDA (1980)(1981) | Rice — Wiens (1980) | Maize — "Reconstructed Official" c/ | Maize — USDA (1980)(1981) | Soybeans a/ — "Reconstructed Official" c/ | Soybeans a/ — USDA (1980)(1981) | Soybeans a/ — Wiens (1980) | Tubers b/ — "Reconstructed Official" c/ | Tubers b/ — USDA (1980)(1981) | Tubers b/ — Wiens (1980) |
|------|------|------|------|------|------|------|------|------|------|------|------|------|------|------|
| 1949 | 21.5 | 21.5 | 22.0 | 25.7 | 25.7 | 26.3 | 10.3 | 11.0 | 8.2 | 8.3 | 8.5 | 7.0 | 7.0 | 7.2 |
| 1950 | 22.8 | 22.8 |      | 26.2 | 26.1 |      |      | 11.5 | 9.6 | 9.6 |      | 7.7 | 7.7 | 7.7 |
| 1951 | 23.1 | 23.1 |      | 26.9 | 26.9 |      |      | 12.0 | 10.8 | 10.8 |      | 8.3 | 8.3 | 8.3 |
| 1952 | 24.8 | 24.8 | 25.3 | 28.4 | 28.4 | 28.9 | 12.6 | 12.9 | 11.7 | 11.7 | 11.9 | 8.7 | 8.7 | 8.9 |
| 1953 | 25.6 | 25.6 | 26.1 | 28.3 | 28.7 | 28.8 | 13.1 | 13.7 | 12.4 | 12.4 | 12.6 | 9.0 | 9.0 | 9.2 |
| 1954 | 27.0 | 27.0 | 27.2 | 28.7 | 28.7 | 29.0 | 13.2 | 13.5 | 12.7 | 12.7 | 12.8 | 9.8 | 9.0 | 9.8 |
| 1955 | 26.7 | 26.7 | 27.0 | 29.2 | 29.2 | 29.4 | 14.6 | 15.4 | 11.4 | 11.4 | 11.6 | 10.1 | 9.8 | 9.8 |
| 1956 | 27.3 | 27.3 | 26.6 | 33.3 | 33.3 | 31.5 | 17.7 | 18.6 | 12.0 | 12.0 | 12.0 | 11.0 | 10.0 | 10.0 |
| 1957 | 27.5 | 27.5 | 27.5 | 32.2 | 32.2 | 32.2 | 14.9 | 15.2 | 12.7 | 12.7 | 11.3 | 10.5 | 11.0 | 10.1 |
| 1958 | 25.8 | 26.6 |      | 31.9 | 32.7 |      | 16.3d/ | 16.5 | 9.8d/ | 9.9 |      | 16.3d/ | 10.5 | 11.0 |
| 1959 | 23.6 | 24.3 |      | 29.0 | 29.7 |      | 13.0d/ | 11.7 | 9.5d/ | 9.9 |      | 11.6d/ | 10.5 | 10.5 |
| 1960 | 27.3 | 26.8 |      | 29.6 | 31.5 |      |      | 11.9 |      | 9.3 |      |      | 16.3 |      |
| 1961 | 25.6 | 24.6 |      | 26.3 | 31.0 |      |      | 12.0 |      | 9.3 |      |      | 12.5 |      |
| 1962 | 25.1 | 24.4 |      | 26.9 | 29.3 |      |      | 12.1 |      | 8.3 |      |      | 13.3 |      |
| 1963 | 23.8 | 24.2 |      | 27.7 | 28.2 |      |      | 12.3 | 8.0d/ | 7.9 |      |      | 14.1 |      |
| 1964 | 25.4 | 25.5 | 25.3 | 29.6 | 29.5 | 28.9 | 15.7 | 12.4 |      | 8.0 | 8.8 |      | 13.2 |      |
| 1965 | 24.7 | 25.5 | 24.0 | 29.8 | 29.8 | 28.2 |      | 12.6 | 8.6 | 8.3 | 7.1 |      | 13.3 |      |
| 1966 | 23.9 | 25.0 |      | 30.5 | 30.3 |      |      | 12.7 |      | 8.1 |      | 11.2 | 12.6 |      |
| 1967 | 25.3 | 25.5 |      | 30.4 | 30.3 |      |      | 12.9 |      | 8.0 |      |      | 13.0 |      |
| 1968 | 24.7 | 25.0 | 24.8 | 29.9 | 30.0 |      |      | 13.0 |      | 8.2 |      |      | 12.6 |      |
| 1969 | 25.1 | 25.3 |      | 30.4 | 30.6 |      | 14.6 | 13.2 | 8.4 | 8.0 |      |      | 12.8 |      |
| 1970 | 25.5 | 25.6 |      | 32.4 | 31.5 |      |      | 13.3 |      | 8.0 |      |      | 12.5 |      |
| 1971 | 25.6 | 25.9 | 25.6 | 34.9 | 32.9 |      |      | 13.4 |      | 8.0 |      | 10.3 | 12.9 |      |
| 1972 | 26.3 | 26.2 |      | 35.1 | 33.6 |      |      | 13.5 |      | 8.3 |      |      | 12.3 |      |
| 1973 | 26.4 | 26.5 |      | 35.1 | 34.4 |      | 16.5e/ | 14.5 | 7.4e/ | 9.1 |      |      | 12.6 |      |
| 1974 | 27.1 | 27.2 |      | 35.5 | 35.1 |      |      | 15.5 |      | 9.1 |      |      | 12.2 |      |
| 1975 | 27.7 | 27.7 |      | 35.7 | 35.5 |      | 19.9 | 16.5 |      | 8.8 |      |      | 12.2 |      |
| 1976 | 28.4 | 28.4f/ |      | 36.2 | 36.2f/ |      | 19.2 | 19.2f/ | 6.7 | 9.1f/ |      | 10.4 | 11.8g/ |      |
| 1977 | 28.1 | 28.0f/ |      | 35.5 | 35.6f/ |      | 19.7 | 19.6f/ | 6.8 | 6.7f/ |      | 11.3 |      |      |
| 1978 | 29.2 | 29.2f/ |      | 34.4 | 34.4f/ |      | 20.0 | 20.2f/ | 7.1 | 6.8f/ |      | 11.8 |      |      |
| 1979 | 29.4 | 29.4f/ |      | 33.9 | 33.8f/ |      | 21.0 | 20.2f/ | 7.2 | 7.2f/ |      | 11.0 |      |      |
| 1980 |      | 28.9f/ |      |      | 33.4f/ |      |      | 19.9f/ |      | 7.3f/ |      |      |      |      |

a/ Soybeans refer to green, yellow, and black soybeans.
b/ Tubers include Irish potatoes, sweet potatoes, cassava, taro and other roots and tubers. Cassava sown area has been around a half million hectares in recent years. Sweet potato sown area has typically occupied about 80 percent of the total area sown to tubers, but may have declined somewhat in recent years.
c/ See Note 2 for definition of "reconstructed official."
d/ These are unsourced CIA reconstructions of official data.
e/ These figures were not given as absolute quantities, but as increments over base years.
f/ USDA figures for 1976-1980, adopted for the most part from official sources, form a discontinuous series with pre-1976 estimates.
g/ USDA has not yet revised its tuber series.

Table A.7. Irrigated Area, 1949–1980

| Year | Shuili Fadian (1957) | Sum of Provincial Data | Great Leap Forward Claims | Ten Great Years (1960) | Treatise on Agricultural Geography (1980) | Annual Economic Report of China 1981 (1981) | Post-1964 "Irrigated Area" Series Based on Published Increments[a] | "Effectively Irrigated Area" | "High & Stable Yield Area" |
|---|---|---|---|---|---|---|---|---|---|
| | | | | | (million hectares) | | | | |
| 1949 | 20.3 | 14.8 | 15.3 | 16.0 | 25.7 | 26.1 | 16.0[b] | | |
| 1950 | 20.8 | 15.3 | | 16.7 | | | | | |
| 1951 | 21.8 | 16.9 | | 18.7 | | | | | |
| 1952 | 23.4 | 19.1 | | 21.3 | | 30.6 | | 20.0 | |
| 1953 | 24.0 | 20.6 | | 22.0 | | | | | |
| 1954 | 24.8 | 21.8 | | 23.3 | | | | | |
| 1955 | 26.1 | 23.4 | | 24.7 | | | | | |
| 1956 | 36.0 | 28.9 | | 32.0 | | | | | |
| 1957 | | 35.7 | 34.7 | 34.7 | 39.8 | 28.2 | 29.1[c] | 27.3 | |
| 1958 | | | 66.7 | 66.7 | | | 40.6[c] | | |
| 1959 | | | 71.3 | | | | | | |
| 1960 | | | | | | | | | |
| 1961 | | | | | | | 60.6[d] | | |
| 1962 | | | | | | | | | |
| 1963 | | | | | | | | | |
| **1964** | | | | | | | | | |
| 1965 | | | | | 35.1 | 35.1 | 33.8 | 33.0 | |
| 1966 | | | | | | | 35.1 | 33.1 | |
| 1967 | | | | | | | 37.8 | | |
| 1968 | | | | | | | | | |
| 1969 | | | | | | | | | |
| 1970 | | | | | | | 40.1 | | 25–30 |
| 1971 | | | | | | | 41.4 | | |
| 1972 | | | | | | | 45.8[b][e] | | |
| 1973 | | | | | | | 43.3[e] | | |
| 1974 | | | | | | | 45.3 | | 33 |
| 1975 | | | | | | | 48.1 | 43.3 | 34 |
| 1976 | | | | | | 46.2 | | | 34 |
| 1977 | | | | | 47.7 | | | | |
| 1978 | | | | | | | 46.7[b][e] | | |
| 1979 | | | | | | 47.7 | 47.3[b] | 45.0 | 22[e][f] |
| 1980 | | | | | | | 48.0[b] | | |

Note: This table includes estimates of irrigated area under various definitions. All estimates are based on material from Chinese publications and are for cultivated not crop area irrigated. The Treatise on Agricultural Geography and Annual Economic Report figures include rainfed paddy, which in recent years is a very small portion of the total. Unfortunately, definitions vary, not only among series, but also for the same series over time.

a/ The post-1964 series is composed of 5 absolute figures (1949, 1973, 1977, 1978, 1979) given by the Ministry of Water Conservancy and estimates based on increments for particular periods. It is not consistent with the Ten Great Years series and presumes that the official criteria for designation of "irrigated area" have changed at least once since the publication of Ten Great Years. All information used in forming this series postdates 1964 and all but the 1964 data postdate 1972. This series illustrates the problems that occur when absolute figures and increments from different sources are combined. The implied declines in irrigated area in 1973 and 1978 are probably due to this problem. All figures have been substantially rounded.

b/ Figures recently reported or endorsed by the Ministry of Water Conservancy. The 1979 figure is not an absolute figure, but is based on an increment of 15 million mu (or 1 million hectares) (assumed to be net) over the 46.7 million hectare figure reported for 1978. At an October 1980 conference attended by members of the Ministry of Water Conservancy, "current" irrigated area was variously given as 710 million mu (47.3 million hectares) and 720 million mu (48 million hectares). It is assumed that these figures refer to 1979 and 1980 respectively.

c/ This figure purportedly represents irrigated area, that satisfied the National Agricultural Development Program (1956) criteria. "Effectively irrigated" area should exceed this figure and "high and stable yield area" should be well below it.

d/ The claimed total increase in effective irrigation from 1958-1960 was over 20 million hectares.

e/ The apparent drop in "high and stable yield area" is probably not real, as different sources were used to assemble these series.

f/ The 1979 figure was approximately the same as the 1978 figure. "High and stable yield area" is described in official sources as "half the irrigated area of 700 million mu" (literally, 23.3 million hectares) and "less than one-fourth of the total cultivated land" (less than 24.9 million hectares).

many projects were hastily constructed, so that actual decreases in irrigated area occurred in the late 1950s and early 1960s. Proliferation of local projects in north China resulted in elevation of the water table and the consequent abandonment of land due to waterlogging and salinization. In particular, projects in the lower sections of the Yellow River had to be abandoned due to silt buildup in irrigation networks. Recovery and expansion proceeded in the middle 1960s when total irrigated area clearly surpassed 1957 levels. Since 1964, total irrigated area has increased by around 3 percent per year, with the largest documented increments occurring in 1964-1966 and in 1972.

Table A.7 includes various irrigated area estimates recorded in Chinese sources. A quick perusal of the data shows that estimates vary widely from series to series. Discrepancies can be attributed largely to definitional differences, although such differences sometimes exist within a single series. Another problem is that definitions have occasionally differed among provinces within a single year.

The estimates appearing in *Shuili Fadian* (Hydroelectric Generation), an official publication of the Ministry of Water Conservancy, are based on irrigation project capacity. In contrast, the *Ten Great Years* series probably narrowed its definition, at the least for the 1949-1950 figures, to include only areas that could sustain crop growth for 30-50 days without rain. Although the *Ten Great Years* series provides more accurate estimates of how much area actually received irrigation water, it is uncertain how precisely lands were assessed. Conversely the 1958 figure from the *Ten Great Years* series and the Great Leap Forward claims are clear overestimates of irrigated area, as they include land within the irrigation project command areas not yet served by canals or tubewells.

By 1960, a further distinction was made between "irrigated area" and "effectively irrigated area," that is land that is actually able to receive irrigation from currently operable facilities. The "effectively irrigated" series show declines between 1960 and 1965. Decline can be attributed to the necessity of terminating irrigation over large tracts of land due to salinization and waterlogging in the north  and to a sustained effort to exclude land that is not "effectively irrigated."

Definitional inconsistencies continue into the 1970s. Chinese officials were careful to stipulate that the 1973 Ministry of Water Conservancy figure (post-1964 "irrigated area") referred to irrigated area "at current standards of measurement." The standards are based on a set of water requirements for each crop in each region. This implies that the inclusion of a particular parcel of land in the irrigated area statistics depends not only on the facilities for irrigation, but also on the distribution of hectarage among crops and the particular strains of those crops currently adopted, as well as average rainfall and cropping intensity. Therefore, the classification of a parcel could be altered without a change in actual irrigation facilities. Additional criteria were introduced with the use of the term "high and stable yield area." Among other requirements, "high and stable yield areas" must have "guaranteed irrigation," that is, they must be effectively irrigated and capable of withstanding 60-80 days of drought.

In 1980, the Institute of Geography published estimated percentages for 1949, 1957, 1965, and 1978 of cultivated land devoted to paddy and to dryland cultivation, together with percentages of irrigated dryland. These data can be used with official cultivated area figures to approximate total irrigated area for these years. The *Annual Economic Report of China 1981* also includes scattered historical estimates for paddy and irrigated dryland. Figures derived from these two publications include area irrigated by manmade means as well as rainfed paddy, and so differ from other irrigated area series, especially during the 1950s. These materials are clearly the most authoritative that have yet appeared, although definitional consistency is still questionable, and the discrepancies between the two sources are still unexplained.

In conclusion, differences between the 1949-1956 (*Ten Great Years*) and the late 1970s definitions may have amounted to an apparent gross loss of 5-10 million hectares of irrigated area. That is, if the 1956 definition was applied to current conditions, "irrigated area" would probably be estimated at 5-10 million hectares above currently published figures. The recent publication of "effective irrigation" figures for 1952 and 1957 at least partially addresses this difficulty. Aside from the 1958 and 1959 overreporting problem, drops in provincial or national estimates, insufficiently substantiated by known deterioration in irrigation facilities, seem to have occurred in the early 1960s, the early 1970s, 1976, 1977, and possibly 1979.

We should keep in mind, however, that drops may not simply indicate a tightening of standards, but instead may be a reflection of: (1) an incorrect assumption or error on the part of the reporting individual, Chinese or foreign; (2) a downward revision of exaggerated claims; (3) the difference between planned and actual facilities completed; or (4) actual deterioration in existing facilities – of which there is some clear evidence.

### Installed Capacity of Irrigation and Drainage Equipment

Data on total horsepower of irrigation and drainage equipment in use are often used as irrigation quality indicators. Although we must note major discrepancies among the various data series, it is apparent that installed capacity, and hence irrigation quality, rose very sharply in the past two decades (Table A.8).

Table A.8.  Irrigation and Drainage Pumps, Tubewells, and Mechanically Irrigated Area, 1949-1980

| Year | Wiens[b] (1980) | Chao[b] (1970) | Groen and Kilpatrick[b] (1978) | Vermeer[b] (1977) | State Statistical[c] Bureau | Agricultural Yearbook of China 1980 (1981) | Electrical Equipment Only Stone[b] (1980) | Number of Tubewells With Pumps | Area Benefiting From Mechanized Irrigation |
|---|---|---|---|---|---|---|---|---|---|
| | Installed Capacity of Irrigation and Drainage Equipment[a] | | | | | | | | |
| | (thousand horsepower) | | | | | | | (thousands) | (million hectares) |
| 1949 | | | | | | | | | |
| 1950 | | 12 | 97 | 100 | | 100 | | | 0.3 |
| 1951 | | | 118 | | | | | | |
| 1952 | | | | | 128 | 128 | | | |
| 1953 | | | | | | 141 | | | 0.3 |
| 1954 | | 176 | 338 | 160 | 176 | 164 | 160 | | 0.4[d] |
| 1955 | | 220 | 508 | 226 | 220 | 208 | | | 0.6 |
| 1956 | | 390 | 560 | 396 | 390 | 385 | | | 0.9 |
| 1957 | 560 | 560 | 1,280 | 545 | 564 | 564 | | | 1.2 |
| 1958 | | 1,610 | 2,535 | 2,145 | | 1,640 | | | |
| 1959 | | 3,380 | 4,145 | 3,345 | | 3,126 | | | |
| 1960 | 1,220 | 5,900 | 4,845 | 5,350 | | 4,814 | | | 5.3 |
| 1961 | 2,230 | 4,500 | 5,800 | 5,300 | | 5,368 | | | 6.1 |
| 1962 | 3,600 | 4,000 | 6,440 | 5,800 | | 6,147 | | | 5.5 |
| 1963 | 5,200 | 6,000 | 7,300 | 6,440 | | 6,934 | 2,040 | | 6.3[d] |
| 1964 | 7,280 | 7,300 | 8,450 | 6,000 | | 7,585 | | | 5.6[d] [f] |
| 1965 | 8,570 | 8,570 | 9,980 | 7,000 | | 9,074 | 7,600[e] | 100 | 8.1 |
| 1966 | | 10,400 | 10,695 | 8,333 | | | | 170 | |
| 1967 | | | 12,742 | | | | | | |
| 1968 | | | 14,790 | | | | | | |
| 1969 | | | 16,911 | | | | | | |
| 1970 | | | 20,000 | | | 18,249 | 15,300 | | 15.0 |
| 1971 | 20,000 | | 24,016 | | | 19,848 | | 590 | 16.6 |
| 1972 | | | 30,000 | | | 24,645 | | 800 | 17.8 |
| 1973 | | | 36,000 | 20,000[g] | | 34,621 | | 1,200 | 19.8 |
| 1974 | | | 43,000 | 28,500 | | 40,865 | 30,000[f] | 1,600 | 21.7 |
| 1975 | 40,000 | | | 40,000 | | 48,666 | | 1,700 | 22.9 |

| | | | | | |
|------|----------|--------|--------|----------|-------|------|
| 1976 | 47,000^f/ | 60,046 | | 47,000^f/ | 1,800 | 24.2 |
| 1977 | | 65,575 | 54,166 | | 2,300 | 24.3 |
| 1978 | | 71,221 | 60,046 | | 2,100 | 24.9 |
| 1979 | | 74,654 | 65,575 | | 2,090 | 25.3 |
| 1980 | | | 71,221 | | | |

a/ With the exception of the "electrical equipment only" column, these data include both electrical and combustion machinery. All figures assumed to be year-end stocks unless otherwise noted.

b/ These estimates by foreign analysts, predating publication of the Agricultural Yearbook of China 1980, are all based on published Chinese materials. Only the Groen and Kilpatrick series includes interpolations and estimates based on production of equipment.

c/ These estimates have been collected from various SSB publications. Some of the figures for the 1950s may be outdated.

d/ This figure includes only area irrigated electrically.

e/ The rapid expansion of electrically driven stock implied by this figure seems doubtful.

f/ These figures do not refer to year-end stocks.

g/ This figure refers to machinery connected with pumpwells only.

The *Agricultural Yearbook of China 1980* includes the first nearly complete series ever published by the Chinese. Previously occasional figures were available, but only on a year-to-year basis. Other included series based on occasional Chinese data illustrate the difficulties of establishing a "reconstructed official" series on the basis of concurrent Chinese materials. Unlike data in other categories, the irrigation and drainage equipment series from the *Agricultural Yearbook* differ for most years from all previously published figures, although sometimes the differences are minor. Over the years, some confusion was introduced when researchers were unable to distinguish between data for total stocks and for stocks of electrical equipment only, and between calendar year-end data and data reflecting stocks at the end of the water conservancy year in September.

Another major problem inherent in capacity figures is that much equipment that is no longer operative is counted. Of the 1.60 million horsepower "in use" in 1958, only 1.04 million horsepower (65 percent) were still in working order by 1962. An additional 11 percent of total horsepower distributed between 1959 and 1961 was probably in disrepair by 1962. In the late 1970s Chinese surveys suggested that about 70 percent of existing stock was actually capable of operating.

Another proxy for quality of irrigation is the area of farmland under mechanized irrigation. There was clearly a downward revision in this category in 1979, probably reflecting a tightening of standards to exclude areas not actually receiving effective mechanization.

In the mid-1960s with increasing shifts to more intensive cropping patterns, tubewell construction helped relieve the constraints of insufficient surface water, as well as waterlogging and salinization problems associated with poorly managed canal irrigation. Over two-thirds of the tubewell construction has taken place in the north China provinces of Hebei, Henan, and Shandong. Most of the remainder has been focused in other north and northeast provinces.

There are two main problems with the tubewell data. First and foremost, stock figures imperfectly reflect the actual stock of operating tubewells because an unknown percentage of wells in good working order do not operate every year. Some are needed only in dry years and some areas find it too expensive in average years to pump water. Federal financial incentives led to unnecessarily dense placement in some localities, and in others, especially around cities, continuous overpumping has resulted in the necessity of closing down some wells. Most importantly, the statistics include an unknown and varying percentage of wells where construction was initiated, but not completed, or where lack of equipment or ancillary facilities preclude operation. The drop in stock between 1978 and 1979 reflects a revision to exclude pumpwells not operating, but certainly the quantity of inoperative wells exceeds the difference between these two statistics plus the estimated quarter million wells for which facilities were completed in 1979. In Shandong an estimated 320,000 (1980) of the 540,000 "completed wells" (1979) were in actual operation. Twenty-two percent of Henan's wells lack ancillary facilities and 228,000 of the 488,000 wells constructed in Hebei (1973–1978) were not operating in 1980. Finally, the SSB and Ministry of Water Conservancy have published different figures for the same years.

### Supply of Fertilizers and Chemical Pesticides

Fragmentary information scattered over a wide variety of sources, as well as incomplete data for different fertilizer types, have made it difficult to obtain reliable estimates of fertilizer production and supply.

Recently, however, an aggregated gross weight chemical fertilizer supply series has been published in the *Agricultural Yearbook of China 1980*. The series appears at least generally consistent with the collection of previously published information on production and imports, although it conflicts for some years with the *Ten Great Years* supply series.

Official fertilizer production data for the 1950s is fairly reliable, and most series are quite similar since total output was modest and confined to a few centralized nitrogen fertilizer plants (Table A.9). Unfortunately the *Ten Great Years* production figures and Kuo's entries through 1958 include only ammonium sulfate. Liu and Chao supplement the *Ten Great Years* series with production estimates for ammonium sulfate and phosphatic fertilizer based on Chinese publications. Estimates for all series for 1959–1977 are intended to include production of all important fertilizers and are based on various Chinese materials giving absolute quantities or growth increments over preceeding years (Table A.9).

Since gross weight figures do not reflect relative changes in average nutrient availability, supply of chemical fertilizer by nutrient weight provides a much more realistic view of total availability (Table A.10). However, official estimates by nutrient weight have appeared for only a few years, so that remaining estimates are dependent not only on gross weight series, but must also use shaky breakdowns for the composition of total fertilizer production by type, and are of necessity based on the optimistic assumption that nutrient contents are up to standard. Although, in general, nutrient weight is a better indicator than gross weight of chemical fertilizer availability, the difference to our understanding of fertilizer production development from comparing these two aggregated series is not very significant since average nutrient content of chemical fertilizers produced in China has remained between 17 and 21 percent. The balance

234

Table A.9. Production and Supply of Chemical Fertilizers and Farm Chemicals, 1949-1980

| Year | Supply of Chemical Fertilizers Agricultural Yearbook of China 1980 (1981) | Production of Chemical Fertilizers | | | | | | Supply of Farm Chemicals a/ "Reconstructed Official"b/ | Production of Farm Chemicals a/ "Reconstructed Official"b/ (active ingredient weight) |
| | | "Reconstructed Official"b/ | Ten Great Years (1960) | Liu (1970) | Chao (1970) | Kuo (1976) | CIA (1978) | | |
| | | (gross weight) | | | | (thousand tonnes) | | | |
| 1949 | | 27 | 27 | 27 | 27 | 27 | 27 | negligible | |
| 1950 | | 70 | 70 | 70 | 70 | 70 | 70 | | |
| 1951 | | 134 | 129 | 134 | 134 | 129 | 137 | | |
| 1952 | 295 c/ | 188 | 181 | 188 | 188 | 181 | 194 | 15 | |
| 1953 | 592 c/ | 249 | 226 | 249 | 249 | 226 | 263 | 19 | 2 |
| 1954 | 802 c/ | 326 | 298 | 327 | 326 | 298 | 343 | 41 | |
| 1955 | 1,255 c/ | 500 | 332 | 353 | 403 | 332 | 426 | 67 | |
| 1956 | 1,608 c/ | 500 | 523 | 601 | 703 | 523 | 663 | 159 | |
| 1957 | 1,794 | 735 | 631 | 858 | 871 | 631 | 803 | 149 d/ | |
| 1958 | 2,708 | 1,500 | 811 | 1,462 | 1,462 | 811 | 1,354 | 478 d/ | 65 |
| 1959 | 2,533 | 2,500 | | 1,777 | 2,227 | 1,333 | 1,876 | 137 | 82 |
| 1960 | 3,164 | 2,500 | | 2,000 | 2,550 | 1,676 | 2,523 | | |
| 1961 | 2,242 | 2,000 | | 1,450 | 2,000 | 1,431 | 1,850 | | |
| 1962 | 3,105 | 3,000 | | 2,170 | 3,000 | 2,147 | 2,775 | | |
| 1963 | 4,483 | 4,000 | | 3,004 | 4,200 | 3,000 | 3,857 | | |
| 1964 | 5,363 | 5,500 | | 4,506 | 5,900 | 3,600 | 5,786 | | |
| 1965 | 8,812 | 8,766 | | 7,660 | 8,900 | 6,400 | 7,600 | 447 | |
| 1966 | 12,582 | 11,500 | | | 11,600 | 8,100 | 9,600 | | 193 |
| 1967 | 13,628 | | | | | | 8,100 | | |
| 1968 | 10,129 | | | | | | 9,500 | | |
| 1969 | 13,611 | 7,500 | | | | | 11,300 | | |
| 1970 | 15,351 | 12,310 | | | 14,000 | 14,000 | 14,000 | | |
| 1971 | 18,142 | 15,000 | | | 16,800 | 16,828 | 16,800 | 321 | |
| 1972 | 20,931 | 17,900 | | | 19,900 | 19,874 | 19,841 | (369) | |
| 1973 | 25,553 | 24,254 | | | 25,000 | 25,000 | 24,801 | (402) | |
| 1974 | 24,051 | 23,000 | | | 30,000 | | 24,900 | 454 | |
| 1975 | 26,579 | 29,000 | | | | | 28,800 | 422 | |
| 1976 | 28,850 | 28,509 | | | | | 24,320 | 389 | |

| | | | | |
|---|---|---|---|---|
| 1977 | 31,920 | 35,807 | | 457/458 [e] |
| 1978 | 43,691 | 42,154 | | 553 |
| 1979 | 52,476 | 52,159 | | 573/523 [e] |
| 1980 | | 60,500 | 38,000 | |

Note: The figures in parentheses are the author's estimates based on official Chinese statements about the growth of production.

[a] Includes pesticides, herbicides, insecticides, and fungicides.

[b] See Note 2 for definition. All post-1955 fertilizer production figures, except those taken directly from The Agricultural Yearbook of China 1980, have been rounded to the nearest 500,000 tonnes. Statistics for production of farm chemicals are clearly given in active ingredient weight terms. However, the supply series may be in gross weight or active ingredient terms. Larger numbers in the supply series may represent the addition of imports plus inventory changes in active ingredient weight, or may simply reflect the use of gross weight terms.

[c] These figures have been taken from Ten Great Years since estimates for these years did not appear in Agricultural Yearbook of China 1980. The 1958 figures from the two sources were identical, but the 1952 and 1957 figures from Ten Great Years were 318,000 tonnes and 1,944,000 tonnes, respectively.

[d] This figure may be substantially exaggerated.

[e] Official sources have conflicting estimates for these years. The noted figures appeared most recently.

Table A.10.   Domestic Production and Imports of Chemical Fertilizers by Nutrient
Weight and Supply of Nutrients from Organic Sources, 1949–1980

| Year | Domestic Production | | Imports | Nutrients from Organic Sources[a] | |
|---|---|---|---|---|---|
| | "Reconstructed Official"[b] | CIA (1978) | CIA (1980) | Chao adjusted[c] (1970) | Tang[d] (1980) |
| | (thousand tonnes) | | | (percent) | |
| 1949 | 6 | 5 | 0 | | |
| 1950 | 14 | 14 | 20 | | |
| 1951 | 28 | 27 | 40 | | |
| 1952 | 39 | 39 | 40 | 99.5 | 99.1 |
| 1953 | 54 | 53 | 80 | 98.9 | 98.7 |
| 1954 | 50 | 69 | 136 | 98.7 | 98.4 |
| 1955 | 50 | 85 | 158 | 98.0 | 97.7 |
| 1956 | 100 | 131 | 270 | 97.5 | 97.2 |
| 1957 | 151 | 159 | 270 | 97.3 | 96.4 |
| 1958 | 350 | 266 | 360 | 96.4 | 96.2 |
| 1959 | 500 | 369 | 270 | 96.1 | 95.3 |
| 1960 | 500 | 495 | 215 | 95.1 | 95.1 |
| 1961 | 450 | 364 | 225 | 93.6 | 94.5 |
| 1962 | 650 | 548 | 240 | 92.0 | 93.2 |
| 1963 | 900 | 757 | 540 | 90.2 | 92.0 |
| 1964 | 1,100 | 1,128 | 357 | 89.0 | 90.3 |
| 1965 | 1,700 | 1,480 | 640 | 85.4 | 89.2 |
| 1966 | 2,250 | 1,882 | 722 | | 87.6 |
| 1967 | | 1,609 | 1,154 | | 86.1 |
| 1968 | | 1,893 | 1,235 | | 84.7 |
| 1969 | 1,400 | 2,243 | 1,315 | | 82.9 |
| 1970 | 2,400 | 2,781 | 1,485 | | 81.3 |
| 1971 | 2,850 | 3,340 | 1,480 | | 80.0 |
| 1972 | 3,300 | 3,944 | 1,550 | | 78.7 |
| 1973 | 4,350 | 4,917 | 1,518 | | 77.4 |
| 1974 | 4,150 | 4,953 | 1,149 | | 76.9 |
| 1975 | 5,200 | 5,734 | 1,201 | | 76.9 |
| 1976 | 5,240 | | 1,009 | | 77.6 |
| 1977 | 7,238 | | 1,523 | | 73.0 |
| 1978 | 8,693 | | 2,173 | | |
| 1979 | 10,564 | | 1,720[e] | | |
| 1980 | 12,320 | | | | |

a/   These figures have been calculated from data on organic and chemical fertilizers.
b/   These data are a combination of official estimates and the author's estimates
based on indirect quantitative data, or ambiguous data from Chinese sources.
All of the author's estimates have been rounded to the nearest 50,000 tonnes.
c/   Percentage estimates appear in Chao's works, but they are not comparable with
other figures because they combine estimates of chemical fertilizer nutrients
supplied with organic fertilizer nutrients absorbed by plants.  Adjustments
have been made on the basis of source material provided in Chao's publications.
d/   These figures are three-year moving averages of Tang's original estimates.
e/   This is a preliminary figure.

among nitrogenous, phosphatic, and potassic fertilizers however, is significant, as is the proportion produced by small plants.

One problem that inadvertently distorts supply series is the long-term availability of plant nutrients incorporated in chemical fertilizers. Because phosphorus and potassium are not prone to evaporation and are not easily leached even in irrigated soils, these nutrients continue to be readily available to plants for several years. However, phosphorus and potassium fertilizers make up only a small portion of total fertilizer production and imports. Historically, more Chinese soils have been deficient in nitrogen, so China has concentrated on production of nitrogen fertilizers. Through time, intensive use of soils has depleted other soil elements so that phosphatic, potassic, and trace element production is currently inadequate. Nitrogen, which dominates both domestic production and imports of chemical fertilizer, has a high rate of evaporation and is easily eroded by water and wind, especially when applied by broadcast methods. In addition, there are significant differences in the volatility of various nitrogen fertilizers. Ammonium bicarbonate produced by small-scale plants tends to be much more volatile than ammonium sulphate or other nitrogen fertilizers produced by large-scale plants.

Estimates of chemical fertilizer nutrient weight have become especially important since the mid-1960s and the development of small-scale production facilities. As small-scale production escalated rapidly, assuming a large share of total production, the quality and accuracy of production statistics became more difficult to maintain, and the assumption that all factory output is up to standard quality is less defensible. In 1974 small plant production constituted 75 percent of total (gross weight) domestic phosphatic production, and 54 percent of domestic nitrogenous output. By 1978 the proportion for nitrogen fertilizers had increased to 70 percent. Although there is pressure to close down inefficient small plants, they will continue to be an important part of China's chemical fertilizer supply for some time.

Chemical pesticides were first produced in 1951 (Table A.9). Since then production and supply have increased moderately. Application is still quite limited and is highly skewed geographically. Early applications of broad-spectrum pesticides, such as DDT, have spawned a variety of associated environmental problems, so that currently more pest-specific chemicals and organo-phosphorus insecticides are favored. In addition to the use of manufactured pesticides, many farmers make extensive use of "indigenous" pesticides. Some of the main varieties include alkaloids, anabasine, rotonoids, Kalanchoe extracts and garlic. In 1958 over 10 million tonnes of "indigenous" pesticides and fungicides were produced in local factories. Today each Chinese county contains at least one such factory.

Because the production level of chemical pesticides is low and highly centralized, production statistics (Table A.9) are apt to be relatively accurate, although quality of the finished product is sometimes deficient. The production statistics included here are in terms of active ingredient weight, as is standard internationally. It is not clear whether supply statistics are larger due only to imports and stock changes, or because gross weights rather than active ingredient weights are the reported quantities.

In addition to the use of chemicals, the Chinese continue to be pioneers in the field of biological and viral control methods, although such methods are used on only about 10 percent of cultivated land. Habitat transformation has also been an important method for controlling some pest species, notably the locust.

Estimates of organic fertilizer nutrients as a percent of total consumption have been made by Chao and Tang (Table A.10). Organic fertilizer estimates include compost, green manure crops, draft animal and hog manures, various oil-seed cakes, nightsoil, river and pond mud, and others. Although estimates of organic fertilizers, by necessity, can be only rough approximations, such exercises may be useful, as organic material still provides a major share of total available plant nutrients. Total organic tonnage may still be growing slightly, although the share of nutrients supplied by chemical fertilizers is certainly rising more rapidly, and future growth potential for organic fertilizer may be somewhat limited. The largest sources of increase still available are human and hog manure, but labor costs for collection, transport, composting, and storing are substantial. One 1965 report indicated that the labor cost of manure containing 100 kilograms of nitrogen nutrient is 35–45 human-labor days and 20–25 animal-labor days. If nitrogen were valued at $0.50/kg (a typical recent world price), the return to labor would be only $0.12 per day without considering animal costs! With shifts to more intensive cropping patterns these large drains on labor at very low returns have become a serious limitation. However, organic materials still provide the bulk of potassium and trace minerals and in some areas are the sole available source.

Assessment of the aggregate organic fertilizer supply involves estimating gross weights available and actually applied in each category. The resulting totals are multiplied by average nutrient content factors and summed to obtain an aggregate. In particular the pattern of change in percentage of available nutrients applied is very important and virtually unknown. The entire estimation process is subject to large errors, but a number of scholars have made serious attempts at quantification for some years. All estimates for the 1960s and 1970s rely on data components of the 1950s and several debatable assumptions. The most notable of these is that the proportion of available nutrients actually applied rose rapidly until the mid-1960s and remained constant thereafter.

## Tractors

Tractors play an important role in Chinese agriculture, although plowing is only one of their functions. Most large tractors are employed in land reclamation and a significant portion of tractor operation time is devoted to rural transportation. Many other mechanized farm tools are also produced, including harvesters, threshers, transplanters, and food processing equipment. Other simpler equipment, such as tractor accessories, wheelbarrows, hand sprayers, and hand carts, have also had a large impact on rural productivity.

Although tractor stock figures are sometimes taken as representative of the level of agricultural mechanization, total stocks of mechanized agricultural equipment (combines, harvesters, grain threshers, rice transplanters, food processing equipment, tractors, and irrigation equipment) may be more appropriate. Statistics are now available for aggregated and disaggregated stocks of mechanized equipment for various years. Of a total stock of 180 million horsepower of mechanized equipment at year-end 1979, irrigation and drainage equipment accounted for 65 million horsepower, and tractors and power tillers about 30 million horsepower.

Reconstructions of tractor stock series are hindered by definitional problems as in other data categories. In the 1950s and early 1960s tractors were aggregated by standard units of 15 horsepower. However, recent SSB figures (1977–1980) seem to list tractor stock by physical units and distinguish between power tillers and large- and medium-sized tractors. It is uncertain exactly when this change in accounting took place and, further, within long-term Chinese data series, it is often unclear as to whether statistics have been adjusted to account for definitional inconsistencies. The *Agricultural Yearbook of China 1980* includes the most extensive tractor stock series to date. Power tiller data have clearly been given in physical units. Large- and medium-size tractor data are labelled "standard units" in the publication, but these figures conflict markedly with standard unit data from the 1950s and early 1960s. Other data suggest that large- and medium-size tractor data are actually recorded in physical units.

Until publication of the *Agricultural Yearbook of China 1980*, the *Ten Great Years* figures in standard units were widely accepted for the 1950s, (Table A.11) although the post-1964 standard unit estimates of all researchers must be regarded as very rough. The 1965 figures in all series (except Tang) are based on different interpretations of a single statement from the *People's Daily*. Because published information about post-1965 estimates has usually been based on multiples of the 1965 figure, ascertaining the exact figure used by the Chinese is most important in this case. In addition, one would question researchers' assumptions that stock increments published by the Chinese between 1970 and 1978 refer to standard units. These stock increments, apparently in physical units, are quite consistent with data for large- and medium-sized tractors only from the *Agricultural Yearbook of China 1980*.

Tang's series, unlike the others included here, is partially based on information about tractor production and attempts to take inventory and depreciation factors into account. There are serious problems with such an approach, as well. For example, Tang's "derived" rate of depreciation is 6.6 percent. Chinese sources place inoperative stock at 23 percent in 1962 and 30 percent in 1979. This suggests a higher actual rate of depreciation than Tang assumes.

Table A.11. Stock of Tractors and Machine-Plowed Area, 1949-1980

| Year | Agricultural Yearbook of China 1980 (1981) | | Total Tractor Stock | | | | | Machine Plowed Area |
| --- | --- | --- | --- | --- | --- | --- | --- | --- |
| | Large & Medium Tractors a/ | Power Tillers | Ten Great Years (1960) | Wiens (1980) | Kuo (1976) | CIA (1978) | Tang (1980) | |
| | (thousand physical units) | | (thousand standard units) | | | | | (million hectares) |
| 1949 | | | 0.4 | | 0.4 | 0.4 | | |
| 1950 | | | 1.3 | | 1.3 | 1.3 | | |
| 1951 | | | 1.4 | | 1.4 | 1.4 | | |
| 1952 | 1.3 | | 2.0 | | 2.0 | 2.0 | 2.0 | 0.1 |
| 1953 | 1.6 | | 2.7 | | 2.7 | 2.7 | 2.7 | |
| 1954 | 2.9 | | 5.1 | | 5.1 | 5.1 | 5.1 | 0.1 |
| 1955 | 4.8 | | 8.1 | | 8.1 | 8.1 | 8.1 | 0.3 |
| 1956 | 11.3 | | 19.4 | | 19.4 | 19.4 | 19.4 | 1.9 |
| 1957 | 14.7 | | 24.6 | 24.6 | 24.6 | 24.6 | 24.6 | 2.6 |
| 1958 | 26.4 | | 45.3 | | 45.3 | 45.3 | 45.3 | 4.7 |
| 1959 | 33.3 | | 59.0 | | 59.0 | 59.0 | 59.0 | 6.2 |
| 1960 | 45.5 | | 79.0 | | 79.0 | 79.0 | 79.0 | 7.2 |
| 1961 | 52.2 | | | 79.0 | | 95.0 | 95.0 | 8.2 |
| 1962 | 54.9 | 0.9 | | 99.0 | 99.0 | 103.0 | 103.0 | 8.3 |
| 1963 | 59.2 | 1.0 | | 103.4 | 100.0 | 113.0 | 115.0 | 10.6 |
| 1964 | 65.9 | 1.3 | | 115.0 | 115.0 | | 123.0 b/ | 12.8 |
| 1965 | 72.6 | 4.0 | | 123.0 b/ | 123.0 b/ | 138.4 b/ | 138.4 b/ | 15.6 |
| **1966** | | | | 130.5 b/ | 154.2 b/ | 153.6 b/ | 156.6 b/ | |
| 1967 | | | | | | | 178.1 b/ | |
| 1968 | | | | | | | 195.4 b/ | |
| 1969 | | | | | | | 216.1 b/ | |
| 1970 | 125.5 | 73.3 | | | 308.3 b/ | 320.1 b/ | 293.0 b/ | 18.2 |
| 1971 | 150.2 | 133.6 | | 200-300 b/ | 700.7 b/ | | 352.7 b/ | 20.8 |
| 1972 | 189.9 | 207.7 | | | 770.8 b/ | 397.0 b/ | 484.1 b/ | 21.9 |
| 1973 | 234.1 | 302.2 | | | | 506.0 b/ | 639.5 b/ | 26.5 |
| 1974 | 280.7 | 421.2 | | | | | 836.2 b/ | 28.5 |
| 1975 | 344.5 | 598.5 | | 613.0 b/ | | 784.5 b/ | 971.8 b/ | 33.2 |
| 1976 | 397.0 | 825.0 | | | | | 1,187.3 b/ | 34.9 |
| 1977 | 467.0 | 1,091.0 | | | | | 1,300.0 b/ | 38.4 |
| 1978 | 557.4 | 1,373.0 | | | | | | 40.7 |
| 1979 | 666.8 c/ | 1,671.0 | | | | | | 42.2 |
| 1980 | 745.0 c/ | 1,874.0 c/ | | | | | | 41.0 |

Note: With the exception of the first two columns, these figures include power tillers or hand tractors as well as large- and medium-sized tractors. One standard unit equals 15 horsepower.

a/ In the Agricultural Yearbook of China 1980 the large and medium tractor stock series is labeled "Standard Tractor Units." However, other data suggests that these figures, like those for power tillers, actually refer to physical units.

b/ These figures are based on indirect quantitative data from the Chinese media.

c/ 1980 figures have been added from the SSB, "1980 Communique."

Table A.12. Aggregate Price Indexes and Price Index Ratios, 1950-1979

| Year | State Purchase Price Indexes of All Farm Goods[a] | Retail Price Indexes of Industrial Goods Sold in Rural Areas | Retail Price Indexes of Industrial Inputs to Agriculture | Composite Price Scissors[b] |
|------|------|------|------|------|
| | | (1950=100) | | |
| 1950 | 100.0 | 100.0 | 100.0 | 100.0 |
| 1951 | 119.6 | 110.2 | | 92.2 |
| 1952 | 121.6 | 109.7 | | 90.3 |
| 1953 | 132.5 | 108.2 | | 81.7 |
| 1954 | 136.7 | 110.3 | | 80.7 |
| 1955 | 135.1 | 111.9 | | 82.8 |
| 1956 | 139.2 | 110.8 | | 79.6 |
| 1957 | 146.2 | 112.1 | | 76.7 |
| 1958 | | | | (72.8) |
| 1959 | | | | 72.1 |
| 1963 | 188.2 | 125.3 | (63.0)[b/c] | 66.6 |
| 1964 | | | | 66.6 |
| 1965 | | | | 62.7 |
| 1966 | | | [d] | |
| 1967 | | | | [d] |
| 1970 | [e] | | [d] | [d] |
| 1971 | 190.0 | | | [f] |
| 1972 | ~200.0 | [d] | | <60 |
| 1973 | 190.0-200.0 | | 33.3-66.7 [g] | ~55 |
| 1974 | 200.0 | | 33.3-66.7 | (53.7) |
| 1975 | >200.0 | | | 53.6 |
| 1976 | 169.0 | | | 55.0 |
| 1977 | 200.0 | 128.0 | | [f] |
| 1978 | 207.0 | | | 64.0 |
| 1979 | 230.0 | | (52.0)[b/h] | [d] 45.5 |

Note: All figures included in this table are "reconstructed official" figures. See Note 2 for definition.

a/ Figures usually include all agricultural and farm subsidiary products purchased by the state.

b/ Price index ratios or scissors are the ratio of the price indexes of industrial goods sold in rural areas to the indexes of state purchases of agricultural and farm sideline production. Numbers have been derived from original source material by the author. Parenthesized values are derived assuming that regardless of what year has been set equal to 100 in Chinese statements, the base periods for the index calculation are actually identical.

c/ 35 percent greater than the 1952 level.

d/ Figure is lower than for the previous year.

e/ Figure is lower than for the subsequent year.

f/ Figure is higher than for the subsequent year.

g/ Includes chemical fertilizer, insecticides and diesel oil.

h/ Includes farm machinery, chemical fertilizer and insecticides.

## Aggregate Price Indexes

From 1949 to 1959, the official purchase price for agricultural commodities, including food grains, rose steadily, whereas the aggregated prices of industrial goods sold in rural areas remained fairly stable (Table A.12). Little is known about the aggregation methods employed in deriving these indexes after the 1950s. They seem broadly consistent with other available data, but may not fully reflect quality changes and could distort the impact of industrial goods not available during the 1950s.

Excessive reliance upon numbers in Table A.12 does not seem well advised, but the existence of several broad trends is undeniable: (1) state purchase prices of agricultural goods rose steadily and substantially up to 1975, and again after 1977; (2) retail prices of industrial goods sold in rural areas have remained roughly constant in the aggregate and may be broken down into two components: (a) prices of industrial inputs to agriculture, which may have risen in the 1950s and early 1960s but fell dramatically at least by the early 1970s; (b) prices of other industrial goods sold in rural areas, which rose less rapidly than prices of inputs to agriculture during the first decade or so but did not experience the dramatic drop over the past 10 to 15 years.

The work of some scholars indicates that the official indexes have somewhat exaggerated the twist in prices in favor of rural areas during the first decade of the PRC's history. Also, it seems clear that the early price structure of the PRC discriminated against rural areas, compared with prewar years. By the PRC's own calculations, purchase prices for agricultural goods relative to sale prices for industrial goods in rural areas were about 22 percent higher in 1930–1936 than they were in 1952. This bias, however, was redressed by around 1957.

Following more progress in the terms of trade in the early 1960s, stagnation occurred during the Cultural Revolution decade (1966–1976). Despite gradual improvement in the early 1970s, rural areas seem to have suffered increasingly in view of the large quantity of industrial goods required in most areas to raise agricultural production further. The ratio of industrial goods sale prices to farm goods purchase prices on a 1950 base (composite price scissors in Table A.12) eased to a pre-1979 minimum in 1974. However the 1977 ratio exceeded even that of 1965, and 1976 may have been higher still. This deterioration in the terms of trade coincided with very poor weather in 1976 and 1977, which culminated in output stagnation. Rural income losses and adverse effects on incentives resulting from the coincident weather and relative price difficulties are surely significant in explaining the major changes in rural policy that became effective in 1978 and 1979.

## Notes

1. Detailed sources for all tables appear in Bruce Stone, *A Review of Chinese Agricultural Statistics, 1949–1979,* Research Report 16 (Washington, D.C.: International Food Policy Research Institute, 1980). This publication provides complete information on sources of data and on series developed by scholars outside the PRC. The reference section at the end of Appendix A lists all English language sources from which series were taken. Only selected Chinese source material is given.

2. The "reconstructed official" series reported in most of the tables are this author's amalgamation of verbatim official statements and estimates based on incremental change given in Chinese media, academic, or government publications.

## References

Sources for statistical series other than "reconstructed official," some Chinese data sets and Table A.12 can be found by author and year below. We suggest that those who are interested in a more detailed description of sources and their use see: Bruce Stone, *A Review of Chinese Agricultural Statistics,* Research Report 16, Washington, D.C.: International Food Policy Research Institute, 1980.

Aird, John. Foreign Demographic Analysis Division. Bureau of the Census, Department of Commerce, 1980, unpublished.

Chao, Kang. *Agricultural Production in Communist China, 1949–1965.* Madison: University of Wisconsin Press, 1970.

Erisman, A. L. "China: Agricultural Development 1949–1971," in *The People's Republic of China: An Economic Assessment — A Compendium of Papers Submitted to the Joint Economic Committee, Congress of the United States.* Washington, D.C.: U.S. Government Printing Office, 1978.

Food and Agriculture Organization. "Production Yearbook Data Tape," 1975 and 1978.

Groen, H. J., and J. A. Kilpatrick. "Chinese Agricultural Production," in *Chinese Economy Post-Mao: A Compendium of Papers Submitted to the Joint Economic Committee, Congress of the United States.* Washington, D.C.: U.S. Government Printing Office, 1978.

Jones, Edwin. "The Emerging Pattern of China's Economic Revolution," in *An Economic Profile of Mainland China: Studies Prepared for the Joint Economic Committee, Congress of the United States.* Washington, D.C.: U.S. Government Printing Office, 1967.

Kuo, Leslie. *Agriculture in the People's Republic of China, Technical Transformation and Structural Change.* New York: Praeger, 1976.

Liu, J. C. *China's Fertilizer Economy.* Chicago: Aldine, 1970.

People's Republic of China, State Statistical Bureau. *Ten Great Years.* Peking: Foreign Languages Publishing House, 1960.

Tang, Anthony, and Bruce Stone. *Food Production in the People's Republic of China,* Research Report No. 15. Washington, D.C.: International Food Policy Research Institute, 1980.

United Nations. *Demographic Yearbook.* New York: 1980, and other years.

U.S., Central Intelligence Agency, National Foreign Assessment Center. "China: Economic Indicators," ER-78-10750. Washington, D.C.: U.S. Central Intelligence Agency, 1978.

U.S, Central Intelligence Agency, National Foreign Assessment Center. "China: International Trade Quarterly Review," Fourth Quarter 1979, ER CIT 80-003. Washington, D.C.: U.S. Central Intelligence Agency, 1980.

U.S., Department of Agriculture, Economics and Statistics Service. "Agricultural

Situation: People's Republic of China Review of 1980 and Outlook for 1981," Supplement 6 to WAS-24. Washington, D.C., 1981, and other years.

Vermeer, E. B. *Water Conservancy and Irrigation in China: Social, Economic and Agrotechnical Aspects.* The Hague: University of Leiden Press, 1977.

Wiens, Thomas. "Agricultural Statistics in The People's Republic of China," in Alexander Eckstein, ed., *Quantitative Measures of China's Economic Output.* Ann Arbor: University of Michigan Press, 1980.

*Zhongguo Jingji Nianjian 1981* (Annual Economic Report of China 1981). Beijing: Jingji guanli zazhi, 1981.

Zhongguo Kexue Yuan, Dili Yanjiu Suo, Jingji Dili Yanjiu Shi. *Zhongguo Nongye Dili Zonglun* (General Treatise on Agricultural Geography). Beijing: Kexue chuban she, 1980.

*Zhongguo Nongye Nianjian 1980* (Agricultural Yearbook of China 1980). Beijing: Nongye chuban she, 1981.

# Sources of
# Additional Information

*Randolph Barker*
*Radha Sinha*
*Beth Rose*

## Readings

The following are readily available general references containing PRC agricultural statistical materials and information about them. Some of the estimates in most of these publications would no longer be used by their authors.

Chao, Kang. *Agricultural Production in Communist China, 1949–65.* Madison: University of Wisconsin Press, 1970.

Chen, Nai-Ruenn. *Chinese Economic Statistics.* Chicago: Aldine, 1967.

Committee on the Economy of China, Social Science Research Council. *Provincial Agricultural Statistics for Communist China.* Ithaca, N.Y., 1969.

Dawson, Owen L. *Communist China's Agriculture.* New York: Praeger, 1970.

Kuo, Leslie. *Agriculture in The People's Republic of China, Technical Transformation and Structural Change.* New York: Praeger, 1976.

Li, Choh-ming. *Statistical System of Communist China.* Berkeley: University of California Press, 1962.

Paine, Suzanne. "Development with Growth: A Quarter Century of Socialist Transition in China." *Economic and Political Weekly,* August 1976, pp. 1349–1378.

People's Republic of China, State Statistical Bureau. *Ten Great Years.* Peking: Foreign Languages Publishing House, 1960.

Perkins, Dwight. *Agricultural Production in China.* Chicago: Aldine, 1969.

Sinha, Radha. "Chinese Agriculture: A Quantitative Look." *Journal of Development Studies,* April 1975, pp. 202–223.

Stone, Bruce. *A Review of Chinese Agricultural Statistics, 1949–1979,* Research Report 16. Washington, D.C.: International Food Policy Research Institute, 1980.

Stone, Bruce. "A Statistical Assessment of China's 1985 Foodgrain Production Target," in Barbara Huddleston and John McLin, eds., *Political Investments in Food*

*Production.* Bloomington: University of Indiana Press, 1979, pp. 143–183.

Tang, Anthony M., and Bruce Stone. *Food Production in the People's Republic of China,* Research Report 15. Washington, D.C.: International Food Policy Research Institute, 1980.

U.S., Department of Commerce. "Full Report of the Visit of the United States Statistical Delegation to the People's Republic of China: November 24 to December 3, 1979." Washington, D.C., April 1980.

Wiens, Thomas B. "Agricultural Statistics in the People's Republic of China," in Alexander Eckstein, ed., *Quantitative Measures of China's Economic Output.* Ann Arbor: University of Michigan Press, 1980.

## Statistical Publication Organizations

The following organizations may be contacted for their most recent estimates or for statistical publications on specific subjects.

China Book Project
M.E. Sharpe, Inc.
901 North Broadway
White Plains, NY 10603

FAO
1776 F Street, N.W.
Washington, D.C.

Institute of Developing Economies
42 Honmura-cho, Ichigaya
Shinjuku-ku
Tokyo, Japan

People's Republic of China Affairs
   Division
U.S. Department of Commerce
Room 4044
14th & Constitution Streets, N.W.
Washington, D.C. 20230

Rand Corporation
1700 Main Street
Santa Monica, CA 90406

U.S. Congress Joint Economic
   Committee
G133 Dirksen Senate Office Building
Washington, D.C. 20510

China Division
Office of Economic Research
Central Intelligence Agency
Washington, D.C. 20505

Foreign Demographic Analysis Division
Bureau of the Census
U.S. Department of Commerce
711 Building, Room 705
14th Street, N.W.
Washington, D.C. 20230

People's Republic of China Section
Asian Branch, IED/ESS/USDA
Room 350
500 12th Street, S.W.
Washington, D.C. 20250

Rural Employment Policies Branch
Research Programme
World Employment Programme
International Labour Office
Geneva, Switzerland

## English Language Periodicals

The following English language periodicals may be perused for the most up-to-date information from the PRC or for detailed information on specific subjects, geographic areas, or time periods.

*Beijing Review* (Peking Review). Distributed by Guoji Shudian, Beijing, China (weekly).

*Chinese Economic Studies*. M. E. Sharpe, Inc., 901 N. Broadway, White Plains, NY 10603. Translations of important articles on the Chinese economy.

*China Reconstructs*. Distributed by Guoji Shudian, Beijing, China (monthly).

*The China Quarterly*. Contemporary China Institute, School of Oriental and African Studies, Malet Street, London WCIE 7HP. An international journal of brief scholarly articles on China, including articles on agriculture and economics.

*Far Eastern Economic Review*. A weekly news publication by Far Eastern Economic Review Limited, Hong Kong.

Foreign Broadcast Information Service — *Daily Report: People's Republic of China*. National Technical Information Service, U.S. Department of Commerce, Springfield, VA 22161. Daily translations of provincial and national radio broadcasts, news releases, newspaper and journal articles.

Joint Publications Research Service — *China Report: Agriculture*. National Technical Information Service, U.S. Department of Commerce, Springfield, VA 22161. A series of translations of broadcasts, newspaper reports, and journal articles.

New China's News Agency (*Xinhua She*). News releases by local radio broadcasting stations, Beijing.

*Selections from People's Republic of China Magazines*. National Technical Information Service, U.S. Department of Commerce, Springfield, VA 22161.

*Summary of World Broadcasts, The Far East Weekly Economic Report*. British Broadcasting Corporation, Reading, England.

*Survey of Chinese Mainland Press*. National Technical Information Service, U.S. Department of Commerce, Springfield, VA 22161.

# The Contributors

**Randolph Barker,** professor of agricultural economics at Cornell University, has a special interest in Chinese grain production and agricultural trade. Although new to the China field he has worked extensively in other parts of Asia, including twelve years' service as an economist at the International Rice Research Institute (IRRI) in the Philippines. His experience brings a valuable comparative outlook to the field.

**Robert F. Dernberger,** professor of economics at the University of Michigan, is chairman of the Subcommittee on Research on China's Economy and is a member of the Joint Committee on Contemporary China (SSRC). He has also been an active participant in several official delegations to China including the American Rural Small-Scale Industry Delegation (1975), the American Economists Delegation (1979), and the Social Sciences and Humanities Delegation (1980). Mr. Dernberger has published widely and is editor of a new book, *China's Development Experience in Comparative Perspective.* His current research interests include economic reforms in China and microeconomic analysis of the farm in China.

**Mark Elvin,** lecturer in Chinese history, University of Oxford and official fellow of St. Antony's College, is a leading sinologist who has published extensively on Chinese social and economic history. Among his major publications are *The Patterns of the Chinese Past, The Chinese City Between Two Worlds* (edited with G.W. Skinner), and a translation of Y. Shiba's *Commerce and Society in Sung China.* He is well versed in both classical and modern Chinese.

**Nicholas R. Lardy** is associate professor of economics at Yale University. His research has focused on China's system of resource allocation and on aspects of agricultural production, consumption, and distribution. His major publications include *Economic Growth and Distribution in China* and *Chinese Economic Planning: Translations from Jihua Jingji.*

**Rhoads Murphey,** professor in the Center for Chinese Studies, University of Michigan, is well known for his work on Chinese geography. Currently he is studying Chinese environmental modification, pollution control, the history and problems of reafforestation in China, and urbanism and the rural-urban balance in China. Mr. Murphey has a long association with China. He lived in China for four years (1942–1946) while working for the International Red Cross and has returned for visits in 1972, 1975, 1979, and 1981.

**Ramon H. Myers,** curator-scholar of the East Asian collection and senior fellow of the Hoover Institute on War, Revolution and Peace at Stanford University, has researched both historical and modern China. His wide range of interests run from customary law and economic development in late imperial China, to land tenure in Republican China, to the modern rural economy. In 1976 he visited China as a member of the wheat studies delegation of the United States. Currently he is preparing for publication a new book, *A Century of Chinese Agricultural Development.*

**Thomas G. Rawski,** professor of economics at the University of Toronto, researches China's economic history and development. He was a member of the Rural Small-Scale Industry Delegation that visited China in 1975. His major publications include *Economic Growth and Employment in China* and *China's Transition to Industrialism: Producer Goods and Economic Development in the Twentieth Century.*

**Beth Rose,** a research assistant at Cornell University, works with Randolph Barker. Her interests include Chinese grain production and distribution and Chinese social and political history.

**Radha Sinha,** reader in political economy at Glasgow University, Scotland, has a long-term commitment to the study of food, population, and development issues in Asia. Some of his books on the subject include *Food in India, Food and Poverty,* and *World Food Problem: Consensus and Conflict.* He is especially interested in the effects of policy on equitable food distribution and consumption in rural China.

**Daniel G. Sisler,** professor of agricultural economics at Cornell University, is especially interested in rural Asia. Other primary research interests include China/United States trade in agricultural products and raw materials and trends in Chinese grain production at the regional level.

**Benedict Stavis,** assistant professor of agricultural economics at Michigan State University, has had a particular interest in institutional aspects of rural development. His major publications include *The Politics of Agricultural Mechanization in China* and *Making Green Revolution: The Politics of Agricultural Development in China.*

**Bruce Stone,** Research Fellow at the International Food Policy Research Institute, has a broad interest in China. Among his most important publications are *A Review of Chinese Agricultural Statistics 1949–1979* and *Shifting the Yangtze North: A Water Transfer Project in China* (with others). Recently he was invited to China by the United Nations University and the Chinese Academy of Science to review the Yangtze–North China Plain interbasin water transfer project. Some of his current research interests include Chinese fertilizer development and agricultural pricing policy in China.

**Frederic M. Surls** is an agricultural economist in the PRC Section, Asia Branch, Economics and Statistics Service, United States Department of Agriculture. He has a very extensive knowledge of Chinese trade, particularly agricultural trade. He also researches connections between grain production, consumption, and procurements and grain trade. He has published extensively on Chinese trade.

**Thomas B. Wiens,** consultant for the World Bank and formerly senior economist at MATHTECH, Inc. is interested in many aspects of the Chinese agricultural economy. He is well known for his work on basic agricultural statistics and for his writings on agricultural technology. In 1977 he visited China as a member of the Vegetable Farming Systems Delegation of the U.S. National Academy of Sciences. He spent 6 months in 1980 in Jiangsu Province, Nanjing, at the Jiangsu Academy of Agricultural Sciences as a research scholar on the U.S.-China Educational Exchange Program. While in China he completed a study of the triple-cropping system in Jiangsu Province in cooperation with Chinese agricultural economists.

**Christine Pui Wah Wong,** assistant professor of economics at Mount Holyoke College, has a special interest in rural industries and the choice of technology problem in China. She has made numerous trips to China and will be spending six months at the Ministry of Agriculture in Peking in 1982 as a research scholar under the auspices of the Committee for Scholarly Communications with the People's Republic of China. She is currently working on a manuscript on rural industrialization in China.

# Index